Things

Things

In Touch with the Past

CAROLYN KORSMEYER

OXFORD
UNIVERSITY PRESS

OXFORD
UNIVERSITY PRESS

Oxford University Press is a department of the University of Oxford. It furthers
the University's objective of excellence in research, scholarship, and education
by publishing worldwide. Oxford is a registered trade mark of Oxford University
Press in the UK and certain other countries.

Published in the United States of America by Oxford University Press
198 Madison Avenue, New York, NY 10016, United States of America.

© Oxford University Press 2019

First issued as an Oxford University Press paperback, 2022

CIP data is on file at the Library of Congress
ISBN 978-0-19-090487-6 (Hbk.)
ISBN 978-0-19-764959-6 (Pbk.)

9 8 7 6 5 4 3 2 1

Paperback printed by Marquis, Canada

Contents

Illustrations

Acknowledgments

During the years that I have been writing this book I have benefited from conversations with many individuals. My husband, David Gerber, introduced me to the controversies surrounding the uncovering of the Erie Canal terminus and other matters of preservation that launched this book. I extend particular thanks to Carrie Tirado Bramen, Ann Colley, and Regina Grol, who tirelessly read through far more chapter drafts than there are chapters. Lynn Hasher passed along tidbits from the news to add to my list of examples. Merril Stevenson and Robin Christopher planned inspirational visits to ruins and other relics from the past, as did Richard Korsmeyer and Renni Ridgeway Korsmeyer, who ventured with me into the Niaux cave. Conversations with many others have been helpful, and I also thank Barbara Andrews, Jeanette Bicknell, Andrew Casper, Renée Conroy, Randy Dipert, Susan Feagin, Charles Ganelin, Ivan Gaskell, David Hershenov, Elisabeth Hodges, Robert Hopkins, Jennifer Judkins, Pascal Massie, Tim Melley, Ron Moore, Ariane Nomikos, Crispin Paine, Andreas Pantazatos, Elisabeth Schellekens, Phil Stevens, and Cathy Ullman. For help rendering images into publishable shape, I owe special thanks to Debra Kolodczak.

Some of the ideas developed here were first presented at lectures where audiences offered insightful criticisms, and I am grateful for such opportunities at meetings of the British Society for Aesthetics; the American Society for Aesthetics; the American Philosophical Association; Durham University; the philosophy departments of the University of Toronto, McMaster University, Guelph University, and the University at Buffalo; the International Congress for Aesthetics; and the Humanities Institutes of Miami University of Ohio and of the University at Buffalo. The Humanities Institute of the University at Buffalo supported this research with a fellowship, and I thank my fellow participants for their helpful suggestions.

While none of this book has been reprinted from earlier publications, I am grateful to have had the opportunity to begin to work out in article form some of the claims made here. Earlier versions of my core arguments, particularly those that appear in Chapter 1, appear in "Touch and the Experience of the Genuine," *British Journal of Aesthetics* (2012); "Real Old Things," *British Journal of Aesthetics* (2016); "Aesthetic Deception: On Encounters with the Past," *Journal of Aesthetics and Art Criticism* (2008); "Genuineness," *Material Religion* (2015); and "Staying in Touch," in *Art and Ethical Criticism*, ed. Garry Hagberg (2008).

Thanks also to Peter Ohlin, editor at Oxford University Press, and to three anonymous reviewers, whose careful comments on the manuscript were helpful in refining my thoughts about the significance of things from the past that remain to us.

This book is for Juliana, who someday may become a keeper of things gone old and precious.

Things

Introduction

In 1998 archaeologists conducting an inspection for the development of the harbor of the city of Buffalo discovered the remnants of the original terminus of the Erie Canal. This structure, known as Commercial Slip, once opened a shipping channel into the Buffalo River and thence to Lake Erie and the west. After a hundred years of use it had been buried and built over, and by the late twentieth century the entire site was overshadowed by elevated highways and empty grain elevators. The redevelopment project was designed to revive the area with recreation and tourist attractions, including a reproduction of a portion of the historic canal district. Even after the original terminus was discovered, plans continued to build a replica nearby, but what remained of the canal itself was to be reburied. Perhaps its outline would be marked on the pavement above to indicate its presence underground. But the historic "feel" of old Buffalo—the "experience" of the nineteenth-century canal town—was to be evoked by a reproduction slip, by an area of newly laid cobblestone streets, and by interpretive centers and signage, all of which would present fewer engineering complications than would resuscitating the original site itself.

To the apparent consternation of officials in charge of the project, this plan met immediate opposition from the vocal majority of citizens, who might have been expected to have no interest in what was at the time a chasm of frozen mud. There were heated public debates, newspaper articles, courtroom hearings, injunctions, and demonstrations for well over a year. Under pressure, the state development plan was revised, and it was decided to uncover, restore, and rewater the old Commercial Slip, retaining not only its site but also the original limestone walls that had been christened with a splash from a bucket by Governor Dewitt Clinton in 1825 when the canal was opened.

What lies behind such fervor to preserve an original object rather than substituting a replica? What is the difference between an encounter with a genuine remnant from the past and a good reproduction that looks the same? What kind of value can we reasonably attribute to old artifacts that they and they alone possess? In this particular case we can set aside instrumental value, inquiring simply what the grounds might be for valuing the ruins of the historical object over a reproduction canal, since neither would be of any use for commercial shipping anymore.

Pursuing such questions reveals the gap between perceptual appearance and historical identity, and within this gap a multitude of complexities and competing values arise. Only the uncovered site, fragmentary and damaged, is (or was) the actual western terminus of the Erie Canal. It not only *represents* but actually *is* a vestige of the past. Because of this, it has claims on attention that a replica would not, even though a replica might *look more like* the original site in its entirety. But why, exactly? After all, an old slip now in ruins isn't much like the way it was when it was whole and functioning. Therefore, surely a good reproduction would catch the imagination and evoke a more convincing encounter with past times—or so it might seem. If one wants acquaintance with the past, wouldn't the greater verisimilitude of appearance better prompt an excursion into a bygone time? The planners of the canal replica project apparently presumed that a reproduction slip and surrounding historical reenactment would have greater popular appeal, but this surmise was wrong. In this book I explore why.

I shall advance the thesis that *genuineness*—being the *real thing*—is a status that possesses a value that has several different aspects. The informational significance of real things for historical understanding is probably obvious, for only true objects from the past stand as evidence of the technology, the art, and the daily life of those who lived before us. As such the importance of their preservation is rarely questioned, assuming that the objects under consideration are sufficiently important (an assessment to be pursued in due course). But in addition to providing evidence for historians and archaeologists, a genuine artifact also has ethical and aesthetic value. The former is evident when cultural artifacts are willfully damaged or destroyed and a moral wrong is perceived to have been done—to the culture that produced them, to those who continue to treasure them, perhaps even to the objects themselves (though this possibility requires careful articulation). The case for aesthetic value comes into focus with the differing appeal of the experience of a real thing as opposed to a replica, though the grounds for that difference are somewhat elusive. This claim probably will raise the most eyebrows, and therefore it receives the greatest scrutiny here.

Two approaches to the past

The stir over the remnants of the Erie Canal is not an isolated phenomenon. It represents one side of two strong and largely opposing tendencies in contemporary culture. The first is toward preservation of the past with its intact remnants protected. That protection can be adamant or flexible. One can be a purist about preservation or accommodate a degree of change, for buildings and other structures can be repurposed in such a way that they take on new uses while deliberately retaining evidence of their original identity and function. Preservation is by no means a universal or transhistorical value, but to many it seems especially urgent these days given galloping losses of land to suburbs and malls, as well as recent events that heedlessly or willfully or vengefully have destroyed older cityscapes, buildings, and historical artifacts. Awareness of receding contact with the past summons concern about what is vanishing in the present. That which is genuine—and rare, for rarity commands attention to things that might once have been common—is foregrounded when so much around us is destroyed.

This is not a concern for professionals alone, though there are many engaged in the laborious and sometimes dangerous safeguarding of the physical remains of past cultures. But in addition, cases like the Erie Canal demonstrate a strong desire among the general public for direct, proximal acquaintance with things that have survived over time. Advocates for protecting artifacts from the past would likely agree with art historian George Kubler's observation:

> In effect, the only tokens of history continually available to our senses are the desirable things made by men . . . Like crustaceans we depend for survival upon an outer skeleton, upon a shell of historic cities and houses filled with things belonging to definable portions of the past.[1]

The wish to retain the presence of authentic historical artifacts is counterbalanced by an opposite of sorts, which might be loosely labeled a simulationist tendency. This contrary inclination offers engagement with objects and the information they convey by means of increasingly effective modes of reproduction and dissemination. It aims at the expansion of experience available through replication of the appearance of artifacts and places that are otherwise difficult or impossible to access. Among its governing premises is recognition that in many instances, the original object simply cannot be preserved in decent condition, and thinking it can be is delusory. Even if the real thing persists (perhaps reburied and safely underground or in a climate-controlled vault) more people can benefit from acquaintance with the past as well as with other cultures if that acquaintance is available by means of images, replicas and other reproductive techniques, or even by amusement enterprises such as theme parks.[2] Good simulations transport visitors to a time and

---

1. George Kubler, *The Shape of Time: Remarks on the History of Things* (New Haven, CT: Yale University Press, 1962) p. 1.

2. This assumes that such acquaintance is always a good thing, but this is contestable. For instance, North American First Nation peoples are often critical of cultural appropriation of sacred objects when they are wrested from context and made public.

place that at the same time they recognize are merely reproductions of what once was. But the artificial past might be presented with spectacular vivacity. While we may know that the thing before us is a contemporary contrivance, its appearance can be so convincing that imagination overtakes knowledge and enthralls with illusion. "To speak of things that one wants to connote as real, these things must seem real," remarks Umberto Eco. "The 'completely real' becomes identified with the 'completely fake.' Absolute unreality is offered as real presence."[3] From this perspective, the simulationist tendency seems to have both the appeal of popular entertainment and democratic values at its back.

The advent of digital reproduction techniques has expanded simulative possibilities to a degree hitherto unimaginable. Virtual worlds offer experiences that the real one lacks, and our expectations for "realistic" encounters are proportionately affected. Dramatic as these technologies have become, reproductive techniques have deep roots. The study of art has for centuries proceeded by means of plaster casts, engravings, copies, even descriptions, as well as by photography, all of which techniques disseminated images and information to a larger public than would otherwise have been possible. What is more, it has always taken more than mere physical proximity to become fully familiar with certain kinds of artifacts. The images on a cupola painting dozens of feet above one's head may be discernible only with the aid of binoculars or the zoom lens of a camera, for example. In the last century the ability to render details of paintings, sculptures, and architecture by means of transparent slide projection vastly aided close peering and magnification. It was also the means by which the history of art was taught to thousands who would never be acquainted with originals. In other words, although digital replications represent dramatic advances for simulation, issues regarding the values of authenticity, genuineness, and direct acquaintance with the real thing have a long history.

George P. Nicholas and Alison Wylie, "Archaeological Finds: Legacies of Appropriation, Modes of Response," in The Ethics of Cultural Appropriation, ed. James O. Young and Conrad G. Brunk (Malden, MA: Wiley-Blackwell, 2009): 11–54, esp. p. 21.

3. Umberto Eco, Faith in Fakes, trans. William Weaver (London: Secker and Warburg, 1986) p. 7.

In a sense the phenomenon of reproduction produces the conditions for which encounters with originals are made notable, rather in the way that only with the introduction of artificial flavors can one extol the virtue of genuine vanilla. Or perhaps it is more apt to say that the possibility of reproduction summons notice of the differing aspects of such encounters. But this observation can give rise to either of two opposite positions: either reproduction summons awareness that one is *not* experiencing the real thing but only a stand-in. Or reproduction provides a convenient and informative means of seeing "through" a copy to its original. The former interpretation can be developed to support the values of preservationism; the latter suggests that simulation is sufficient and even advantageous. To choose between the two we need to ask a further question: Does, or can, the experience of reproductions—the copies, the images, the simulacra—supplant the experience of originals altogether?

Many museums now make their collections available on websites, a boon to those unable to travel or who desire information quickly. Constraints of time mean that for many of us, the virtual form is the only one that we shall ever encounter. Indeed, some museums are themselves only virtual, possessing no material counterpart at all. Certain archaeological sites are being reconstructed virtually while leaving their material vestiges alone, a technique that actually might benefit the preservation of the original substances. What is more, when artifacts such as ancient ruins are destroyed, the record of what they once were can be preserved in detail, and their appearance prior to destruction can be resurrected by means of digitally produced replicas.[4] One could argue that perhaps the past is actually better preserved by means of extraordinary simulacra that circulate information about its qualities, because the experience we can have by means of representations of all sorts is both available to many and fuller in content compared to encounters with whatever fragile fragments might still persist.

This last point is important even without worries about the utter destruction of historical artifacts, for it is easy to be misled

---

4. For a vigorous advocacy of the importance of digitally produced records and replicas, see the Institute for Digital Archaeology: http://digitalarchaeology.org.uk/ (Accessed 8.3.16). This technique is discussed in more detail in Chapter 4.

about the material legacy that remains to us. Even if some original object is preserved—the Erie Canal, the Ishtar Gate, the Mostar Bridge, the Sistine Chapel ceiling—it may require massive restoration, including replacement of missing or damaged components with replica parts. As they accumulate, those replacement parts become the immediate objects of experience, even if we are right before an original site. As a consequence, people frequently fool themselves about being in the presence of the real thing, if by that is meant the exact original object. Therefore a case can be made that an outright simulation—replica, model, mock-up, virtual tour—is superior both because it is fuller and more detailed and because it is less deceptive.

In spite of the cogency of the above considerations, however, and with due recognition of their importance, I am going to argue that simulacra can by no means completely supplant the importance of the genuine article. This is probably no surprise, for few actually want to jettison originals altogether. But my point runs deeper than a taste for preservation, for I claim that the *experience* of the genuine is *in principle* not transferable to its representations, no matter what form they may take. In this endeavor I defend some concepts that may appear to be relics of a bygone era whose values are no longer relevant, but I contend that the retention of the genuine object from the past, the authentic, the original, the *real* one, is just as valuable as ever—possibly even more so. The impetus for this position goes beyond nostalgia. However, firm reasons that underwrite it are not easy to come by, for the ones that seem most obvious are readily undermined, as we shall see in the course of this study.

The thesis in brief

My argument on behalf of the authentic, original, genuine, real artifact will take some time to develop, though to anticipate, I intend to show that:

(1) The property *authentic* or *genuine* is both a descriptive and an evaluative property. The value it possesses can be cognitive, aesthetic,

or ethical, or all three at once, depending on the type of thing in question. It is particularly tricky to vindicate genuineness as an aesthetic property, but this feature actually underwrites aspects of both ethical and cognitive value, a claim that implicitly builds in Chapters 2 and 3 and that is explicitly amplified in Chapter 4.

(2) Unlike other, more familiar, aesthetic properties, such as *beautiful, powerful, delicate, vivid,* or *dynamic,* genuineness is not directly perceptible, nor is it dependent upon descriptive perceptual properties such as shape, color, or design. As a consequence, in principle it is not reproducible. Not even the most accurate copy or replica can retain it.

(3) Therefore, the experience of an object by means of some other object that merely stands in for the real thing, including one that is perceptually indiscernible from the original, is never identical to an encounter with the genuine.

(4) While genuineness is not a perceptual property, the senses are fully engaged in its experience. Experience is almost always multisensory and encounters with artifacts usually involve sight, but the sense that I foreground is touch. Touch is not a standardly recognized aesthetic sense, and in many situations where one confronts something that is old and rare, actual contact is prohibited. Nonetheless, touch performs a covert but indispensable operation with the appreciation of the real thing.

All of these points are presented in Chapter 1 and elaborated throughout the rest of the book.

As the opening anecdote indicates, this study will proceed with a heterogeneous set of examples, including historical artifacts, nature, and works of art. Some of these are famous objects that have virtually uncontested global significance and are recognized as such by having become national treasures or world heritage sites. These are artifacts that so define a stage of culture that they have become not only evidence for but also emblems of history.[5] Such momentous

---

5. The British Museum launched a project to find in their collection 100 objects with such standing. The result was a popular television program and also a book by the same title: Neil MacGregor, *A History of the World in 100 Objects* (New York: Viking Press, 2011). See also Laurel Thatcher Ulrich, Ivan Gaskell, Sara J. Schechner, and Sarah Anne Carter, *Tangible Things: Making History through Objects* (New York: Oxford University Press, 2015).

significance by no means completely describes the importance of the real thing, however, and even more of the examples that I invoke are modest, having only local, domestic, or personal significance. The arguments that I present pertain equally to any object that carries its past into the present, whether humble or grand. A few examples are drawn from narrative fiction, but I avoid the invention of examples by means of the sorts of thought-experiments so frequently employed by philosophers. Actual events provide numerous cases that are dramatic, poignant, riveting, whimsical, and bizarre, sometimes outright goofy—presenting even more complexity than philosophic imagination is likely to conjure. Readers will be able to supply even more examples, for almost every city has some older structure valued for its history, and virtually every community, household, or even closet contains some fragment of the past that is treasured for reasons both common and idiosyncratic.

Anticipated objections

Despite widespread evidence that people value encounters with genuine things, as numerous accounts—to be sampled later—testify, a defense of this value faces some immediate objections. Here are four.

First of all it may be pointed out that holding old things dear enough to keep may be just a contemporary whim based on nostalgia and a taste for the antique that is entirely culture bound. Not all societies hang on to old things and mourn their loss.[6] Progress is frequently valued over preservation. After all, some European cities were built using the wrecked materials of antiquity, and icons of modern architecture such as some of Frank Lloyd Wright's houses were demolished for commercial reasons before being protected as historic sites. Granted, the value of artifacts is not always recognized before it is too late. Certainly multitudes of smaller objects have been lost through neglect and carelessness, and few tears have been

---

6. Interest in the past waxes and wanes, as David Lowenthal recounts in *The Past Is a Foreign Country* (Cambridge: Cambridge University Press, 1985) p. xvi and chapter 3.

shed over their loss. The historical moment in which old things are valued is certainly not permanent, and it would be foolish to deny that not everyone values the past in the way that I intend to defend. So yes, staying in touch with the past is "culture bound," if by that is understood "related to cultural values"—which are subject to change. But what else could it be? Both we and the artifacts we keep are products of culture, and the reasons why some things are considered worth preserving are complex and variable. Despite the lack of universality with which such value is held, we can still ask: When something old is preserved because its loss would be regretted, what lies behind that sentiment? What does it mean to say that the past is carried by or embodied in a thing? What kind of experience does it afford? These are the questions that interest me.

Second, it may be claimed that seeking authenticity is a deluded enterprise because there are no truly authentic artifacts left in the world. Time and history have changed everything and continue to do so. At present, it is the mere appearance of age that is trendy, nothing more. Distressed denim clothing or furniture that is painted and then sanded to look worn and old—both currently popular styles—provide evidence that authenticity is merely a *look*—a surface value that we can confidently predict will not endure beyond the fashions of the market. What is more, the world has changed and homogenized, and no culture has been untouched by others. Therefore, no cultural artifact can be considered truly authentic.[7] This objection presumes that in order to have any meaning at all, terms like "authentic" and "genuine" must be *pure*, must properly describe only things that are entirely unaffected by anything other than some remote originating conditions. Such a requirement would be doomed, violating both common sense and ordinary usage as well as the facts of commercial and artistic exchange that have characterized different societies since ancient times. Cultures are rarely static, nor do they develop in isolation from one another. Therefore, the notion of genuineness explored here is far from

---

7. Pico Iyer, "Keeping it Real," *T: The New York Times Style Magazine*, November 15, 2015:37–38. This article features a picture of Indonesian tourists being photographed with members of New Guinea's Dani tribe, a "stone age" culture that charges a fee to be in such photos.

purist. In any event, no such requirement is necessary. As we shall see, genuineness admits of degrees, and recognizing gradations and different meanings of what it means to be a real thing does not undermine the significance of the concept.

This objection is related to a third, which questions the accuracy of the vocabulary in use with preservationist values: "Authentic," "original," "real," and "genuine" are related but not synonymous terms, and all of them raise problems of meaning and application. Employing any of these terms invites an array of familiar puzzles: ontological, epistemic, ethical, and aesthetic. What counts as genuine or authentic for an object that inevitably changes over time, for example, especially one that has been damaged and restored? Given such change, by what means do we recognize genuineness? The notion of being original provokes similar skepticism. With many cultural products, including the opening example of the Erie Canal (or any very large artifact, such as Notre Dame Cathedral or China's Great Wall) it is impossible to pinpoint the exact moment—or even year—when the object came into being. Therefore, how does one situate the notion of an original thing? And furthermore, how can one justify the claim that a reproduction does not provide the same experience as the real thing if in fact they cannot be told apart? What does the ontological state of an object matter if it delivers a full and enjoyable experience? While not inseparable, these questions are sufficiently connected that responses to one have consequences for the others, and I hope that satisfactory answers will unfold in the course of this book.

I use all of these terms to conduct this study, including "genuine" and—more riskily—"authentic."[8] (The latter is particularly open-ended because of its many uses in existential accounts of the self.) All these terms have wide currency that lends them a degree

8. "Authentic" is used with striking breadth of connotation in philosophy, anthropology, and culture at large. As Charles Lindholm observes of the term, "At a minimum, it is the leading member of a set of values that includes sincere, essential, natural, original, and real." *Culture and Authenticity* (Malden, MA: Blackwell, 2008) p. 1. Lindholm is particularly enlightening about the many meanings of "authentic." For a sampling of other analyses see also Lionel Trilling, *Sincerity and Authenticity* (Cambridge, MA: Harvard University Press, 1971); Charles Guignon, *On Being Authentic* (London and New York: Routledge, 2004); and George E. Newman and Rosanna K. Smith, "Kinds of Authenticity," *Philosophy Compass* 11:10 (2016): 609–618. 10.1111/phc3.12343.

of ambiguity. But short of inventing an entirely new vocabulary, one must simply commandeer the available language, wending through different meanings and emphases in the course of discussion. The term that I actually like best is "real"—or Real, for I sometimes capitalize for emphasis. "Real" is a deceptively colloquial word that is also metaphysically fraught. But it is particularly apt for this study because *real* invokes the brute, material presence of artifacts and the bodily, palpable encounters with them that bring the past alive.[9] The emphasis I place on the sense of touch makes attention to physical presence especially pertinent.

Finally, there is a fourth objection that has received extensive scholarly treatment, namely, that originality and authenticity are outdated notions that harken back to premodern values. This objection folds together the first three into a fuller and more subtle rejection of the value of singularity or genuineness for cultural artifacts, as well as a skepticism about what is sometimes called the *aura* of special objects.

Aura

Authenticity, acquaintance, and presence are concepts that are all related to the elusive quality that Walter Benjamin famously dubbed "aura." The idea that artworks are no longer regarded as unique and singularly located was analyzed by Benjamin in his 1934 essay, "The Work of Art in the Age of Mechanical Reproduction," in which he argued that the ability to replicate objects—through images, sounds, films, print—disperses aesthetic objects throughout the range of the technique of reproduction, in effect detaching the object of appreciation from its origin. "The presence of the original is the prerequisite to the concept of authenticity," he remarked; but the authority of the object is diminished by multiplication.[10] Reproduction

9. In a similar vein (though for a different purpose), Jesse Prinz notes that "real" refers to "properties that can be truly and falsely ascribed . . . discourse about the real is truth-apt." Prinz, "Really Bad Taste," in *Knowing Art: Essays in Aesthetics and Epistemology*, ed. Matthew Kieran and Dominic McIver Lopes (Dordrecht: Springer, 2006): 95–108, on p. 96.

10. Walter Benjamin, "The Work of Art in the Age of Mechanical Reproduction," *Illuminations*, trans. Harry Zohn (New York: Harcourt, Brace, Jovanovich, 1968) p. 222.

compromises singularity and reduces that sense of being set apart from ordinary things that gives rise to aura.

> That which withers in the age of mechanical reproduction is the aura of the work of art . . . One might generalize by saying: the technique of reproduction detaches the reproduced object from the domain of tradition. By making many reproductions it substitutes a plurality of copies for a unique existence. And in permitting the reproduction to meet the beholder or listener in his own particular situation, it reactivates the object reproduced.[11]

There is a paradoxical aspect to the experience of aura, which Benjamin describes as a "phenomenon of distance." For an atmosphere of otherness persists even when one is in the presence of an object whose singularity and rarity impart a sense of occupying its own sacrosanct space, apart from the ordinary world of objects for which multiples are typical. However, when a replica can transmit the qualities of the original, the value of genuineness becomes obsolete. Therefore, says Benjamin with more than a whisper of regret, what remains of aura is its sentimental residue: a misplaced reverence for relics, a worship of the cult of the artist. In other words, if notions such as aura pertain to unique, nonreproducible art and artifacts, and if all aspects of art and artifacts are now in principle reproducible, then aura—and with it authenticity or genuineness—adds nothing to aesthetic encounters. In fact, it is more likely a product of overheated imagination. "Aura" connotes something mysterious and occult, a glow or shimmer like a halo; but also like a halo it possesses dubious ontological status.

Several elements of aura are suggested in Benjamin's text. Absent the ability to replicate an object, in order to perceive it one must be in its presence. If the object is of special importance, that experience also inspires reverence. The religious overtones of such encounters carry political implications, for aura inspires a giving-over of agency to the authority of the object. Hence with artifacts

11. Benjamin, "Work of Art," p. 223.

such as films and photographs for which there is no single original object, Benjamin projects a possibility of greater independence
of critical thought. At the same time, there is a loss of something
unique. For all its progress, the forward-looking present leaves behind something precious in the traditions of the past. In certain
respects aura is a retrospective phenomenon. Changes in technology bring about changes in our affective attention, and lost with
aura is wonder and awe at the singular, one of a kind object.[12]

Benjamin's ideas and politics were adjusted and simplified for
a later generation by John Berger in the popular 1972 BBC documentary and book, both titled *Ways of Seeing*. Berger agrees that
ease and accuracy of reproduction diminish the aesthetic potency
of the genuine. He endorses Benjamin's idea that human perception itself changes with advances in technology. "During long
periods of history," Benjamin wrote, "the mode of human sense
perception changes with humanity's entire mode of existence."[13]
Therefore, Berger asserts, what once was cherished as an aspect of
aesthetic encounters is no longer salient. Valuing the unique original is mere "mystification," he says, and it prompts an attitude that
envelops art in "an atmosphere of entirely bogus religiosity."[14] Even
more radically, Jean Baudrillard argues that postmodern societies
themselves are organized wholesale by means of simulacra.[15]
From such perspectives the concept of the unique original thing
is otiose and obsolete. I do not reject these observations completely
as characterizations of contemporary technological outcomes.
Nonetheless, I believe that a core of importance for genuineness is
ineradicable.

Benjamin's own views are particularly complex and ambiguous, sufficiently redolent with nostalgia to make his declarations

12. See also Stephen Greenblatt on wonder in "Resonance and Wonder," *Exhibiting Cultures: The Poetics and Politics of Museum Display*, ed. Ivan Karp and Steven D. Lavine (Washington, DC: Smithsonian Institution, 1990): 42–56.

13. Benjamin, "Work of Art," p. 224.

14. John Berger, *Ways of Seeing* (London: BBC/Penguin Books, 1972) p. 21; see also p. 34.

15. Jean Baudrillard, *Simulacra and Simulation* (1981), trans. Sheila Faria Glaser (Ann Arbor: University of Michigan Press, 1995). Whereas premodern society engaged in symbolic exchange and modern society is characterized by production, postmodern society is wholly determined by images and signs.

about the demise of aura far from triumphant.[16] Both his work and the concepts of authenticity and aura are widely employed in a variety of scholarly enterprises, sometimes in ways that are relevant to this study and sometimes in ways that are not.[17] My own references to aura will occasionally resonate with Benjamin's tantalizingly opaque text and in other ways will represent an independent usage of the term.[18] Despite the occasional wiftiness of its connotations, I find the term appropriate to pick out the sorts of objects that are the focus of this study. If some valuable properties are hidden from perceptual discernibility, then they are in principle not reproducible. For this and other reasons, the sense of singular encounter captured by the term "aura" has not been expunged by the ever-increasing possibility of indistinguishable simulacra. In the course of this study I shall pursue the nature of genuineness as a property that warrants the value attached to the notion of aura, which properly understood is far from mere mystification. Rather, it aptly describes encounters with objects notable for their age, rarity, or singularity, and only Real Things qualify.

Encounters thus characterized are never simple perceptual events; they involve the exercise of imagination, background knowledge, and immediate sensory experience. A major theme of this book concerns the sense of touch. I speculate that underlying encounters with the genuine is the operation of touch, which philosophers from Aristotle to the present have considered the sense that, while not infallible, gives us the most reliable access to external physical reality. The urge to touch is common when encountering objects singled out for their age and historical uniqueness. (As one

16. As many have noted, Benjamin's attitude toward aura is ambiguous. I have emphasized the nostalgia for aura here rather than his anti-fascist politics. For nostalgia as a component of postmodernism, see Jean-François Lyotard, *The Postmodern Condition: A Report on Knowledge,* trans. Geoff Bennington and Brian Massumi (Minneapolis: University of Minnesota Press, 1984).

17. Benjamin engaged in debates with other members of the Frankfurt School regarding modes of artistic production and freedom to resist the authority of state-sanctioned culture. Although this scholarship represents one context in which the issue of authenticity has an important role, it is not directly relevant to this study. On the relationship among Benjamin, Brecht, and Adorno in postmodernist debates see Robert Kaufman, "Aura, Still," *October* 99 (Winter 2002): 45–80.

18. Thomas Leddy has also revived a use of "aura" in *The Extraordinary in the Ordinary: The Aesthetics of Everyday Life* (Peterborough, Ont.: Broadview Press, 2012).

writer to the *Buffalo News* declared when it appeared that the Erie Canal terminus would remain buried: "The trip back would be so much easier for me if I could reach out and touch the walls of the Commercial Slip."[19]) Touch provides a sense of being in the very presence of an object—within touching distance. This is the case, I maintain, even though the reigning requirements maintained by museums and other places where objects or rarity or age are on display usually prohibit handling their objects. Their very nearness stands in place of actual touch, and proximal acquaintance is the event to savor, a point defended in Chapter 1. In all such encounters, touch plays a crucial, delicate, and sometimes treacherous role. It is crucial because certain aesthetic responses can only occur before an object that is what one takes it to be—in other words, that is genuine. It is delicate because genuineness is not an all or nothing affair. And it is treacherous because one can make so many mistakes about objects whose identity is presumed with little direct evidence.

My emphasis on the role of touch leads to a focus on material things, remnants of history that still take up space, can be visited and, in theory at least, handled. Other sense modalities offer their own routes into bygone times. A man hiking by ancient petroglyphs in Utah recounts a moment when amid the silence he heard the whoosh of a bird's wing nearby: "It stopped me in my tracks. The past has never left us. It is present to this day, and I heard the past come back alive."[20] Hiking through what remains of wilderness areas can seem to erase the immediacy of the urban present by means of the sheer physical effort of making one's way through unmanaged nature. The open-minded listening demanded by many kinds of music may bring the pasts of different cultures to our ears, prompting us to wonder if we hear now as we would have in another historical era.[21] Old records preserve for us the voices of singers long

19. Jack Kempf, "Reburying the Canal Doesn't Make Sense," "Viewpoints," *Buffalo News*, August 30, 1999, p. 3B.

20. Malcolm Lehi, Ute Mountain Ute tribal council member, quoted in Jack Healy, "Remote Utah Enclave Becomes Battleground Over Reach of U.S.," *New York Times*, Sunday, March 12, 2016, pp. 1 and 16. Quoted on p. 16.

21. Peter Kivy, *Authenticities: Philosophical Reflections on Musical Performance* (Ithaca, NY: Cornell University Press, 1995).

dead, and the scratches and jumps of their recordings are not just technical flaws but also poignant signs of the gap of time between listener and singer. Similar impressions emerge from the flickers of early films or the faded edges of photographs. Objects of taste and smell are harder to preserve, but these senses also provide routes that promise to take one into the past. The currently popular revivals of ancient recipes and vanished cuisines represent attempts not only to replicate older style foods but also to enter into worlds of taste long gone. In other words, remnants of the past come in many different forms and engage different sense modalities both individually and together. Here I examine what it means to be a genuine or real thing whose material presence summons the past it endured. As we shall see, touch is frequently invoked with such encounters; and because it is a relatively under-analyzed sense in aesthetics and in philosophy generally, it will be the focus of my inquiries.

I begin in Chapter 1 by laying out the main argument of the book, including the idea that "genuine" names a perceptually indiscernible aesthetic property, a thesis that disputes the common notion that the latter term refers chiefly to qualities of appearance. I am hardly alone in rejecting the idea that aesthetic properties are all surface properties available immediately to the senses. Many theorists have argued that one must presume certain facts about works that are not immediately apparent to inspection in order to categorize and assess them properly. However, I think that one of the most compelling reasons to look beneath the surface tends to be neglected because of the habit of thinking of the so-called aesthetic senses in terms of vision and hearing, a habit I hope to correct with some reflections on the sense of touch. Although this sense obviously registers tactile properties such as smooth or sticky, it also has a nonsensuous role to play in experiences with the genuine. From there I shall assemble arguments from several directions, including some observations about emotions, until discovering the core of aura and the assortment of values it signifies.

Doubtless many of the objects valued as genuine are not what we believe them to be, and the phenomenon that I call "aesthetic deception" is the focus of the second chapter. In defending the values attached to objects of special, even singular, significance, one must also acknowledge the many missteps, mistakes, delusions, and bald stupidities that can befall misdirected admiration. Examination of both the legitimate and the mistaken will thus proceed in tandem. From the mere fact that one can be deceived about valuing something because it is genuine—because it is what one takes it to be— we cannot conclude that there is no force to the value. While the main point of this study is to make that case on behalf of physical objects, the argument is enhanced when one notices that precisely the same phenomenon of valuing and deception occurs when the object of one's attention is another human being. Chapter 3 pursues this point by considering genuineness as a quality of persons. This parallel explores genuineness as a basic aspect of human relations both with one another and with things, preparing the way for an exploration of the ethical dimension of being the real thing. Here also is introduced the role of emotions in valuing both persons and artifacts in their singular identity, an affective phenomenon that I believe substantially illuminates both the aesthetic and the ethical standing of genuineness.

While the arguments of the first chapter focus on the claim that genuineness is an aesthetic property, it is more apt to speak of it as a general value property that has an aesthetic aspect. Chapter 4 shows how it can be both an aesthetic and an ethical property at one and the same time, especially, though not exclusively, when one considers objects that serve as memorials. Memorial sites convey a sense of history and place, where those who lived before us suffered, endured, or perished. This chapter also explores why the destruction or mistreatment of artifacts can be morally wrong. Destruction takes various forms; artifacts become worn from use and damaged not only by accident but also by intent, especially when they become targets of warfare and revenge. Mistreatment can even be well intentioned, a fact that introduces controversies over preservation and restoration. Repair both returns an object to its former appearance and reduces the physical integrity of original materials. This inescapable fact opens a fissure in the object of perception, that is, between what can be seen and what can be touched. By this point it will be clear that preserving the authenticity of objects is no mean feat, and I shall argue on behalf of the necessity of compromised standing— inevitable but important in considering what it means to be genuine.

The discussion builds toward a picture of what terms like "genuine" or "authentic" mean when they are applied to objects, as well as to the experiences we have of old things. It will be evident as the argument progresses that there are numerous zones of ambiguity, partiality, and compromise that arise with the standing that is accorded objects from the past. Only after pondering the range and diversity of such things are we in a position to address the issues covered in Chapter 5: an account of the conditions of identity of objects that are valued for their singularity, their rarity, or their age. The diversity of things that permit us to visit the past advises a complex ontology that accommodates change, and with it flexible criteria for something remaining the real thing over long stretches of time. I do not attempt here to formulate a complete ontology of the genuine. However, the picture of real things that builds throughout this study is apt to raise a few metaphysical eyebrows. Therefore, the final chapter anticipates some objections that might be raised when my account seems to violate some common metaphysical assumptions. In the course of answering those, a general picture of the parameters of genuineness emerges.

At the end as well as the beginning I again address the role of touch in encounters with the genuine. Attention to this sense complicates an account of identity through time, for touch conveys the impression of contact with the past, and yet the object in the present is often not physically identical with the one in the past, having been damaged and restored to such a degree that most or all of its parts have been replaced. Not only persistence of physical matter but also the role of practice and tradition will figure intermittently but importantly in an account of objects valued because they are genuine. The pursuit of the Real Thing thus takes a crooked path.

During the years that I have been writing this book, the world has seen a tragic upsurge of armed conflict and the brutal, deliberate destruction of persons, populations, and cultural artifacts that have been treasured as embodiments of history for centuries. A few of these examples are discussed here, and doubtless as time goes by there will be more to add to the tally. Authors usually welcome the timeliness of their subjects, but in this case, I wish it were otherwise.

Even without the urgency of war, questions of destruction, replacement, and preservation confront every expanding society on earth. I hope that this meditation will shore up the importance of genuineness even while granting its various degrees and often its partial status. Not everything can or ought to be saved. But it is difficult to make judgments about what is worth saving without investigation of the nature, meaning, and value of the things that linger from the past. This study will not answer all of the questions that arise in practice, but I hope it will provide a framework within which real issues about saving and discarding, nostalgia and practicality, preservation and change might be illuminated.

1

Touch and the Genuine

In this chapter I put forward the idea that genuineness possesses an aesthetic aspect. As will become clear, this is not a standard use of "aesthetic," but I think it is the best available concept to understand the thrill of encounters with things that are prized for being original, authentic, rare, very old, or unusually special. To ready us for the fray, let us consider another example that confirms widespread public interest in the real thing.

In early 2009 on the occasion of the two-hundredth anniversary of Abraham Lincoln's birth, it was reported that

> When the Library of Congress put the original Gettysburg Address on display, the line was blocks long. But when they submitted a "modern facsimile so accurate that the naked eye of an untrained person could not tell the difference" . . . there was no line. People wanted to see the authentic document, the one that Lincoln touched.[1]

---

1. "Lincoln's Manuscripts Reveal a Constant Reviser," National Public Radio, February 12, 2009. At www.npr.org/templates/story/story.php?storyId=100531323 (Accessed 2.12.09). The internal quotation is from Library of Congress Archivist John Sellers.

As has been indicated already, this account of public enthusiasm for an original, unique artifact contains a puzzle. If the eye cannot discern a difference between the original Gettysburg Address and a faithful copy, what is it that people want to see? In many such situations there is no perceptual means to distinguish the original object from a skillful replica. Is there, then, no defensible difference between the experience of a genuine object and good copy? Does only the original broadcast an aura, to invoke Benjamin's famous term? Without the ability to distinguish original from copy, how could we tell which one has the aura?

Those visiting the Library of Congress cherish the opportunity just to encounter a physical object that is identified as *the* Gettysburg Address. They are not there to read it. Indeed most have already read it (though now the referent of "it" has shifted to one of the text's many copies). They likely are already familiar with the battlefield where it was delivered; and if they want to learn about the American Civil War, a history textbook is easy to find. There is nothing to learn by seeing the paper that Lincoln held and no moral message to ponder that could not be prompted by other means. The only reason to view the Gettysburg Address is just to do so—to see an important artifact penned by this particular president. It is this phenomenon that suggests that there is an aesthetic dimension of genuineness.

However, counting genuineness among the properties that arouse aesthetic admiration may seem in principle unlikely, because it pertains to a fact regarding origin that is itself perceptually undetectable. Even an expert can be fooled by a fake, at least for a while. Objects of dubious provenance require scientific testing before they can be authenticated. As a rule, genuineness is part of the understanding that audiences bring to encounters with artifacts, but it is presumptive rather than noticed in the moment. What is more, according to a prevailing analysis, aesthetic properties are dependent upon other observable characteristics of objects. Since physical artifacts and their perceptible characteristics are replicable, good copies should have the same aesthetic appeal as originals. But they do not. This claim is widely noted. Replicas do not draw crowds when on museum display, for instance. The general public flocks to visit things that would be overlooked if copies stood in for originals, even though good copies are both informative about and can completely duplicate the appearance of original real things. As a writer for the *New York Times* remarked about the charm of genuine artifacts, "These traces have a powerful effect partly because we know they are authentic. Reproductions, even if expertly made, would disappoint."[2] But what does knowledge or belief contribute to perceptual appearance?

A glimpse of the answer is provided by Georg Simmel, who speculated about the importance of vestiges of the past in his famous essay, "The Ruin." Simmel is most interested in architectural ruins, but his comments extend to smaller artifacts as well.

> In the case of the ruin, the fact that life with its wealth and its changes once dwelled here constitutes an immediately perceived presence. The ruin creates the present form of a past life, not according to the contents or remnants of that life, but according to the past as such.
>
> This also is the charm of antiquities, of which only a narrow-minded logic can assert that an absolutely exact imitation equals them in aesthetic value. No matter if we are deceived in an individual case: with this piece which we are holding in our hand, we command in spirit the entire span of time since its inception; the past with its destinies and transformations has been gathered into this instant of an aesthetically perceptible present.[3]

This forceful assertion contains the three points that I want to pursue: that encounters with artifacts of great age or special rarity possess an aesthetic dimension; that no substitute or replica can possess that dimension (though we can certainly be fooled in the individual case); and that the sense of touch plays an especially central role in the encounter: *with this piece that we hold in our hand the past is gathered into an aesthetically perceptibly present.*

---

2. Edward Rothstein, "Artifacts with a Life All Their Own," *New York Times*, May 29, 2014: 5/31/2014 NYTimes.com. Print version May 30, 2014, p. C21.

3. Georg Simmel, "The Ruin," trans. David Kettler, in *Georg Simmel, 1858–1918: A Collection of Essays, with Translations and a Bibliography*, ed. Kurt H. Wolff (Columbus: Ohio State University Press, 1959): 259–66, on pp. 265–266.

But again, whether or not one holds an original thing or a deft copy may not be determinable by scrutiny in the moment, which is a predictable aspect of the fact that being genuine is not a perceptual property. Of course, if a replica or reenactment is amateurish and badly done, the discrepant styles between the original and the bad copy are evidence for absence of genuineness. But there are plenty of excellent copies, not to mention misattributed objects, which command admiration that is withdrawn when they are discovered not to be the real thing. And yet there is no perceivable difference to separate the object of early admiration from the later reassessment. Perhaps, therefore, the charm of the genuine is merely the fantasy of a fervid imagination. Those who follow the line of thought expressed by Benjamin and Berger, discussed in the Introduction, may well dismiss such sentiments as a residue of the cult of the artist or a superstition akin to regard for magical talismans.[4] Defending encounters with the genuine requires two lines of address: one concerning what is meant by "aesthetically perceptible" and the other analyzing touch.

Touch and the aesthetic

The invocation of touch as an aesthetic conduit may seem odd at first, for not only is actual touch usually prohibited to anyone but the expert scholar or the lucky discoverer of an artifact, tactile qualities are not the focus of admiration in the encounters being considered.[5] Simmel is not talking about the sorts of sensible qualities that touch is designed to transmit—smooth, sticky, prickly, curving, and so forth. This is not to say that tactile

4. To update this sentiment: Roger Michel of the Center for Digital Archaeology observes that in the west we are "fetishistic about originality. We want to touch the object that the master touched." He relates this "fetishism" to the medieval Christian cult of relics. (Interview with Scott Simon, NPR Weekend Edition, April 2, 2016: http://www.npr.org/programs/weekend-edition-saturday/2016/04/02/472784684/weekend-edition-saturday-for-april-2-2016?showDate=2016-04-02.) This view is discussed further in Chapter 4.

5. For a study of the changing role of touch in museums, see Fiona Candlin, *Art, Museums and Touch* (Manchester: Manchester University Press, 2010).

qualities themselves have no aesthetic role, which is clearly false. Certain objects, such as the small *netsuke* of Japan, are made for tactile admiration.[6]

But in the cases examined here, it is simply the *realness* of an artifact that is the target of admiration, and being real doesn't have any distinctive tactile qualities. Rather, touch seems to be invoked because it registers a singular thrill of contact with something old and rare. Such a thrill was reported by a treasure hunter diving off the Florida coast who plunged his hands into the sandy seabed and grasped a handful of Spanish doubloons. "Being the first person to touch something in over 300 years, there's a euphoric feeling that you'll never forget. . . . I couldn't believe what I was holding in my hand."[7]

Here are some more accounts that confirm the peculiar delight of encounters with the real thing and that also draw attention to the role of touch in this kind of experience.

Dan Lewis, the Senior Curator of the History of Science and Technology at the Huntington Library in California, describes the thrilling privilege of handling books housed in that collection, including Newton's own copy of the *Principia*, a first edition of Darwin's *Origin of the Species*, and Benjamin Franklin's manuscript autobiography. Lewis, who does not wear gloves, says that being able to handle such rare documents is like "being present at the moment of creation." "Just to be in their presence is an honor."[8] Such experiences evoke an impression that gaps of time have been momentarily bridged, bringing the past into the present. As one hiker tramping the route of Lewis and Clark remarks, "Walking in Meriwether Lewis' footsteps makes

6. Edmund De Waal, *The Hare with Amber Eyes: A Hidden Inheritance* (New York: Farrar, Straus, and Giroux, 2010). De Waal evokes not only the potency of touch in apprehending *netsuke*, but also the urgency of touch to retrieve the past. See also Yuriko Saito, *Everyday Aesthetics* (Oxford: Oxford University Press, 2007) esp. Ch. 4. And Gregory Currie, "Empathy for Objects," in *Empathy: Philosophical and Psychological Essays*, ed. Peter Goldie and Amy Coplan (Oxford: Oxford University Press, 2009): 82–96.

7. Brent Brisben, quoted in "Vacationing Family Finds Treasure Off Florida's Coast," July 30, 2015, National Public Radio Morning Edition, reported by Steve Inskeep. http://www.npr.org/2015/07/30/427648600/vacationing-family-finds-treasure-off-florida-s-coast (Accessed 8.21.2015).

8. "Paging through History's Beautiful Science," Joe Palca, National Public Radio Weekend Edition, Saturday, November 15, 2008. At npr.org. https://www.npr.org/templates/story/story.php?storyId=96957080 (Accessed 3.20.12).

my feet tingle."[9] This comment does not express appreciation of a pedal sensation but rather is a way of drawing attention to the fact that, quite apart from any of its manifest sensory qualities, touch furnishes a sense of being in actual, literal contact with something, or in this case some event, from the past. Similarly, a visitor to London noted, "I went through a door Shakespeare once went through, and into a pub he knew. We sat at a table . . . and I leaned my head back against a wall Shakespeare's head once touched, and it was indescribable."[10] Commenting on this phenomenon, David Lowenthal observes that "The shiver of contact with ancient sites brings to life their lingering barbarity or sanctity, and merely touching original documents vivifies the thoughts and events they described."[11]

At sites of old places, including both those that endure in their function and those that have become ruins, whole environments embody the material presence of the past. This passage from Nathaniel Hawthorne's novel *The Marble Faun*, though fictional, sums up the experience vividly:

One of the immense gray granite shafts lay in the piazza, on the verge of the area. It was a great, solid fact of the Past, making old Rome actually sensible to the touch and eye; and no study of history, nor force of thought, nor magic of song, could so vitally assure us that Rome once existed, as this sturdy specimen of what its rulers and people wrought.[12]

This description from another novel vividly evokes the experience of taking something in one's hands: "As many times as I've worked on rare, beautiful things, that first touch is always a strange and powerful sensation. It's a combination between brushing a live wire and stroking the back of a newborn baby's head."[13] The hand

---

9. Stephen Ambrose (quoting his wife), "Join Us on the Trail," *National Geographic Traveler* 19:2 (March 2002): 63.

10. Helene Hanff, quoted in David Lowenthal, *The Past Is a Foreign Country* (Cambridge: Cambridge University Press, 1985) p. 246.

11. Lowenthal, *Past*, p. 246. It should be noted that Lowenthal is somewhat skeptical about these shivers. His views are discussed further in Chapter 2.

12. Nathaniel Hawthorne, *The Marble Faun*, Ch. 16.

13. Geraldine Brooks, *People of the Book: A Novel* (New York: Penguin, 2008) p. 13.

FIGURE 1.1 *Reaching Through Time.*
Grand Gulch, Utah, 2007. Photo Mark
Pennington.

reaching to match the print of an ancient petrograph in Figure 1.1 illustrates the impulse to place oneself in literal contact with a trace of something from long ago. In this case the impetus to touch is amplified by the fact that the object is the outline of another hand.[14] Touch here is vividly a give-and-take affair, as the past seems to extend a hand into the present. In the case of a handprint this old, left for reasons we can only guess, it is unlikely that whoever left the original mark envisioned a matching touch so far in the future. However, there are cases where precisely that is intended. On the Cornell University campus sits a stone bench overlooking a long slope and a glimpse of the town below. The bench was erected in 1892 and bears these lines on its back:

> To those who shall sit here rejoicing
> To those who shall sit here mourning
> Sympathy and Greeting
> So have we done in our time.
> 1892 A.D.W – H.M.W.[15]

The lines invite one to sit in the same place and position where others have done, and to ponder lives from the past, not only through the words they left but also by means of the touch of the stone where they rested.

14. On the top of Biaterek tower in Astana, Kazakhstan, is a gilded handprint of the president Nazarbayev. http://www.cnn.com/2012/07/13/world/asia/eye-on-kazakhstan-astana/ (Accessed 9.26.16). There are reportedly queues lined up to touch it. I thank Robin Christopher for this tidbit.

15. The initials are those of Andrew Dickson White and his wife, Helen Magill White. http://ezra.cornell.edu/posting.php?timestamp=1176789600 (Accessed 1.21.13).

The phenomenal character of such encounters is hard to describe precisely, though I hope that readers will recognize what I am talking about: a shiver, a thrill, a poignant acknowledgement, a small dose of awe in the presence of the real thing—if, of course, that thing merits attention in the first place, a separate problem to be noted again later. Moreover, it is important to note that genuineness is aesthetically important not just for works of art but for artifacts of all sorts. The urge to touch extends beyond artifacts over an enormous range, including objects that nature produces such as fossils and giant redwood trees. I recall reading that after the meteor explosion over Chelyabinsk in 2013, many people scavenged to find fragments of meteorites, desiring to hold in their hands something that came from outer space.

The zone of appreciation I emphasize includes, for the most part, artifacts from the past that command attention for their rarity or singularity, evoking thrill, wonder, or awe. A feature of that thrill involves a heightened awareness of the passage of time such that for a moment history is present before one. Hence the title chosen for this book, for *things* can put us in touch with the past in an immediate and palpable way. All of the accounts mentioned here seek to describe a special moment of attention when in the presence of something unique, rare, or special. These thrills or shivers signal what I am calling an aesthetic encounter, a claim that requires some explanation.

What counts as aesthetic?

I anticipate an initial skepticism with this project. Why consider the experience of the genuine *itself* to be aesthetic at all? Perhaps the aesthetic qualities of objects simply don't travel well and diminish without the real thing to examine. One might visit another country to view works of art, the reproductions of which do not yield the objects' full aesthetic features. The tapestries of the *Lady with the Unicorn* series in Paris, for example, are more vivid and expressive in the subdued lighting of their special rotunda in the Cluny Museum than they are in any of the reproductions one encounters. But if this is all that is meant by the aesthetic value of genuineness—that originals have a better quality than copies—then genuineness would be simply a precondition for maximum excellence, not a quality that yields experience on its own. If this were the whole story, however, how could we explain the opening account of interest in the Gettysburg Address or the desire to visit historical sites and relics? Still, why insist that these encounters are examples of *aesthetic* experiences? Genuineness is already established as an important quality of objects as *historical* artifacts. Isn't this enough? I believe that the historical aspects of an object also have an aesthetic valence, one that is in fact implicit in the value of genuineness.

The extension of the term "aesthetic" to genuineness is not standard, but it isn't off the graph either, and in proposing this extension I employ an experiential account of the aesthetic, maintaining that the character of the encounter warrants the label. This approach is sometimes criticized on several grounds, including that there is no common affect that all instances of aesthetic experiences share; that reference to experiential quality does not allow for indifferent or negative aesthetic assessments; and that noticing aesthetic properties of objects can be done competently in the absence of any particular appreciative response at all.[16] However, I am by no means proposing any particular affective quality as the definitive mark of the aesthetic. Aesthetic experience describes extremely broad territory, making it unlikely that any single characterization can furnish the grounds for definition of the concept. Nonetheless, there is room to note that there are certain qualities that are characteristic of the response to objects of significant age or rarity. It is here that I would situate the thrill of an encounter with the genuine, and the term "aesthetic" does as well as any to describe it.

---

16. Noël Carroll criticizes experiential accounts of the aesthetic in *Beyond Aesthetics: Philosophical Essays* (Cambridge: Cambridge University Press, 2001) pp. 41–62. See also Carroll, "Art and the Domain of the Aesthetic," *British Journal of Aesthetics* 40:2 (2000): 191–208 and "Recent Approaches to Aesthetic Experience," *Journal of Aesthetics and Art Criticism* 70:2 (Spring 2012): 165–177. Carroll's own characterization of the aesthetic centers on art works, an approach that would narrow the scope of aesthetic encounters with artifacts to those exhibiting admirable design. For a defense of an experiential approach, see Alan H. Goldman, "The Experiential Account of Aesthetic Value," *Journal of Aesthetics and Art Criticism* 64:3 (2006): 333–342. See also Gary Iseminger, *The Aesthetic Function of Art* (Ithaca, NY: Cornell University Press, 2004).

Encounters such as these represent a kind of apprehension that has a singular affective intensity, directness, and immediacy, during which attention focuses upon the thing itself and the past it embodies, registering what art historian Alois Riegl singles out as age value. As he puts it, "Age value manifests itself immediately through visual perception and appeals directly to our emotions."[17] Although the two often come packaged together, age value is importantly different from historical value. The latter engages quests for information and knowledge about previous ways of life, whereas age value prompts a kind of wonder at the thing itself—marvel for its very being. Indeed, *wonder* is frequently invoked to describe this particular sort of experience.[18] Stephen Greenblatt suggests this account of the resonance that certain objects possess and the wonder they can inspire.

> By *resonance* I mean the power of the displayed object to reach out beyond its formal boundaries to a larger world, to evoke in the viewer the complex, dynamic cultural forces from which it has emerged and for which it may be taken by a viewer to stand. By *wonder* I mean the power of the displayed object to stop the viewer in his or her tracks, to convey an arresting sense of uniqueness, to evoke an exalted attention.[19]

The character of encounters with the genuine confirms their aesthetic aspect and—equally important—the difference between the

---

17. Alois Riegl, "The Modern Cult of Monuments" (1928), trans. Kurt W. Forster and Diane Ghirado, *Oppositions* (1982): 21–52, on p. 33. I extend the phenomenon to touch. Riegl himself did not hold touch in the highest esteem in an aesthetic role, as Candlin notes in *Art, Museums and Touch*, Ch. 1.

18. Jesse Prinz identifies wonder as an aesthetic emotion in "Emotion and Aesthetic Value," in *The Aesthetic Mind: Emotion and Psychology*, ed. Elisabeth Schellekens and Peter Goldie (Oxford: Oxford University Press, 2011): 71–88. See also Prinz, "Wonder Works: Renovating Romanticism about Art" blogpost at *Aesthetics for Birds*, August 5, 2013. http://www.aestheticsforbirds.com/2013/08/wonder-works-renovating-romanticism.html#more (Accessed 8.27.15).

19. Stephen Greenblatt, "Resonance and Wonder," in *Exhibiting Cultures: The Poetics and Politics of Museum Display*, ed. Ivan Karp and Steven D. Lavine (Washington, DC: Smithsonian Institution Press, 1991): 42–56 on p. 42.

experiential value of a replica and of the thing itself. And although I am identifying an experience as aesthetic partly on the basis of what it feels like (thrilling, shiver producing, awesome, marvelous[20]) there is no need to demand uniformity of phenomenal character for the event. It may be reverent, awed, wondering, or merely curious.[21]

There is an obvious cognitive prerequisite for this sort of experience, which requires that one believe one has correctly identified its object. The value of an encounter may be erased upon discovery of an error (a common phenomenon that is analyzed further in the next chapter). This need not entail, however, that one possess complete understanding of the nature of an object or its purpose. While correct or at least plausible interpretation is needed to discern many types of aesthetic properties, sometimes brute presence is affecting in itself. An element of encounters with old things is their strangeness and their resistance to being understood, what one archaeologist—invoking sublimity—calls "the ineffable otherness of the past."[22]

Descriptions of such encounters match several commonly mentioned features of the aesthetic. First of all, appreciating an object for just being itself has no purpose other than a kind of reverence for its presence. A relatively contemplative moment that is savored for itself rather than for any outcomes it might produce is one of the standard descriptions of experiences accorded aesthetic value, a concept that is often contrasted to moral, religious, economic, or strategic value because of its relative purposelessness. Or rather, for the fact that its purpose is just the experience it yields, for the term "purposeless" (borrowed from Kant) is intended to direct attention to the savoring of experience itself, not to dismiss it as useless, frivolous, or dispensable.

---

20. Kendall Walton, "How Marvelous! Toward a Theory of Aesthetic Value," *Journal of Aesthetics and Art Criticism* 51:3 (1993): 499–510.

21. For a brief on behalf of an aesthetic role for curiosity, see Carolyn Korsmeyer, "A Lust of the Mind: Curiosity and Aversion in Eighteenth Century British Aesthetics," in *Suffering Art Gladly: The Paradox of Negative Emotions in Art*, ed. Jerrold Levinson (Aldershot, UK: Ashgate, 2014): 45–67.

22. "The sublime is that mixture of terror and fascination experienced in the spectacle of stormy sea. In archaeology, for me, it is the experience of difference, the ineffable otherness of the past, and its fascinating presence to me now." Michael Shanks, *Experiencing the Past: On the Character of Archaeology* (London: Routledge, 1992) p. 191.

Second, genuineness occasions a response that engages both emotions and perception in the way that more standardly recognized aesthetic experiences do. (This point is elaborated in Chapter 3.) And like a fairly traditional account of aesthetic assessment, the experience of the genuine requires that we grant a version of the so-called principle of acquaintance.[23] According to the latter, no aesthetic judgment can be made unless one perceives first-hand the object being assessed. Just as one cannot judge the flavor of a soup without tasting it, one cannot confidently assess a musical performance without actually hearing it. No second-hand account can substitute for the first-hand experience. Critics of acquaintance deny that discernment of aesthetic properties always requires direct encounters with the original object; reliable judgments about at least some sorts of works may be made on the basis not only of reproductions but also of competent descriptions and surrogates.[24] Regardless of one's stand on acquaintance in general theories of the aesthetic, encounters with objects valued because they are genuine clearly do require first-hand experience. As Alexander Nehamas puts it, "A feature is aesthetic not because it is perceptual but because we can't be aware of it unless we perceive or experience directly . . . the object whose feature it is."[25] In cases of the genuine, acquaintance is not so much a prerequisite for sound assessment as a condition of having the experience at all. After all, encounters with things that embody their pasts evoke a sense of *presence*, of *being there*. Acquaintance is part of being there.

23. Richard Wollheim, *Art and Its Objects*, 2nd ed. (Cambridge: Cambridge University Press, 1980) p. 233.

24. Paisley Livingston analyzes various versions of the acquaintance principle and the arguments for and against in "On an Apparent Truism in Aesthetics," *British Journal of Aesthetics* 43:3 (July 2003): 260–278. See also Malcolm Budd, "The Acquaintance Principle," *British Journal of Aesthetics* 43:4 (October 2003): 386–392; Noël Carroll dismisses direct acquaintance with the example of conceptual art in "Aesthetic Experience: A Question of Content," in *Contemporary Debates in Aesthetics and Philosophy of Art*, ed. Matthew Kieran (Malden, MA: Blackwell, 2007): 69–97. Even if appreciation of conceptualism does not require direct experience, this kind of case would not pertain to other aesthetic encounters. Jerrold Levinson refers to direct acquaintance as a "shibboleth," but again this does not indicate that it never pertains: "Aesthetic Properties II," *Aristotelian Society Supplementary Volume* 79:1 (July 2005): 211–227.

25. Alexander Nehamas, *Only a Promise of Happiness: The Place of Beauty in a World of Art* (Princeton, NJ: Princeton University Press, 2007) p. 94.

Nonetheless, one may still doubt that these thrills and shivers are warranted by any quality of the object; rather, they may simply be the effect of an imagination that projects a difference between genuine and copy where no perceptually relevant distinction exists. Although I am approaching the concept of the aesthetic by way of its (plural but related) phenomenal characteristics, it is not the case that the mere experience in the moment suffices to ground encounters with the real thing. The status of the object is equally important. This demand also requires some further defense, including an evaluation and rejection of some older but intransigent attitudes.

At its etymological root "aesthetic" refers to perceptual admiration ensuing from sense experience, and for that reason some philosophers have concluded that aesthetic properties rest on the perceivable surface of objects—the way they look or sound, and the effects of their appearance on emotional response, imagination, or insight. If this be the case, the perceptual experience of an object encompasses its aesthetic properties in their entirety. No perceptual difference would entail no aesthetic difference. An influential article from the mid-twentieth century by J. O. Urmson, for some time widely anthologized and taught, defines aesthetic qualities as those that are presented immediately to the eyes or ears and thereby prompt affective response. According to this analysis, *appearance* in aesthetic situations is sufficient; *reality* is beside the point. As Urmson puts it, "What makes the appreciation aesthetic is that it is concerned with a thing's looking somehow without concern for whether it really is like that."[26] His declaration echoes that of a venerable predecessor, Kant, who asserts that pure aesthetic pleasure is aroused by appearance only and is indifferent as to whether the object in question even exists.

26. J. O. Urmson, "What Makes a Situation Aesthetic?" in *Art and Philosophy*, ed. W.E. Kennick (New York: St. Martin's, 1964 [1957]) p. 562. For an extension of this view to museum display see Curt John Ducasse, *The Philosophy of Art* (New York: Dover, 1966 [1929]) p. 10. Hilde Hein notes that museums are increasingly substituting visually indiscernible replicas to display in place of fragile artifacts, supplementing the objects with teaching tools such as virtual tours and interactive videos. Hilde Hein, "Museums—from Object to Experience," in *Aesthetics: The Big Questions*, ed. Carolyn Korsmeyer (Malden, MA: Blackwell, 1998): 103–115.

Defending genuineness as an aesthetically salient property requires rejecting the idea that aesthetic properties are all surface properties, and I have many allies in this cause.[27] Quite a number of theorists have argued that one must presume certain facts about works of art that are not immediately apparent to inspection in order to understand and assess them properly—indeed even in order to *see* or *hear* or *read* them properly. Kendall Walton has influentially argued that critical assessment of artworks implicitly places them in an appropriate category and context, and only then do their aesthetic properties become evident.[28] For example, if you look at a painting by Giotto without knowing anything about the history of spatial representational that came after him, you will not notice the depth or solidity of his works.

Genuineness has also received considerable attention with regard to the aesthetic status of forgeries, copies, or misattributions. Forgeries and fakes quite obviously have different economic value than do originals, and it is equally clear that they are morally problematic. The debatable philosophical question concerns claims about aesthetic differences between original and fake when the two might be perceptually indiscernible. If aesthetic properties are entirely manifest in the appearance of a work, what grounds do we have for valuing an original over a forgery that looks equally good? Indeed, if one is readily mistaken for the other? Reflecting on this question reveals the mistake of thinking that mere appearance covers all aspects of aesthetic value. A work of art is the result of a deliberate human action and may be considered a performance of sorts.[29] Unless one presumes accurately what kind of action or

---

27. Positions that locate aesthetic properties exclusively on what might be termed the perceptual surface of objects have been dubbed "aesthetic empiricism." As Gregory Currie describes this approach (which he goes on to criticize): "Empiricism finds its natural expression in aesthetics in the view that a work—a painting for instance—is a 'sensory surface'. What is aesthetically valuable in a painting can be detected merely by looking at it. Features that cannot be so detected are not properly aesthetic ones." Gregory Currie, *An Ontology of Art* (London: Macmillan, 1989) p. 17. More arguments against aesthetic empiricism are advanced by David Davies, *Art as Performance* (Malden, MA: Blackwell, 2004) Ch. 2; and R. A. Sharpe, "The Empiricist Theory of Aesthetic Value," *Journal of Aesthetics and Art Criticism* 58:4 (Fall 2000): 321–332.

28. Kendall Walton, "Categories of Art," *Philosophical Review* 79 (1970): 334–367.

29. For example, Denis Dutton, "Artistic Crimes," *British Journal of Aesthetics* 19 (1979): 304–314. Dutton argues that all art works are accomplishments in the manner of

performance a work represents, one is incapable of appreciating it for its period style or position in the history of creative development. To value a work for being innovative, for example, requires that it be among the first of its kind and situated in the right historical sequence, ruling out mere copies, whether or not they are intended to deceive. Besides, as Nelson Goodman has acutely observed, perceptually manifest qualities may not always be immediately apparent. Looking at a complex object such as a painting takes time and expertise before one can be certain that every single feature has been noticed. In his words, "The fact that I may later be able to make a perceptual distinction between the pictures that I cannot make now constitutes an aesthetic difference between them that is important to me now."[30] In other words, one should not be too confident about claims of perceptual indiscernibility.

Genuineness is thus already established as a property with many zones of value: historical, moral, economic, and—at least in a supporting role—aesthetic. By "supporting role" I mean that genuineness is deemed aesthetically relevant chiefly because it grounds the correct ascription of certain other properties, being presumed for the proper attribution of descriptions such as "path-breaking" or "representing the pinnacle of Baroque composition." This function, however, does not explicitly grant genuineness its own aesthetic standing. I maintain that genuineness—being the real thing—is also a property that commands attention in itself, and that this attention yields an experience that qualifies as aesthetic, though this term by no means describes its only value. My position, however, must wrangle with the apparent absence of perceptual foundation for this experience, given that an original object and a fine replica can be quite indistinguishable. Moreover, the use of indiscernible replicas to prompt appreciative experience is no doubt expedient in many situations. If in the absence of actual deception there is no moral disvalue, then what does it matter (aesthetically speaking) if

performances. See also Matthew Kieran, *Revealing Art* (London: Routledge, 2005) Ch. 1. For a more comprehensive theory of performance, including its relevance to forgeries, see Davies, *Art as Performance* (Malden, MA: Blackwell, 2004).

30. Nelson Goodman, *Languages of Art: An Approach to a Theory of Symbols* (Indianapolis: Bobbs-Merrill, 1968) p. 104.

the real object is carefully put away and an indiscernible copy is made available for public display? Or even if the real thing is lost and good substitutes remain?

The crucial question is whether experience is detachable from its object in such a way that a substitute produces a comparable experience. Alan Goldman is one of many who claim that "the aesthetic value of an artwork cannot come apart from the value of the experience of it," but he is equally adamant that the reverse is also true, that the value of the experience cannot be detached from the work itself.[31] A veridical aesthetic experience is one that is based upon an adequate understanding of the nature of the work before one. "An object itself would not be valuable for the experience it provides if it were not in large part causally responsible for that experience."[32] Experience must possess sufficient connection to its object to sustain the aesthetic value located therein. Of course, one can be fooled, as with any perceptual encounter. But being fooled constitutes a flaw in the experience itself, even if the flaw goes unrecognized. Granting this point further attaches experience to its intentional object, for the experience recognizes a value, and if the object of value is misidentified and does not possess the value (e.g., being rare or ancient), then the recognition that is part of the experience is ill-founded.

The next section pursues on different grounds the defense of a property—genuineness—that is in principle unperceivable yet legitimately affects the experience of an object. Most discussions of indiscernibility focus on whether one can *see* a difference between a real thing and a copy. But at the heart of encounters with the genuine, as the testimonies assembled here indicate, is the implicit operation of a sense often overlooked: touch. To be sure, experience in general is multimodal, and proximity can be registered by other senses as well: looming objects of vision, increased volume of sound, and so forth. Yet it is the sense of touch that provides us with a clue to the deepest attachment with the genuine, one that is compelling and perplexing in equal measure.

---

31. Goldman, "Experiential Account," p. 340. Also Matthew Kieran, *Revealing Art*, p. 14: "What matters regarding our attitudes to something is not just a function of what its inherent qualities are, but also a matter of the relations in which the object stands to us." I shall return to this idea in Chapter 4.

32. Goldman, "Experiential Account," p. 340.

Touch and presence

Touch is one of the so-called bodily senses (along with smell and taste) that are traditionally excluded from aesthetic operation, since the pleasures to be gained from tactile sensation allegedly qualify as merely sensuous and hence nonaesthetic. Philosophical thinking about the bodily senses is becoming more permissive, but my argument does not require that I elevate sensuous tactile experiences to aesthetic status, because the role of touch in the experience of authenticity is almost entirely non-sensuous.

Why is touch readily invoked when in the presence of things that have endured from the past? Perhaps because touch is the sense that is particularly attuned to the unmistakable presence of material objects. Philosophers from diverse perspectives have singled out touch as the sense that furnishes the most reliable confirmation of external physical reality. Aristotle regarded touch as the most basic sense in that it is necessary for the existence of any animal, and unlike sight and hearing, it has no external medium interposed between organ and object of perception.[33] "It is touch that gives us our sense of reality," remarks Bertrand Russell, ". . . our whole conception of what exists outside us, is based upon the sense of touch."[34] Russell observes how widespread is this intuition about touch by quoting Shakespeare, for when the dagger appears before Macbeth, he tests its reality by the sense of touch:

> Is this a dagger which I see before me,
> The handle toward my hand? . . .
> Art thou not, fatal vision, sensible
> To feeling as to sight? Or art thou but
> A dagger of the mind . . . [35]

In order for touch to sense its proper objects, it is necessary that one be in the physical presence of those objects. Indeed that one be sufficiently close that the two bodies might meet. Writing of Aristotle,

---

33. Aristotle, *De Anima* II: 421a–424a.
34. Bertrand Russell, *The ABC of Relativity* (London: Allen and Unwin, 1969 [1925]) p. 10.
35. *Macbeth*, Act II:1.

Pascal Massie notes that "Touch . . . is the sense of materiality par excellence; and this can occur only if the experience of presence is an experience of co-presence."[36] That is, one senses another object as being close to one's own body. The combination of physical presence and the solidity of contact means that the perceiver is intimately engaging the sense of touch, with or without actual contact (more on this below).

Since the aesthetic role I am attributing to touch has little to do with qualities of sensation, it is rather minimally illuminated by the venerable iconography associated with this sense.[37] Nonetheless, that iconography is interesting to consider insofar as it underwrites the presumption that touch puts us in more immediate contact with the physical world than do other senses. Jan Brueghel the Elder and Peter Paul Rubens's allegorical painting of Touch, for example, is filled with objects of manual use, such as tools and armaments; objects whose weight and shape are distinctive; tactile sensuousness is depicted in the caresses of Amor and Psyche (Figure 1.2).

Among the paintings depicted hanging above the latter is one of the standard images of touch: a blind man groping his way with the aid of outstretched hand and cane. Not only is this a familiar image, for it is indeed one means by which people with visual limitations can make their way in the world, it also indicates the coordination of touch and vision, for touch grasps in proximity what sight apprehends at a distance. The sense of touch is valued not only for the particular tactile qualities that it apprehends but also for the fact that it confronts objects as such—physicality in its most resistant, undeniable mode. As Steven Connor observes, "Touch is unlike the other senses in this, that it acts upon the world as well as registering the action of the world on you."[38] Touch provides an

---

36. Pascal Massie, "Touching, Thinking, Being: The Sense of Touch in Aristotle's De Anima and Its Implications," Existentia 23 (2013): 155–174; on p. 168. See also Robert Hopkins, "Re-Imagining, Re-Viewing, and Re-Touching," in The Senses: Classic and Contemporary Philosophical Perspectives, ed. Fiona Macpherson (Oxford: Oxford University Press, 2011): 261–283.

37. Robert Jütte, A History of the Senses from Antiquity to Cyberspace, trans. James Lynn (Cambridge: Polity Press, 2005) p. 74.

38. Steven Connor, The Book of Skin (Ithaca, NY: Cornell University Press, 2004) p. 263.

FIGURE 1.2 Brueghel, Jan the Elder (Velvet) (1568–1625) and Peter Paul Rubens. *Touch* 1617–18. Oil on panel. 0.64 x 1.11 m. Copyright of the image Museo Nacional del Prado / Art Resource, NY.

affectively powerful experience of presence—an encounter with material reality.

Such a role for touch has long been acknowledged, though more in epistemic than aesthetic situations. It is indicated in the old English saying, "Seeing's believing, but touching's the truth," which suggests that sight is prone to illusion that is correctable by extending the hand. Dr. Johnson defied Berkeley's idealism by kicking a stone and declaring: "I refute you thus!"—implying that the sheer contact of touch, the direct apprehension of a primary quality, belies the illusions cultivated by philosophers preoccupied with vision. Those who research the development of the sensorium observe that touch was the first sense to evolve and remains a foundation for an organism's orientation toward the world.[39]

Philosophers as diverse as Johann Gottfried Herder, George Berkeley, Maurice Merleau-Ponty, and more recently Mark Johnson, Brian O'Shaughnessy, and Matthew Fulkerson have taken note of

---

39. Even in individuals, according to Ashley Montagu, touch is the first sense to develop and the last to extinguish. *Touching: The Human Significance of the Skin* (New York: Harper and Row, 1986) p. 270.

the role in perception of the body and its movement, for we are not static creatures but move around, making contact with the world.[40] This fact, so basic that it sometimes falls beneath attention, is central to the shape of conscious experience. Herder regards touch as the reliable coordinate of vision when he remarks that "our sense of touch remains the solid foundation and guarantor of seeing."[41] O'Shaughnessy provides an update of sorts to Aristotle when he contends that touch, along with the body-sense of proprioception, is primordial. Touch is the fallback sense that is used to confirm evidence of the other four; indeed, touch is in general veridical.[42] This does not mean that we always accurately perceive the tactile qualities of objects, but we are seldom deceived about their presence, and as O'Shaughnessy says, "Tactile sensation is inessential to tactile perception."[43] This latter comment is especially relevant for my purposes, for it acknowledges the operation of the sense to produce an apprehension of position without haptic sensation of any sort. Even without sensation, touch is the sense of position and presence.

> In touch we become aware of extra-bodily objects through becoming aware of the unique body-object. That is, in touch we gain epistemological access to the world at large through immediate epistemological access to one small part of it: our own body.[44]

40. Johann Gottfried Herder, *Sculpture: Some Observations on Shape and Form from Pygmalion's Creative Dream*, trans. Jason Gaiger (Chicago: University of Chicago Press, 2002); George Berkeley, *An Essay towards a New Theory of Vision* (London: Dent, 1910 [1709]); Maurice Merleau-Ponty, *The Phenomenology of Perception*, trans. Colin Smith (London: Routledge and Kegan Paul, 1962); Mark Johnson, *The Body in the Mind* (Chicago: University of Chicago Press, 1987) and *The Meaning of the Body* (Chicago: University of Chicago Press, 2007); Brian O'Shaughnessy, *Consciousness and the World* (Oxford: Clarendon Press, 2000); Matthew Fulkerson, *The First Sense: A Philosophical Study of Human Touch* (Cambridge, MA: MIT Press, 2014). See also Suzanne Langer, *Feeling and Form* (New York: Charles Scribner, 1953) Ch. 6. Anthropologist Robin Dunbar speculates that touch is indispensable for social cohesion, and while he has the actual sensation in mind one could extend the idea in this direction: Dunbar, *Grooming, Gossip, and the Evolution of Language* (Cambridge, MA: Harvard University Press, 1996) Ch. 3.

41. Herder, *Sculpture*, p. 38. See also Andrew Benjamin, *Art's Philosophical Work* (London and New York: Rowman and Littlefield, 2015) Ch. 8.

42. O'Shaughnessy, *Consciousness*, p. 656, pp. 671–673.

43. O'Shaughnessy, *Consciousness*, p. 662.

44. O'Shaughnessy, *Consciousness*, p. 662.

I offer this eclectic set of observations to confirm several presumptions that seem to be at work in the idea that there is something important about experiencing the real thing. While for sighted people vision is usually a significant aspect of encounters with artifacts, literally *seeing* the thing does not do all the work in the encounter with the genuine. It is the covert operation of touch that sustains the sense of being in the presence of the real thing.

Proximity

When physical objects last longer than we do, their lingering existence seems to put their own pasts within reach—literally, if we are close enough to touch. But often actual touch is not possible. Touching is usually prohibited by institutions that house old things, for fragile and rare objects are sensibly protected from many hands.[45] In such cases, proximity must suffice. And it is often sufficient, indicating that a sense of nearness does not require literal physical contact. I surmise that proximity can serve in place of literal touch in part because the role of touch in the experience of the genuine is almost entirely nonsensuous and because of the function of this sense to register bodily position. These factors are mutually reinforcing.

One could distinguish at least three "degrees" of touch, as it were: actual touch (when one is in physical contact with an object), possible touch (where one is near enough that one might reach out a hand to touch but does not), and hypothetical touch (where one could touch an object under certain circumstances—for example if a display case were opened). The absence of actual contact does not erase what we might think of as implicit touch, which is shorthand for possible or hypothetical contact.[46] Even though they themselves cannot touch the Gettysburg Address, visitors desire to visit the document whose words were inscribed by Lincoln's own fingers. Such

45. This is a modern prohibition, as Constance Classen reviews in "Touch in the Museum," in *The Book of Touch*, ed. Constance Classen (Oxford: Berg, 2005): 275–286. See also Candlin, *Art, Museums*.

46. See also Christopher Perricone on nearness and tactile imagination in "The Aspiration to the Condition of Touch," *Philosophy and Literature* 30:1 (April 2006): 229–237.

behavior suggests that proximal acquaintance with these objects is the event to savor, even though one rarely is permitted actual touch.

The thesis that proximity can serve in place of actual contact requires some probing reflection. I extend the role of touch to include proximity from the fact that so many people who express their thrill of encounters with the real thing invoke the sense of touch. But when actual touch is not permitted or possible, proximity is the best one can do. I posit that touch is still at work in such encounters because touch carries such a high degree of bodily awareness—specifically of position and location in relation to an object. Thus mere nearness can suffice to bestow a sense of presence. As one philosopher puts it, "touch . . . is unlike the other senses in displaying a duality of the proximal and the distal, since it informs us both of the condition of our own bodies and of the properties of external things."[47] And as another observes, "All tactile perception, while opening itself to an objective 'property' includes a bodily component; the tactile localization of an object, for example, assigns to it its place in relation to the cardinal points of the body image."[48] In other words, even when one falls short of actual contact, one's bodily position in the vicinity of an object is implicit in experience (an observation confirmed by several of the theorists mentioned above). Position includes being near—within touching distance of—an object. It supplies the sense of being in the very presence of something special, to invoke one of the contested terms of debate. In short, the sense of touch can operate vividly absent the perception of characteristic sensible properties.[49]

Furthermore, touch is comparatively immune to illusion; you might mistake the identity of the thing that you trip over in the dark, but there is no doubt that there is something in your path. Touch engenders physical resistance between perceiver and object, and for that reason, as another philosopher puts it, "touch is the true test of reality."[50] One is palpably aware that one is bodily near

47. Fulkerson, *First Sense*, p. 77. See also Hopkins, *"Re-*Imagining," pp. 261–283.
48. Merleau-Ponty, *Phenomenology of Perception*, p. 315.
49. O'Shaughnessy, *Consciousness*, pp. 661–662.
50. Hans Jonas, "The Nobility of Sight," *Philosophy and Phenomenological Research* 14:4 (1954): 507–519; on p. 516. For some historical views on the reliability of touch, see Jütte, *History of the Senses*, pp. 98–99.

something else—something solid and unarguably *there*. Thus even proximity serves to impart a sense of being in the presence of a thing that embodies its past. Combined with the necessity of first-hand acquaintance for encounters with real things, these factors provide grounds for allowing that proximity functions as part of the operation of touch in aesthetic encounters with the genuine.

Appearance and reality

Full experience involves all the senses as well as imagination and belief, and at least for sighted people encounters with the genuine typically also arouse awe at the sight of something rare or old. I am stressing touch because it is a seldom-noticed aspect of this kind of experience and provides grounds for valuing the real material object over a replica. Still, the passage of time does leave its visibly perceptible record: chips, cracks, breaks, wear. The visible appearance of things is certainly part of the experience they arouse, and I do not mean to discount its power.[51]

There are aspects to the appearance of old things that are aesthetically notable precisely because they have accrued over time. Simmel describes the effects of nature on products of human endeavor that gradually become ruins, and also that produce the marks of age such as the skin of years that form a patina.

> If in this way there emerges an aesthetic significance, it ramifies into a metaphysical one in the manner revealed by patina on metal and wood, ivory and marble. In the formation of patina, too, a natural process takes place on the surface of a human product and produces a growth of skin which completely covers up the original one. That the product becomes more beautiful by chemical and physical means; that what has been willed becomes,

---

51. Though some do: one skeptical historian declares that "Aesthetic defence of history's erosions is simply quixotic passion for *pentimenti* and limbless torsos." Lowenthal, *Past*, p. 186.

without intention or force, something obviously new, often more beautiful, and once more self-consistent—this is the mysterious harmony which is the fantastic fascination of patina; and it cannot be wholly accounted for by analyzing our perception of it.[52]

Of course, that patina can be faked and a replica can look as old as a real thing. But when we learn that the patina was not earned, as it were, the thrill of contact with antiquity diminishes.[53]

While marks of age may be simulated, they do not have the same effect as something that is truly aged—that came to be the way it is now by the long process that altered it from the way it was when it was first made. Indeed, reflection on the marks of age can be developed into an entire sensibility, as with the *wabi* aesthetic of traditional Japan.[54] Damage—real damage not simulated damage—can be moving, an affective element of this sort of encounter. For objects are vulnerable and, like ourselves, can be, in Stephen Greenblatt's words, wounded.

> Wounded artifacts may be compelling not only as witnesses to the violence of history but as signs of use, marks of the human touch, and hence links with the openness to touch that was a condition of their creation.[55]

52. Simmel, "Ruin," p. 262. A related reflection on ruins comes from Paul Zucker: "Whether we perceive a ruin primarily as an expression of an eerie, romantic mood, as a palpable documentation of a period in the past, or as something which recalls a specific concept of architectural space and proportion, the ruin evokes in us a feeling of the impact of history on the living." *Fascination of Decay* (Ridgewood, NJ: Gregg Press, 1968) p. 3.

53. Robert Elliott makes a similar observation about the very concept of "restoring" aspects of nature that have been destroyed. "Some of the value of the earlier rainforest derives from a property it possessed that cannot possibly be replicated. Specifically, the distinctive, natural genesis or origin of the earlier rainforest contributed intensely to its value. The earlier rainforest had naturally evolved, whereas the later rainforest is the direct produce of human artifice." *Faking Nature: The Ethics of Environmental Restoration* (London: Routledge, 1997) p. 79.

54. Yuriko Saito reflects on *wabi* as well as the aesthetic dimension of age in general in Ch. 4 of *Everyday Aesthetics*.

55. Greenblatt, "Resonance and Wonder," p. 44.

FIGURE 1.3 Chariot ruts, Ostia Antica, 2014. Photo by author.

Touch invoked again, both the originating touch of the maker of an artifact and the damaging touch of time. Touch seems to recognize an implicit continuity, a temporal chain that includes the touch that fashioned the original object, the touch of those who lived with it in the past, and the touch of those who discover and continue to value its being.[56] Signs of touch with things that have been used are expected and even comforting, and their absence can be unsettling.[57]

The scope of this kind of encounter is enormous, for it includes not only human artifacts but also other things that retain traces of the past. For example, the worn grooves in the stone streets of Ostia Antica, the ancient port of Rome, invite one to step in the very places where Romans once drove their chariots (Figure 1.3). Tripping over a chariot rut is rather thrilling and quite different from tripping over a pothole. Just for a moment you have stumbled over—almost into—the past. The sheer physicality of the experience and the movement of one's own body are elements of the aesthetic operation of touch. If you want to travel even further back in time and tread the path of a dinosaur, you can visit fossils and stand in their footprints. A plaster cast of such a thing hardly has the same appeal or phenomenal impact. Inviting genuineness into the company of other aesthetic properties thus demands an approach

56. Simon James argues that old things embody narratives of past lives and events. See "Why Old Things Matter," *Journal of Moral Philosophy* 14:4 (2013): 313–329.

57. Architectural historian Witold Rybczynski writes of a chair made from materials that resist signs of age: "While the wooden armrests of my banker's chair are pleasantly worn where countless hands have rubbed them, I've written nine books in my Aeron, and its rubber armrests look exactly the same as the day I bought it. Such mechanical perfection is slightly intimidating, rather than endearing." *Now I Sit Me Down: From Klismos to Plastic Chair* (New York: Farrar, Strauss and Giroux, 2016) p. 190.

that does not model aesthetic encounters on the apprehension of artworks, as the admiration for all sorts of archaeological remains testifies. There are many kinds of artifacts as well as natural objects that rivet attention on the pasts that they have weathered.

The transitivity of touch

One more aspect of the role of touch needs exploration: the sense that in touching something old, one makes contact with others who have touched it before. Handling old things evokes an almost mysterious sense of intimacy, an experience that is succinctly summed up in this anecdote from poet Helen Macdonald:

> I once asked my friends if they'd ever held things that gave them a spooky sense of history. *Ancient pots with three-thousand-year-old thumbprints in the clay*, said one. *Antique keys*, another. *Clay pipes. Dancing shoes from WWII. Roman coins I found in a field. Old bus tickets in second-hand books.* Everyone agreed that what these small things did was strangely intimate; they gave them the sense, as they picked them up and turned them in their fingers, of another person, an unknown person a long time ago, who had held that object in their hands. *You don't know anything about them, but you feel the other person's there*, one friend told me. *It's like all the years between you and them disappear. Like you become them, somehow.*[58]

That sense of communion with the past spreads to the maker of the object and to those who experienced it before us. This account from Frederick Douglass also eloquently describes such an encounter:

> Of all the interesting objects collected in the museum at Genoa, the one that touched me most was the violin that belonged to and had been played upon by Paganini, the greatest musical genius of his time.... There are some things

---

58. Helen Macdonald, *H Is for Hawk* (New York: Grove Press, 2014) p. 116.

and places made sacred by their uses and by the events with which they are associated, especially those which have in any measure changed the current of human taste, thought, and life, or which have revealed new powers and triumphs of the human soul. . . . So this old violin, made after the pattern of others, and perhaps not more perfect in its construction and tone than hundreds seen elsewhere, detained me longer and interested me more than anything else in the museum . . . This was his old violin, his favorite instrument, the companion of his toils and triumphs, the solace of his private hours, the minister to his soul in his battles with sin and sorrow. It had delighted thousands. Men had listened to it with admiration and wonder. It had filled the concert halls of Europe with a concord of sweet sounds . . . [59]

In the case of Paganini's violin, the instrument joins Douglass not only with the musician but also with all those who heard him play, though Douglass admits that nothing before him signals perceptually that the violin is at all special.

The impression that touch somehow transmits the touch of others is an additional idea that requires investigation on behalf of the real thing. Skeptics about aura, as noted earlier in the Introduction, disapprove of the odor of the magical, the illusory halo, that often attends that notion. Benjamin refers to antique cults of saintly relics; Berger derides aura as bogus religiosity. Certain aspects of touch illuminate these sentiments, for this sense does seem to harbor a certain odd power that even our postmodern era has yet to shed.[60] Touch, for a host of reasons that

59. Frederick Douglass, *The Life and Times of Frederick Douglass* (New York: Dover, 2003) pp. 417–418.
60. "In many of the European languages that are descended from Indo-Germanic, there is a striking semantic kinship between psychic feeling and the touching of the skin: whether the heart is touched or the skin is touched by a breeze, whether one speaks of being seized by something or seizing someone's hand, whether one feels cold toward something or something feels cold, whether one is moved by something or one moves a chair, the same verb is always used for both events." Claudia Benthien, *Skin: On the Cultural Border between Self and the World* (New York: Columbia University Press, 2002) p. 186.

probably include the possibilities of infection or contamination, is also enjoined in the midst of the sacred. One can be in the presence of the holy and yet be forbidden from drawing too near, the final approach halted before actual contact is possible. Philosopher Jean-Luc Nancy joins many anthropologists in noting that in holy places, there is almost always a prohibition against touching sacred objects. He ruminates on the statement of the risen Christ to Mary Magdalene: *Noli me tangere*. Do not touch me, do not try to touch me, do not wish to touch me.[61] In such a circumstance, presence stops short of actual touching, observing a perpetual distance but also retaining proximity. Perhaps this idea echoes and sustains Benjamin's observation that aura is a "phenomenon of distance," even though it implies physical proximity. Although admittedly opaque, these remarks indicate something of the reverence for the genuine that I defend, though I hope now to demystify it somewhat, if not entirely.

The experience of being in contact with the real thing conveys an impression that the act of touching possesses a sort of transitivity: that by touching, one becomes a link in a chain that unites one with some original object, with a creative hand, with a remembered or historical event, or with others who have touched the same thing, rather in the way that a magnet transmits its attraction through a chain of paperclips or nails. The impression of transitivity, however, is more than a little difficult to justify on rational grounds. The chain of paperclips or nails occurs because of magnetism, not perceptually discernible in itself but known to be in operation. But what can we posit as the equivalent of magnetism with transitivity of touch? The value of genuineness and the accompanying evocation of presence with art and historical artifacts suggest a variety of what has been labeled "magical thinking," a term with ambiguously pejorative connotations.

61. Jean-Luc Nancy, *Noli me tangere: On the Raising of the Body*, trans. Sarah Clift, Pascale-Anne Brault, and Michael Naas (New York: Fordham University Press, 2008) pp. 13–14, 37. See also Nancy, *The Birth to Presence*, trans. Brian Holmes et al. (Stanford, CA: Stanford University Press, 1994); Jacques Derrida, *On Touching—Jean-Luc Nancy*, trans. Christine Irizarry (Stanford, CA: Stanford University Press, 2005) esp. Chs. 3–4, 6.

"Magical thinking" refers to tendencies of mind that systemati-
cally attribute properties to objects that they actually do not possess.
First explored as a symptom of so-called primitive mentalities and
placed in contrast with modern scientific thinking, magical thinking
was commonly derided for the absence of rational grounds, as we
can see in some influential writings of the last two centuries.[62] In
his popular analysis of religion and magic, *The Golden Bough*, James
Frazer identified several elements of magical thinking, including
the tendency to misunderstand the effects of touch on objects. One
type of magical thinking, labeled contagious magic, describes a way
of thinking that conceives of touch as imparting some quality from
one object to another, thereon capable of being passed to the next
generation of those who touch.

> Contagious magic proceeds upon the notion that things
> which have once been conjoined must remain ever
> afterwards, even when quite dissevered from each other,
> in such a sympathetic relation that whatever is done in the
> one must similarly affect the other.[63]

Similar thinking is evident in beliefs such as the healing power of
the king's touch or the laying on of hands, as well as some enduring
religious practices, such as the Apostolic Succession of the Roman
Catholic Church, wherein ordination of popes requires the transfer
of touch from one bishop to the next, a practice that is believed to be
continuous from the time of St. Peter, first bishop of Rome.[64]

Contagious magic, however, turns out not to be confined to
primitive or antique societies. Nor can it be understood merely as
the retention of practices for traditional or sentimental reasons,
absent any explicit belief in transitivity. It has turned up in

62. Earlier analyses of magical thinking as a phenomenon of primitive stages of
human culture include Edward Burnett Tylor, *The Origins of Culture* (1871), James Frazer,
The Golden Bough: A Study in Magic and Religion (1890), and Marcel Mauss, *A General
Theory of Magic* (1902–3).

63. Frazer, *The Golden Bough*, vol. 1 abridged (New York: Macmillan, 1935) p. 37.

64. For a history of such touch practices, especially those of the Christian
Middle Ages, see Constance Classen, *The Deepest Sense: A Cultural History of Touch*
(Urbana: University of Illinois Press, 2012) esp. Ch. 2.

contemporary psychological experiments and is now surmised to be a fairly widespread feature of certain kinds of affective responses. According to psychologists Paul Rozin and Carol Nemeroff, one form of magical thinking follows the same sort of "law" of contagion that Fraser remarked on, whereby the touch of one object imparts an indelible quality to another. It seems to operate on an intuitive principle that maintains that "when objects make physical contact, essences may be permanently transferred."[65] This means that things once touched appear to retain the effects of that contact—once touched always touched. With such objects, "their history, which may not be represented in their appearance, endows them with important properties."[66] This seems precisely to be at work in the distinction between rapt attention before an object that one believes to be the real thing—that is, to have the history one believes it to have—and the more casual interest taken in a replica so exact that it is perceptually indiscernible from the original.[67]

Those who decry magical thinking may claim that the sense of presence that touch conjures up is merely a projection from the imagination of the beholder onto an object. Matthew Hutson remarks (of the piano on which John Lennon composed "Imagine"):

> How is it that an object, such as Lennon's Steinway, can carry meaning around with it, independent of its material

65. Paul Rozin and Carol Nemeroff, "Sympathetic Magical Thinking: The Contagion and Similarity 'Heuristics'," in *Heuristics and Biases: The Psychology of Intuitive Judgment,* ed. Thomas Gilovic, Dale Griffin, and Daniel Kahneman. (Cambridge: Cambridge University Press, 2002) p. 201. Many of Rozin and Nemeroff's studies of contagious magic have focused on disgust responses. Contact with a foul substance can render an object psychologically repellent even in the face of knowledge that it is quite clean. One can see the artistic employment of contagion in David E. Scherman's famous 1945 photograph of journalist Lee Miller bathing in Hitler's tub. This picture virtually demonstrates the law of contagion with the *frisson* of revolt directed at the idea of water that bathed a monster surrounding her naked body. Or more specifically, the touch lingering in the bathtub that invades the water that touches her body.

66. Rozin and Nemeroff, "Sympathetic Magical Thinking," p. 202.

67. There is a certain parallel between this topic and Arthur Danto's famous arguments about indiscernibility between works of art and mere real things, though I do not pursue this issue here.

composition? To attribute personal value—a subjective property—to a lump of atoms: that's magical thinking.[68]

In other words, the implication is that the impression of transitivity projects one's own thoughts (subjective) on the actual (objective) properties of a thing. Hence magical thinking is based on confusion, and by extension valuing things because of the sense that they put one in touch with past lives is not rationally founded.

Nonrational it may be, but Paul Bloom claims that there is a universal, transcultural value for the importance that touch can impart to objects. This phenomenon is traceable to the tendency of the human mind to adopt what Bloom terms "essentialism," that is, to believe that objects (both categories of objects and individual objects) have essences. This is less a metaphysical position than a description of common intuitive assessment, for under certain circumstances most people believe—or more precisely, behave as if they believe—that the essence of one object can transfer to another by means of touch.[69] This accounts for the values that lead us to preserve certain objects from the past long beyond their use, for the histories of objects become part of their essence. For example, the essence of Chopin transfers to the musician's piano, such that people revere the piano for the traces of Chopin that it retains. ("A mere thing that has been touched by a special person gains value, which is one reason why people pay a lot for objects such as JFK's tape measure.")[70] Of course, there are multiple layers of value assumed by such sentiments, including those that concern the value of the original object or person that generates the transfer of essence by touch. If the original is sufficiently significant, even fragments remain precious, providing that those fragments are really the remains of the original. Casting that sentiment in even more extreme terms, Jesse Prinz asserts that "If the *Mona Lisa* burnt in a fire, we'd sooner visit the ashes than a perfect replica."[71] (This

---

68. Matthew Hutson, *The 7 Laws of Magical Thinking: How Irrational Beliefs Keep Us Happy, Healthy, and Sane* (New York: Plume, 2013) p. 13.

69. Paul Bloom, *How Pleasure Works: The New Science of Why We Like What We Like* (New York: W.W. Norton, 2010) Ch. 1.

70. Bloom, *How Pleasure Works*, p. 79.

71. Jesse Prinz, "Emotion and Aesthetic Value," p. 84.

may sound preposterous, though we shall revisit the notion of ashes and fragments in later chapters.)

Referring to the transitivity of touch as a variety of magical thinking might suggest that this phenomenon of evaluation is fundamentally irrational and represents a throwback to unscientific thinking. Bloom maintains it is neither irrational nor rational; it just is the way that the human mind works. Be that as it may, this claim strikes me as a retreat from pursuit of a better explanation for the impression that touching possesses a sort of transitivity that other senses lack. There really is something to be explained about the aura attributed to special objects saved for their rarity, age, or cultural or personal significance, and if touch plays a role here, as I claim it does, then that sense may provide a clue to the impression of transitivity (or contagion, to use the older term). After all, not everything from the past is treasured, and if the law of contagion just reflects an innate mental predisposition, it ought not to discriminate between that which is important to save because of some originary touch and that which is not.[72] I hope that we can find more particular grounds to vindicate genuineness, for the intrepid skeptic will doubtless feel that this embrace of magical thinking is rather cavalier, and that we should resist phylogenetically primitive tendencies that would not be endorsed by rational reflection. If the aesthetic standing of the genuine cannot survive such reflection, genuineness would still be an important quality to assess for historical analysis, authentication, honesty of presentation, and so forth. But its aesthetic element might diminish with an embarrassing absence of foundation. How to deal with this problem?

Even if the impression of transitivity qualifies as a type of magical thinking, it remains intelligible, at least what Peter Goldie calls "primitively intelligible."[73] Rozin and Nemeroff speculate that magical thinking may indeed be a basic feature of human mentality, part

72. See also Gregory Currie's reservations about Bloom's analysis of contagion in "Aesthetic Explanation and the Archaeology of Symbols," *British Journal of Aesthetics* 56:3 (July 2016): 233–246, esp. pp. 242–243.

73. "An emotional thought or feeling is primitively intelligible if it cannot be better explained by anything else other than the emotion of which it is a part." Peter Goldie, *The Emotions* (Oxford: Oxford University Press, 2000) p. 43.

of a set of "natural and intuitive modes of thought."[74] Bloom agrees; magical thinking, at least the sort that attributes the transfer of essences by touch that seems to underlie the value of the genuine, is an attribute of the human mind that must be granted without condemnation as irrational or primitive. As such, magical thinking is understandable and not crazy, but it is still not especially well grounded to merit the sometimes intense value ascribed to being in the presence of the real thing. We need to pursue the importance of touch further to understand how it operates with encounters with the genuine and how it warrants aesthetic standing. Transitivity involves both sensory and affective responses. Therefore, my strategy, both here and in the next two chapters, is to point out ways in which transitivity is similar to aspects of these other experiential phenomena, thereby to muster some observations in its vindication. This chapter concludes with some speculations and assertions that are intended to validate the influence of belief on aesthetic perception.

Defending transitivity

We know now that disease can spread from contact that leaves behind bacteria, not to mention traces of DNA. But such recent discoveries cannot account for the antiquity of the belief that touch bestows something of the original toucher onto an object. Magic is not, however, the most obvious explanation for the intuition that touch can leave a trace of itself behind. Touching is a bodily activity, and as such it can leave a physical imprint on certain materials. Think of footprints in wet sand or a cushion that retains the impression of the last sitter—even for a short while the warmth of the body that rested upon it. Seeing something leaves no such trace behind, nor does hearing or tasting. Scents can linger after the smelly object departs, as any dog can attest, but this is different from the protracted effects of touch. It is the scent of a person or an object that remains, not the outcome of an act of smelling. Only

---

74. Rozin and Nemeroff, "Sympathetic Magical Thinking," p. 203. See also Richard A. Shweder, "Likeness and Likelihood in Everyday Thought: Magical Thinking in Judgments about Personality," *Current Anthropology* 18:4 (1977): 637–658.

with touch does the sensory act (i.e., the act of touching) leave behind a mark that others can sense in their turn. This fact does not completely explain the power of transitivity of touch, but it does offer a common sense observation that reduces the irrationality that attaches to magical thinking.

FIGURE 1.4
Müller-Lyer
Illusion

Also at issue is the degree to which perception, including aesthetic perception, occurs independently of ideas held about the object of perception. One possible route of explanation pursues the cognitive penetrability of perception and belief. Cognitive *im*penetrability is a thesis about the modularity of perception, such that what we believe about an object does *not* affect how that object immediately appears to the senses; perceptual experience persists even in the face of knowledge to the contrary. A familiar example of cognitive impenetrability is the Müller-Lyer illusion, where lines that one knows measure the same appear to be of different lengths because of the angle of arrows placed at their ends (Figure 1.4).

Whether perception, especially perception at a basic or "low" level of sense experience where the data of the senses is first received, is ever cognitively penetrable is a matter of some contention. We need not tangle with that controversy because aesthetic encounters with artifacts are certainly not low level; they involve at least some engagement with context and history. Nonetheless, there is a line of thought that Fiona Macpherson has explored about the possibility of low-level penetrability that provides a productive way to think about the difference between a real thing and an exact replica.[75]

Macpherson argues that the perception of color, though low level, may be penetrable. Two pictures colored the same hue may appear different depending on the object depicted. Red, for instance, may appear more intense when it is presented as the color of an apple as opposed to a cloud. However, if it is the thought of

75. I first explored cognitive penetrability and the transitivity of touch in "Touch and the Experience of the Genuine," *British Journal of Aesthetics* 52 (2012): 365–377. I no longer am confident that this approach offers a sufficient explanation of transitivity, and so the argument here is more modest than the earlier one.

the redness of an apple in nature that induces subjects to consider its color more intense than another shape of exactly the same hue, this is not a mere perceptual illusion. It is a case of some doxastic state affecting a perceptual experience. Macpherson argues that such cases of penetrability require an indirect, two-step explanation, whereby cognitive states cause some nonperceptual state with phenomenal character to come into being, and then to affect the phenomenal character and content of perceptual experience.[76]

This thesis can be adapted for my purposes. Suppose that the nonperceptual cognitive state of believing an object to be genuine has a particular phenomenal character, and that character penetrates the perceptual experience of that object, occasioning the aesthetic encounter and giving rise to a thrilling experience. I believe that this accounts for the shift of value that ensues upon discovering that one has made an error about the identity of an object. Perhaps my thesis is made more readily acceptable by the fact that aesthetic encounters are "high level," involving relatively sophisticated and reflective acts of perception, and thus are rather remote from the simple reception of sensation. In such cases the cognitive state one brings to encounters with the genuine—namely a belief that one is in the presence of the real thing—itself has a value, a value that affects the phenomenal character of the perceptual experience of that object. And if that doxastic state changes and belief is withdrawn, so the perceptual value changes as well. In other words, the belief that one is in the presence of a real thing (of sufficient rarity and value) is a nonperceptual, doxastic state with phenomenal character. And the perceptual experience of the thing itself is altered by this cognitive state. There are no "bare" perceptual differences

76. Fiona Macpherson, "Cognitive Penetration of Colour Experience: Rethinking the Issue in Light of an Indirect Mechanism," *Philosophy and Phenomenological Research* 84:1 (January 2012): 24–62. Macpherson discusses a body of psychological research, including J. L. Delk and S. Fillenbaum, "Differences in Perceived Color as a Function of Characteristic Color," *American Journal of Psychology* 78 (1965): 290–293. In extracting her argument and adapting it for my purposes, I am considerably simplifying Macpherson's analysis. For a hypothesis about cognitive penetrability and aesthetic evaluation, see Dustin Stokes, "Cognitive Penetration and the Perception of Art," *Diacritica* 68:1 (2014): 1–34. For a set of recent essays on cognitive penetrability, see John Zeimbekis and Athanassios Raftopoulis, eds. *The Cognitive Penetrability of Perception: New Philosophical Perspectives* (Oxford: Oxford University Press, 2015).

between a copy and the real thing, for a covert switch of replica for original would likely not be noticed. Nonetheless experience of the latter, penetrated as it is with belief that one is within touching distance of something rare and awe-inspiring, is affectively different from the former.

This claim will be disputed by those who would separate the perception of an object from judgments about what it is, such that perceptual qualities alone fully describe the immediate experience of an object, and other qualities emerge as a result of interpretation.[77] This returns us to the question of the limits of direct experience. As Peter Lamarque aptly notes, a lot depends on what counts as experience, an observation that clears the way for the effects of cognitive penetrability on aesthetic experience. Without using the term, Lamarque effectively endorses this possibility when he notes that "our aesthetic responses are thoroughly determined by our beliefs about what kind of thing we are looking at."[78] Absent a presumption of genuineness, certain experiences simply do not happen. Indeed, all it takes to reduce the thrill of the genuine is discovery that objects are not as one took them to be. This subject is pursued further in the next chapter.

With or without the language of cognitive penetrability, one can advance a similar point by observing that certain experiences are based on a *correct* grasp of an object's identity, whereas others are misled. In the moment of encounter, the experience of a replica that is wrongly taken to be genuine is thrilling. If that thrill disappears when belief is corrected, this is entirely appropriate because one *ought* to respond to objects with certain valuable

---

77. For example, Noël Carroll, *On Criticism* (New York: Routledge, 2009) p. 59. However, he also notes that we value reality over simulated experience (p. 58). For a set of arguments on related issues see the Symposium on the "Historicity of the Eye," articles by Arthur Danto, Noël Carroll, Mark Rollins, and Whitney Davis, *Journal of Aesthetics and Art Criticism* 59:1 (2001): 1–44.

78. Peter Lamarque, *Work and Object: Explorations in the Metaphysics of Art* (Oxford: Oxford University Press, 2010) p. 132. Lamarque's comment is directed to debates over so-called aesthetic empiricism. I have conscripted it to support my claim about presumed genuineness and ensuing experience. His description of differences among experience is also apt for my purposes: "E is a (qualitatively) different experience from E' just in case there is some (non-trivial) characterisation true of E that is not true of E'" (p. 32).

standing.[79] There is a normative weight to value judgments, which ideally are based on proper understanding of their subject matter. While an aesthetic encounter is not a judgment per se in the sense of being a deliberative assessment, it does represent a grasp of its object, an understanding that is partly responsible for the thrill it occasions. These can be well or ill founded, grounded in correct belief or misunderstanding. Inasmuch as correct belief is a superior cognitive state to misunderstanding, encounters that presume the former are to be preferred to the latter.

This argument is best developed by means of considering examples of the sorts of errors to which aesthetic encounters with the genuine are prone. For without immediate perceptual confirmation, the presumption that one stands before some real thing with claims for rarity, age, or unusual history is taken on trust in the moment of encounter. It is a trust that frequently turns out to be groundless, and discovery of this fact compromises and often erases the perceived value of the experience altogether. The next lines of inquiry to pursue in order to amplify the circumstances that make genuineness a valuable property include the troubled reverence for things wrongly believed to be genuine, the various grounds on which one might hold the real thing to be precious, the (limited) conditions under which valued objects might be substituted, and the identity of things that embody the past. Chapter 2 begins these explorations by considering the many mistakes, illusions, and deceptions to which valuing the real thing is prone.

79. This line of thought is rather roughly adapted from Robert Hopkins, "Aesthetics, Experience, and Discrimination," *Journal of Aesthetics and Art Criticism* 63:2 (Spring 2005): 119–133. I thank Robert Hopkins for useful exchanges on these issues.

2

Tarnished Halos

In the previous chapter I began to examine the complex significance of genuineness and argued that the experience of the genuine can be understood as an aesthetic encounter. But we have yet to get a clear enough idea of what it means to call something genuine—specifically, the conditions that render an object sufficiently important that it qualifies for the positive evaluation implicit in the term. There are innumerable objects that *really are* what they *appear* to be, and if that were the only criterion they would seem to qualify. A textbook used in third-grade classes in 1990; floorboards from a house built in 1950; a hinge holding a door for years in the same house; or—as I once found in an elderly relative's storage unit—jars of pickles inadvertently packed with household items and sent to a warehouse, then forgotten for half a century. When they finally came to light, the mummified pickles were barely visible through brine that had turned a murky black. Real pickles, but who cares?[1]

---

1. The pickles were thrown out, but similar oddities have had a more formal disposition; the Hockey Hall of Fame in Toronto, for example, has acquired several nosebleed seats from Buffalo's old Memorial Auditorium, carefully preserving the wads of chewing gum stuck on their undersides.

All these things are genuine in the sense that they are neither reproductions nor passed off as something they are not. Yet in
these cases, *genuine* is hardly the first adjective that comes to mind,
at least insofar as the term connotes anything of value meriting
preservation. At best they are curiosities, though most of the time
they are dispensable detritus. There might be situations that would
render them worth saving, such as accidents that make them suddenly rare or emblematic of a special moment, or if they last long
enough to attain great age. But absent such special circumstances,
these things are unlikely treasures. It is obvious that criteria for
genuineness need to extend beyond the fact that objects have particular, even unusual histories (like the pickles), because too many
things will qualify and the items valued as genuine will proliferate
unreasonably.[2] After all, given sufficiently fine-grained description, many things will count as unique. Therefore, part of the task
of defending genuineness requires that we get closer to understanding what makes an object sufficiently valuable that it deserves
singling out for being an original or authentic object worthy of
attention.

Fair warning: this is an issue that will prove exceedingly difficult to pin down.

The discussion now must expand from a focus on genuineness
as an aesthetic property to include other aspects of its value and to
scout out the sources of that value. One angle to pursue concerns
objects whose merit is withdrawn, because the reasons for that
change of evaluation are enlightening. At the same time, they per-
petuate a problem regarding the role of sentiment in evaluation.

It is common to reassess an object when one discovers it is
not what it was first believed to be. Appreciating a real thing just
because it is what it purports to be is prone to error that is not always correctable simply by refining one's discerning capabilities.
The information prompting this event is likely to stem from "external" sources, such the historical record or an arrest for fraud.
To repeat a point raised at the conclusion of the last chapter: Since

2. The "proliferation problem" is examined by Erich Hatala Matthes, "History,
Value, and Irreplaceability," *Ethics* 124 (October 2013): 1–30.

nothing perceivable changes about the object of attention when new information comes to light, one might be inclined to claim that the experience of genuineness is the product of psychological projection.[3] Projection is a phenomenon that attributes to an object some quality that is imagined to be there but really has its sole source in the mind of the beholder. This is pertinent to assessing what occurs when one discovers an error regarding an object and its aura fades and dissipates.[4] One might try to separate experience from object such that the experience can still be authentic even if the object turns out to be misidentified. It is not clear to me what "authentic experience" under this description means, other than that the experience is intense and meaningful to the beholder, which could well be the case. By this way of thinking, if the mistaken identity or significance of an object is never discovered, the value of the experience it prompts should not be questioned. This would be a clear case of ignorance being bliss, and it is a mistake.

Although valuing of any sort usually engages sentiments (pride, affection, admiration), genuineness cannot be considered a characteristic projected from those sentiments. Rather, it is an objective property—property of an object—that refers to the conditions under which it came into being. In this respect it escapes the subjectivism that besets analyses of other aesthetic properties such as beauty. It is not directly perceptual, but we do not value things only because of how they seem to us but also because of what they *are*. Naturally, we can make mistakes. But the very phenomenon of imposters, fakes, or copies actually sustains the importance of genuineness. The experience of real things is valuable because the objects themselves are valuable under correct description. When errors are discovered, affective responses change; when they are not discovered, the affective response is like an undetected lie: still bad. One can be deceived about the object of one's encounters with the genuine just as one can be deceived about the object of any kind of intentional activity.

3. In this section I am thinking of "projection" in its colloquial sense and am not addressing philosophical projectionist theories of value.
4. The frequency with which this occurs is examined in Part III of David Lowenthal, *The Past Is a Foreign Country* (Cambridge UK: Cambridge University Press, 1985).

The very possibility of deception indicates the importance of genuineness as a presumption of having an encounter of the relevant sort. In short: if we admit that deception is possible (and it undeniably is), then—on the assumption that being deceived is an undesirable state—it follows that genuineness remains important even in the breach.

The argument of this chapter proceeds by way of examples. They are chosen because they represent different kinds of errors that can be made about objects, and thus they aid in investigating the value of the genuine more closely. The first set includes examples that attribute aura—which is the term I employ as shorthand for the special nature of encounters with the genuine—to objects of dubious desert. A second set of examples confronts deceptions and other mistakes about the identity of objects, and a third presents issues regarding reproductions, restorations, and substitutes, a complicated subject that is taken up again in Chapter 4. The complexities of genuineness now come into brighter light, for when it comes to selecting objects for their authenticity, their originality, or their status as real, it is clear that genuineness is hardly an all or nothing affair.

Misplaced auras and shifting sentiments

Many objects become cherished enough to save solely because of the affection someone has toward them, endowing them with a significance that is invisible to others. In cases such as these, it may indeed be misplaced sentimentality that is the culprit in mistakes about evaluation. As I argued in Chapter 1, to cherish the possibility of contact with an object seems to be centered on the impression that the act of touching possesses a kind of transitivity, that by literally being in contact with an object, one establishes or retains a sort of remote contact with others who have touched the same thing. While there are numerous cases where this impression can be vindicated as the foundation for an encounter of value, it can have ludicrous consequences as well. This is one of the treacheries of aura, for sentimental attachments can easily go awry.

In Jane Austen's novel *Emma*, the ingenuous Harriet Smith, having been disappointed in her hopes for a union with the perfidious Mr. Elton, ritually disposes of some private keepsakes from her doomed romantic attachment. Emma looks on with puzzlement as Harriet removes two little objects from a box labeled "Most Precious Treasures." First to appear is a piece of court-plaster (a kind of band-aid). Surely you remember, insists Harriet, when Mr. Elton cut his finger with a pen knife and I gave him some of my court-plaster,

> but it was a great deal too large, and he cut it smaller and kept playing some time with what was left before he gave it back to me. And so then, in my nonsense, I could not help making a treasure of it; so I put it by never to be used, and looked at it now and then as a great treat.

Emma must suppress a smile. But Harriet is not done with her revelations.

> "Here," resumed Harriet, turning to her box again, "here is something still more valuable, I mean that *has been* more valuable, because this is what did really once belong to him, which the court-plaster never did."

Emma was quite eager to see this superior treasure. It was the end of an old pencil, the part without any lead.

> "This was really his," said Harriet. "Do not you remember one morning . . . he wanted to make a memorandum in his pocket-book . . . but when he took out his pencil, there was so little lead that he soon cut it all away, and it would not do, so you lent him another, and this was left upon the table as good for nothing. But I kept my eye on it and, as soon as I dared, caught it up and never parted with it again from that moment."[5]

5. Jane Austen, *Emma*, vol. III, ch. 4 (New York: New American Library, 1964) pp. 268–269.

Her revelations complete, Harriet throws her foolish keepsakes into the fire. The reader is amused, as is Emma, and also pleased that this naïve girl is recovering from an inappropriate infatuation.

But just where does Harriet's silliness reside? Some of it has to do with the fact that Mr. Elton is an unworthy object of her affection, but suppose he were a more commendable person? Would the fact that a virtuous man had played idly with a band-aid endow that object with any greater value? How about the pencil stub? Would Harriet seem less foolish if she had saved his clerical collar, an emblem of his occupation, or his Bible? How important does an object or its owner have to be in order to warrant saving? Because these objects are so very trivial, one might say that they themselves are simply not important enough to cherish, no matter what their histories of touch. This, however, would be a mistake, as triviality can disappear with rarity when a small thing comes to be the last of its kind. At the same time, being the last of its kind and therefore unique does not guarantee significance beyond individual whim. G. A. Cohen, for example, confesses attachment to a worn bit of eraser that has been with him for years.[6]

What is more, mundane, domestic objects can have their own aura.[7] It is precisely these sorts of things that Orhan Pamuk assembled for his Museum of Innocence.

> The more I looked at the objects on my desk next to my notebook—rusty keys, candy boxes, pliers, and lighters— the more I felt as if they were communicating with one another. Their ending up in this place after being uprooted from the places they used to belong to and separated from the people whose lives they were once part of—their loneliness, in a word—aroused in me the shamanic belief that objects too have spirits.[8]

6. G. A. Cohen, "Rescuing Conservatism: A Defense of Existing Value," in *Reasons and Recognition: Essays on the Philosophy of T. M. Scanlon*, ed. R. Jay Wallace, Rahul Kumar, and Samuel Freeman (New York: Oxford University Press, 2011): 203–230.

7. Tom Leddy argues for the presence of aura in everyday objects in *The Extraordinary in the Ordinary: The Aesthetics of Everyday Life* (Broadview, 2012).

8. Orhan Pamuk, *The Innocence of Objects*, trans. Ekin Oklap (New York: Abrams, 2012) p. 52.

There is a rather more down-to-earth explanation that might be advanced for saving items of the sort that Harriet does, and that is simply that they act as *reminders* of someone or something cherished. But the pencil stub and the court-plaster are not presented in the novel just as reminders for Harriet of Mr. Elton, although they attained their value through her temporary sentimental attachment and then lost it when she no longer wanted the reminders around. Although saved objects often do remind us of their pasts and the people who held them, the phenomenon of aura cannot be explained fully in terms of reminding. For one thing, valued encounters often occur when confronting objects with which one shares no past, so there is nothing to be reminded of. (Think of chasing after meteorites or finding an arrowhead.) And even in Harriet's kind of case, this explanation cannot account for why particular objects themselves are cherished. All sorts of tags can serve as reminders: jottings in notebooks, diary entries, photographs, and so forth. But once the reminding is accomplished, those *aide-mémoires* can be set aside and memories explored. Practically speaking, it is far more efficient to keep a simple reminder than an object—a photo rather than a thing, a picture of a wall rather than a chunk of it for instance.[9] But a photograph or a memo may be *only* a reminder, though it can be valued for its own sake as well. If the thing itself, or even a fragment of the thing, is valued, it is because it not only *reminds*, it *embodies*— carries the past in its very being. It is the relation of embodiment that sustains the transitivity of touch, the impression of physical contact with the past and the histories that an object lived. Strictly speaking, of course, objects do not live at all, but this context seems to demand anthropomorphic terms: lived, endured, suffered.

Reminding is a relevant comparison to pursue, however. Like reminding, embodying has a recipient: someone to whom the object embodies something important. Someone to whom its aura appears, not in a glow but in the pang of recognition of an object for having its own particular history. To Harriet Smith, the pencil stub and court-plaster temporarily had aura. It was finally withdrawn

---

9. Consider fragments of the Berlin Wall saved after it came down; or the flakes chiseled away from the John Lennon Peace Wall in Prague.

after Mr. Elton proved himself to be unkind, and besides he married someone else so her early hopes were unfulfilled. Was it, then, only Harriet's silly sentimentality that contributed aura?

This question turns out to be surprisingly hard to answer. Harriet *was* foolish, and the withdrawal of her sentiment *did* lead her to disvalue the objects she had purloined. And since she was the only one who took note of them, their consignment to the fire was no loss. In a case such as this, the attachment is entirely individual, and one is tempted to attach the qualifier "mere" in front of "sentimental." But the fact that some objects are precious to only one person cannot be the sole factor in dismissing them from deep importance. Both individuals and families often keep objects of loved ones that mean nothing to anyone else, though their keeping does. This probably indicates that those items will not be kept for more than a generation, although if sufficient time passes the fact that they were kept so long can become reason enough to continue keeping them. The passage of time can bring about strangeness, endowing trivial objects with aura just because they are still here. The proliferation problem again looms here, as does the hazard of hoarding.

Harriet's little collection of treasures represents items with only personal value. But at the same time they are similar to the sorts of things that might become socially recognized keepsakes, forming a genre of sorts. For example, the once fashionable mourning brooches that featured locks of hair in tiny frames mounted as jewelry meant something personal to the individuals

who wore them (Figure 2.1). But in addition, at the time of their popularity this display of private affection was recognized as a public type of memorial. The oddity of Harriet's treasures is not solely traceable either to the inconsequence of the objects she saved or to the misdirection of her sentiment. Her objects, however, are idiosyncratic, as comparison with a mourning brooch indicates. The

FIGURE 2.1 Mourning Brooch, 19th century. Photo by author.

brooch pictured here occupied my grandmother's jewelry box for years, but it came from an even earlier generation. As I handle it now, I marvel at the miniscule, tightly woven mat of fine, light brown hair framed behind glass. I wonder if it belonged to a child or to a soldier lost in battle, facts I have no way of checking. It is not for me an occasion of mourning, and yet it still evokes an oddly impersonal intimacy. The fact that what lies in my hand once grew on someone's head is a portion of that intimacy, as it imparts a mildly weird sense of contact. Equally important is the fact that I recognize what kind of thing the object is. There is an institutional practice it represents, a genre of mourning jewelry to which it belongs. There was an established precedent to its making, unlike the happenstance that landed the court-plaster and the pencil stub in Harriet's box of treasures.

Even so, preexisting practice cannot alone provide a general account for what is recognized as being worthy to save and to harbor. Sometimes keepsakes and memorials are made from the most accidental remains. After Pan Am flight 103 exploded over Scotland in 1988, residents of Lockerbie collected fragments of the sad detritus that had fallen from the cabin. They cleaned and repaired things that were whole enough to be recognized and returned them to the families of the bombing victims, realizing that even small objects would be cherished under those terrible circumstances.

Although no catastrophic tragedy endowed Harriet's objects with significance, at least there was a true affection lying behind her little relics, as Emma calls them. What is more, Harriet was deceived about Mr. Elton but not about the objects he had held. She correctly identified her treasures as items that possessed the property of having-been-touched-by-Mr. Elton. But she reassessed the man who had touched them, which led her to disclaim them. Her sentiment, foolish as it may be, was directed to the right objects, but she was mistaken in her judgment of the one who had touched them, which altered their worth for her.

Here is another object for which sentiment might be questioned, though for quite different reasons. What do we make of a splinter taken from the *Titanic*, framed with a certificate of authenticity and sold for years by no less a vendor than the *New York*

Times shop? Most of what is contained within the frame is mechanically reproduced print material, but the fragment of wood at the bottom supposedly *is* a *true* piece of the *Titanic*. The splinter would be positioned near to the one who purchased this item and would be possible to touch, although touching would require dismantling the frame. The splinter by itself could reside in a thimble, but it needs to be surrounded by documentation for display purposes in order to distinguish it from any other tiny wood fragment. Thus the display depends for its value on that splinter—the genuine relic of the real ship.

But . . . a *splinter*?

The value of this little object is different from Harriet's courtplaster because the *Titanic* was a mighty ship and its dramatic sinking a tragedy of human loss and engineering miscalculation. Therefore perhaps—just perhaps—these tiny, dispersed slivers deserve the aura that their marketing anticipated. On the other hand, unless the purchasers lost a forebear when the ship went down, they are unlikely to have the personal attachment to the fragment that Harriet possesses for her relics, and in this way she seems to have better grounds for treasuring her little keepsakes. Does the fact that some beam or board was deliberately reduced to fragments in order to mount splinters for sale enter into the assessment of this object? Might the purchaser of this relic lack the right kind of relationship to the object, turning the aesthetic encounter into a kind of collector's stunt? I leave these questions in the air. The point to bear in mind is that, while neither Harriet's treasures nor splinters for sale are central paradigms for genuine artifacts, they are not entirely off-target either. The affection attached to the first was strong; the miniscule piece of the second was once part of something grand.

Quite aside from its size, the *Titanic* splinter raises an important matter pertaining to this study, for it represents an important category of the genuine: a *fragment*. Fragments of things are often cherished when the whole original is gone. A fragment is a piece of original material that is not repaired or reconstructed. It is damaged and partial, and yet it still is able to bring the past into awareness with vivid immediacy. Broken bits of sculpture, archaeological ruins, and pages torn from letters are all examples of fragments that can matter enough to be kept and even treasured as relics from the whole that they once formed. As a rule, a fragment is more powerful if it bears a trace of the original whole and is recognizable as a part of a thing now destroyed, as are the pieces of pediments from the Parthenon, for example. But in a case such as this, the splinter is so reduced that external testimony is required to identify what it is—hence the necessity of surrounding news reports. (Although the many pieces of the true cross that circulated for centuries may have been no larger.) This kind of case foregrounds the need for knowledge of what one is confronting in order for an encounter of the sort under discussion to occur, a matter pursued at length in the next chapter. What is more, fragments can become the foundation for repairs that restore something back to its whole form, as for example when a wall of a collapsed building is retained and new walls attached. Here the old acts as an anchor of sorts to the past, remaining still within reach amid restoration.

These first examples are knit together by virtue of the fact that the objects in question do indeed have the histories they represent, and therefore they rightly can be said to embody those histories and to possess whatever value they have just because they are what they are. The court-plaster really was handled by Mr. Elton, the hair in the mourning brooch really came from the head of a person long dead, the fragment of wood really did come from the *Titanic* (even though not much of it). Touch, both actual and implicit, operates in all cases, summoning the presence of the past embodied in these physical, real things. Now let us address a set of examples where that reality is more contestable.

The next kind of error involves an intense encounter but a mistake about the identity of its object. In 2002 the news spread of the discovery in Israel of an ancient ossuary purported to contain the bones of James, the brother of Jesus. Not only was this an archeological find of stupendous importance, one that would provide the first material evidence of the existence of Jesus, it also became an object of widespread veneration, drawing hundreds of visitors on the few occasions that it was displayed. Alas, the James Ossuary turned out to be a carefully executed fraud.[10] The ossuary itself was genuine. But first-century ossuaries are relatively

10. Although some continue to defend its genuineness.

common, and this one had little to distinguish it from others of its kind—except for the inscription indicating whose bones had once lain within. Analysis of the small surfaces of the incised letters revealed a different patina from that on the outside of the stone, one that could not have accrued over the same span of centuries. The inscription was deemed fraudulent. With doubt cast on its inscription, and hence on the identity of what it had held, the crowds eager to visit the ossuary drifted away.[11]

Touch is quite obviously at work in the case of the ossuary: the wrong bones had rested inside, the wrong body left its final touch; and to continue the chain of contact, whoever had lain within had not himself touched a brother who was Jesus. In addition, there is an amusing coda invoking transitivity of touch in the case mustered against the perpetrator of the fraud, for magical thinking's law of contagion affected not only the reassessed aura of the object but also the evidence gathered to disprove its authenticity. One of the signals that the authorities cited to prove that the owner of the ossuary knew it was a fraud was that he had hidden the artifact in a dirty toilet.[12] Presumably nothing truly regarded as even remotely sacred would have been carelessly sullied by such contact, and so the man who placed it there must have been a knowing perpetrator of deception.

Responses to these disparate objects indicate a range of scope for what merits being considered genuine. (One, of course, comes from fiction, but I believe that the situation Austen describes is readily recognized in real cases.) Sentiment does enter into aesthetic encounters with objects prized because of what they are and the histories they have undergone. Consequently, there will be inevitable disparity in the appreciative audiences for aura. It might be utterly private and personal, which is the area most apt to be labeled *merely* sentimental. Or it could be a family that hands down heirlooms or remnants of a past, especially if that past suffered displacement or disruption as with immigrants or refugees—where

---

11. Nina Burleigh tells the story of the ossuary and uncovering of the fraud in *Unholy Business: A True Tale of Faith, Greed, and Forgery in the Holy Land* (New York: Har-perCollins, 2008).

12. Burleigh, *Unholy Business*, p. 202.

again things saved or salvaged can become important tokens of a past left behind, no matter how small or trivial they seem. An appreciative audience could be a group, civic or cultural. Or it could be larger—national or even global. Practical issues of preservation and display chiefly arise as one proceeds along this list from individual to larger audience. But I suspect that the reasons to value objects for the encounters they can yield grow from similar sources, at least with regard to the aspects of aura that summon the presence of something really persisting from the past. To be sure, works of architectural grandeur, monuments, major art works, and other objects of splendor are also singled out and valued because of the achievements that they represent, their beauty, or their momentous cultural position. Nothing that grand can be claimed for small domestic objects, nor need it be. Their worth resides in the embodiment of far more modest bits of the past. Nonetheless, the importance of the persistence and continuity of that which is tangible pertains to the lowly and the lofty alike. Touch is a great equalizer in this respect.

Partly genuine

The examples discussed above are relatively clear cases of genuineness or its opposite: misattribution or fakery. But there are numerous other instances where the nature of an object is more equivocal, and the experiences gained therefrom are more difficult to analyze. Examples such as the James Ossuary, which are revealed as fakes and therefore do not legitimately occasion the experience they pretend to provide, are not only aesthetic deceptions but also legal frauds; they are historically misleading and morally corrupt. Straightforward replications, however, are invitations to imagine rather than attempts to cheat. They raise their own puzzles about encounters with the past.

In 2001 a researcher at the Vatican archives discovered the lost record of the papal investigation into the charge of heresy against the Knights Templar that took place in 1308. The *Processus contra Templarios* reveals that, even though they continued to be persecuted as heretics, the Knights were actually absolved of the charge of heresy. After the discovery and the subsequent correction of the historical record, the Vatican authorized 799 "authentic reproductions" of the manuscript known as the Chinon Parchment. It was meant to be sold to archives around the world for €5000 and to be exhibited at historical societies for all to see.

The idea of an authentic reproduction is only superficially oxymoronic; it simply indicates a true copy, which looks exactly like the original and has the seal of approval of the owner. The reproductions "recreate the folds, faded ink and mold stains found on the original," for example.[13] In other words, the copies not only replicate the text but also all the perceptual qualities of the original parchment. Randall Dipert characterizes reproduction (with art in mind, but the terms serve for other artifacts as well) like this: "A reproduced artifact is an object created by agents intending to follow, and succeeding in following, the intentions of an artist or intentionally copying the physical aspects of the artifactual features of the original artifact."[14] As such, a reproduction can look and even feel just like the original and can thus be interesting to examine and to contemplate because of its perceptual similarities.

However, this claim from the Director of the Masonic Library in Manhattan needs some examination: "People who are fascinated or intrigued by history can come up and touch something that represents a document from 700 years ago. That tactile experience of history is an important part of education."[15] There is some ambiguity in this statement about what would come of this "tactile experience of history," but it would certainly not yield an encounter with the genuine of the sort I am investigating. Of course, one can touch a document that *feels like* old parchment, but touching an authentic reproduction can be at best only an imaginative aid in thinking about what it might have been like to create or to handle the original. But because authenticity does not possess any sensory dimension, touch in the foundational role that aura demands must

13. Jay Tokasz, "Separating History from Legend," *Buffalo News*, October 26, 2008, p. C2.

14. Randall Dipert, *Artifacts, Art Works, and Agency* (Philadelphia: Temple University Press, 1993) p. 123.

15. Thomas M. Savini, quoted in Tokasz, "Separating History."

permit contact or a degree of proximity with the real thing. There is no transitivity of touch that can operate with a reproduction, no matter how accurate.

A reasonable interpretation of this statement about the Vatican's reproductions of the Chinon document is this: Touching a reproduction imparts a sense of what it would have been like to write in a culture quite unlike our own—one in which the written word is literally *written*. The materials in use are very different from our keyboards, ballpoint pens, paper, and printers. The production of a document on parchment is painstaking and slow. Errors require careful effacement or, worse, recopying the whole thing. Literacy is limited to a few, so the finished product would doubtless have a more exalted status than our multiply produced texts. Not to mention the fact that in this case, the meaning of the words is of considerable historical and religious importance.

Handling a reproduction Chinon Parchment might indeed aid the imagination through a trip to the fourteenth century. Certainly, it couldn't hurt, and it is not an example of deception. Note, however that apparently one goal of touching the reproduced document is to experience circumstances as if one were momentarily living in the past. An attempt to go back in time. Setting aside whether such reenacted experience is even conceivable, we can see that this is quite different from valuing an encounter with a historical artifact *as an object that has the history that it does*. The latter encounter retains the knowledge that we are ourselves living *now*; and the artifact before us was produced *back then*. There is no attempt to reenact being there ourselves when we keep the pastness of antiquity in mind. Encounters with objects that embody their histories are not experiences of time-travel where the present disappears but rather are moments of palpable notice of the past.

This example foregrounds a difference between an object that *has historical value* and an object that is *valued for its history*. While it may seem that these two phrases express essentially the same idea, they do not. The categories *having historical value* and *valued for its history* overlap. Many things that are not of much historical weight in that they are not important evidence for past event, are still valued for the histories they have, keepsakes and heirlooms among them. And copies of old things can contribute to our understanding of history and as such have historical value. Many things occupy both categories. Both the reproduction Chinon parchments and the original have historical value of some sort, but only the latter can be valued for its own unique history. The reproduction parchments *represent* the original, but they do not *embody* the past as the real Chinon parchment does—its age having carried that past into the present, so to speak.[16] To speak of embodiment is another way to note that when an object is Real it actually *is* a thing from the past; it does not merely represent, describe, or remind us of that thing.

The very term "embody" summons the sense of touch and the enduring physical presence of the past in the object before one. Hence, a person savoring the aura of what appears to be the parchment itself would be disappointed to discover one of the reproductions in his hands instead. At the same time, I grant that through a reproduction one can often get a whiff of something that does exist elsewhere, though appreciation is derivative. One appreciates that there is a genuine item safely secured somewhere that matches—indeed grounds—the one before you; even if, disappointingly, it is not here. In my experience, this is the response to displays of the maps and documents at the Karpeles Manuscript Museums, which feature only objects held in their collections, but place on exhibit copies distributed among the originals at their nine widely dispersed sites. All the objects look genuine, but visitors pore over the identification tags to separate the old ones from those that are merely apparently old. Though all the displays are interesting and informative, visitors tend to cluster around the items that not only *look* old but *really are* old. Therefore, just as the thrill of aura needs to be kept distinct from a reminder of another time, so it is distinct from an imaginative prompt that aids us in thinking about what it would be like to inhabit other times and places. Granted, encounters with old things can prompt all of these experiences simultaneously, and the above distinctions are meant to disambiguate phenomena that might be confused with aura. Real old things

16. This comment is in keeping with Leon Rosenstein's characterization of an antique as an object that is capable of generating a world that "evokes and preserves for us the image of a world now past." *Antiques: The History of an Idea* (Ithaca, NY: Cornell University Press, 2009) p. 17.

certainly stimulate the imagination, but they also anchor it in the history embodied in the thing before one.

Here is another way to make the point: implicitly, those who seek the real thing among things that merely appear real are acknowledging a distinction between what we might call the properties *of* an object and the properties that are *characteristic of* an object. Properties of an object include those that are sensibly discernible such as shape, color, size; they also include aesthetic properties of the so-called surface of an object: whether or not it is vivid or intense or elegant or Italianate. They may be simple and easy to see (red) or arcane (fifteenth-century Venetian). Some properties may also be characteristic of an object and as such can be replicated. That is to say, they present to the senses—in this case vision—the characteristics of artifacts created at a certain time and place. A replica object may be just as red as the original and just as sweepingly majestic; it cannot be fifteenth-century Venetian, though it may be in the style of that period and manifest the same characteristic features.

In many circumstances, the distinction between "of" and "characteristic of" is inconsequential. Suppose you want to flavor a custard dish with vanilla, but you don't have any fine vanilla extract on hand so you use artificial vanilla. Your custard will taste more or less vanilla-y, but you will not have cooked something that tastes of vanilla, even though conversationally one speaks like this. Rather, you will have made a dish whose flavor is characteristic of vanilla but tastes instead of some chemical compound that is vanilla-like. If you just want a yummy dessert, then both custards might taste equally good. If you are seeking to eat the very dessert your great-grandmother prepared, you are in a potentially deceptive situation, possibly disappointing when discovered.

I have an august ally in defense of this claim, for Kant makes a similar point when he observes the difference between enjoyment taken in the song of a nightingale and resentment after finding that the melody was but the imitative whistling of a trickster.

> What do poets praise more highly than the nightingale's enchantingly beautiful song in a secluded thicket on a quiet summer evening by the soft light of the moon? And

yet we have cases where some jovial innkeeper, unable to find such a songster, played a trick—received with greatest satisfaction [initially]—on the guests staying at his inn to enjoy the country air, by hiding in a bush some roguish youngster who (with a reed or rush in his mouth) knew how to copy that song in a way very similar to nature's. But as soon as one realizes that it was all deception, no one will long endure listening to this song that before he had considered so charming.[17]

The following anecdotes further illustrate the difference in value between properties that are characteristic of an object and those that are also of that object. I once visited a Swedish natural history museum to see a display of the carcass of a baby mammoth recently released from glacial ice. I found the mammoth resting in a huge climate-controlled glass cube. He was black and rubbery looking, collapsed on his side, and rather squashed. It was a peculiarly moving experience, and I stood vigil for a while. Although as far as I could see he might have been made from a deflated inner tube, I trusted that I was in the presence of a creature so old and rare as to be now nearly unique.

Suppose I was wrong. Suppose the Swedish caption to the display (which I could not read) announced that the actual mammoth carcass was still in a freezer somewhere, and what lay before me was a polymer replica. (Implicit in this supposition would be a replica of a refrigeration unit as well for added verisimilitude.) Would my experience change if someone translated the caption for me? Undoubtedly. Sometimes there is interest, charm, and enjoyment in viewing a good reproduction of something important, such as a work of art, and often a reproduction is as close as one can get. Indeed, sometimes copies are themselves "works." (Think of all the Roman versions of Greek statuary.) But I cannot imagine why one would ponder a lopsided lump of dark plastic in order to imagine what the remains of a mammoth look like. The same can be

17. Immanuel Kant, *Critique of Judgment*, trans. Werner S. Pluhar (Indianapolis: Hackett, 1987 [1790]) p. 169.

said of numerous other artifacts, such as the kidney stones from a Neolithic gravesite I encountered in an Uppsala museum: large, jagged mineral deposits that tortured someone thousands of years ago. Unless the object is actually a baby mammoth or a real kidney stone and not just a replica with all the visible characteristics of those things, the trip to the museum is hardly worth it.

Purism about the real thing is hard to maintain in all circumstances, however. If an object is made to appear as something did in the past, and if that appearance is announced openly and not hidden, deception—perhaps now the better term is illusion—can be induced in a willing audience. The commonest type of perceptual deception is also an outcome of valuing an object sufficiently that it is preserved for posterity and continued use. Many, indeed most, old objects and ancient sites have required substantial restoration in order to endure. That restoration might take place over a long period of time, in which case portions of an object are repaired and replaced gradually. Or, as is the case with the next example, restoration might be wholesale, requiring complete reconstruction. This raises another type of case where the edges of the genuine are difficult to discern with confidence.

When the armies occupying Warsaw fled the advancing Russian army in 1944, they mined what remained of the city, which already had been heavily damaged from earlier bombing. The final detonations reduced it to acres of rubble (Figure 2.2). After the war the city was rebuilt to look much as it had before, and the famous Old Town, an urban center since the Middle Ages, now attracts thousands of visitors a year. They walk within a section of Warsaw that was painstakingly reconstructed with the aid of drawings, paintings, photographs, and memories to the way it appeared around the seventeenth century. There is an important sense in which one does indeed *see* the old city while traversing narrow, twisting streets evocative of urban growth from long ago. For those who like their aesthetic encounters to include visits to the past, it is a compelling experience (Figure 2.3).

However, the tourist leaning against a wall of the old city, sharing a contact with generations past as her palms press against stone where many hands have lain, might in fact be leaning against what was once part of the city of Szczecin far to the west or Wrocław

FIGURE 2.2 Warsaw Old Town Square, 1945. Wikimedia Commons image from Marek Tuszyński's collection of WWII photos.

FIGURE 2.3 Warsaw Old Town Square, 1994. Photo by author.

to the south, for fragments of those cities were utilized in rebuilding the oldest sections of Warsaw.[18] There is a strong sense in which she visits old Warsaw, and no sense in which she visits Szczecin or Wrocław. Yet what does she touch? Has she touched Warsaw? Well, it is Warsaw *now*, though presented as Warsaw *then*. Has she touched either of the other cities (though clearly not seeing them)? Compare touching tiny fossils of ancient creatures caught in stone. If one's attention is directed to a building, the geological features of the stone are not in the aesthetic frame, so to speak, though they might be in another. But the agedness of the historical artifact—an aspect of this stone wall that is the best candidate for being the closest continuer in the preservation of old Warsaw's identity through time—is in the frame of aesthetic relevance.[19] Hence the conundrum, for it is the right property in the wrong frame, as it were, and is therefore a prompter of perceptual deception. This is the case in spite of the fact that guidebooks are quite clear that the city was rebuilt, and if there is deception there is also mutual complicity with those who enjoy their trip back in time. Furthermore, the choice in this case is not between the "real" Old City and a rebuilt one, but between the rebuilt area and something of a style altogether different that not only does not embody but also does not represent, reproduce, replicate, or even refer to, the past.

The different sense modalities (sight and touch) that are at play in the experience of a place that was destroyed and rebuilt are complicated and, in this case, somewhat at odds with one another. One sees old Warsaw, one touches fragments of the walls and buildings of other towns that now stand in place of—are surrogates for—the original Old City.[20] Willing deception there may be, though it

18. This account vastly simplifies the complex set of decisions over rebuilding the old city, which utilized materials from various sites in Poland. See David Crowley, "People's Warsaw/Popular Warsaw," *Journal of Design History* 10: 2 (1997): 203–223. The example of Szczecin is variously reported and somewhat controversial, and I thank Elizabeth Peña, Jean Dickson, and Sławomir Józefowicz for research and advice on this question.

19. A closest continuer theory of identity through time is defended by Robert Nozick, *Philosophical Explanations* (Cambridge, MA: Harvard University Press, 1981) Ch. 1. I discuss the ontology of genuineness in Chapter 5.

20. If one were really trying to re-experience an ancient place and time, the smells, tastes, and sounds of antiquity would also need to be introduced.

still makes a difference that the rebuilt city is made from other old places rather than from cement casts or polymer replicas, even if neither sight nor touch could detect the latter. But if a substitute is permissible at all, why does the material substance or the actual age of that which constitutes the substitute matter? There are two angles that explain why old materials are preferable. One notes that the use of old materials to rebuild something of roughly the same age is likely to yield a more successful reconstruction, that is, one that is more like the original than would be produced using entirely different kinds of building materials. The other notes, in addition, that the more successful reconstruction is, in some sense, *truer* to that which once existed. The desideratum is not just something that looks like the first or that can fool the unwary, but that is closer to its characteristic features. Thus accuracy of period materials is called for—the old in place of the old. This observation returns us to further reflections on the value of age itself.

Age value again

As is now evident, genuineness of historical artifacts is bound up with a number of values. Being the genuine, the "right" thing, means having the right history and being the right age. Age itself is among the features of artifacts such as old cities, as well as the host of other historical artifacts.

I return now to the art historian Alois Riegl, whose earlier remarks, when elaborated, will help to draw together the preceding observations. Riegl wrote at the turn of the twentieth century about monuments and artifacts from the past that accrue two distinct sorts of value, which he labeled "historical value" and "age value." Every work of art (and, we can add, artifact) is also an historical monument because it represents a specific stage in the development of culture. As Riegl states, "in the strictest sense, no real equivalent can ever be substituted for it."[21] While both bring temporal location

---

21. Alois Riegl, "The Modern Cult of Monuments: Its Character and Its Origin," trans. Kurt W. Forster and Diane Ghirardo, *Oppositions* Fall, 1982 [1903]: 21–52, on p. 22.

to mind, age value is to be found in objects that embody the passage of time and that show the marks of their antiquity, whereas historical value attaches to objects insofar as they represent a stage of cultural creativity. Consequently, historical value invites preservation of artifacts, restoring them as much as possible so that they retain the characteristics of their time. Some might contend that an encounter with an object from the past ideally yields an experience as though time is erased and one experiences the object as a contemporary would. Among the several confusions implicit in this notion is failure to recognize that the object is of a time that we do not share. Neither historical nor age value imply a collapse of temporal consciousness. They are distinct inasmuch as one—historical value—aims at preserving an artifact the way it was *back then*, whereas the other—age value—permits an artifact to devolve to a state of *now*, a state that manifests wear and decay. Therefore, there arises a tension with acute practical consequences between historical value and age value, since age value displays the mark of time, and time eventually destroys.

> The cult of age-value, then, stands in ultimate opposition to the preservation of monuments. Without question, nature's unhampered processes will lead to the complete destruction of a monument. It is probably fair to say that ruins appear more picturesque the more advanced their state of decay: as decay progresses, age-value becomes less extensive, that is to say, evoked less and less by fewer and fewer remains, but is therefore all the more intensive in its impact on the beholder. Of course, this process has its limits. When finally nothing remains, then the effect vanishes completely. A shapeless pile of rubble is no longer able to convey age-value; there must be at least a recognizable trace of the original form, that is, of man's handiwork, whereas rubble alone reveals no trace of the original creation.[22]

22. Riegl, "Modern Cult of Monuments," pp. 32–33.

While no one disputes that many artifacts and artworks have substantial historical value insofar as they provide indispensable information about the past, many theorists would separate (extrinsic) historical from (intrinsic) aesthetic value. This is not a simple distinction to draw, for artworks and other artifacts have historically situated properties, such as being a manuscript illumination, that are also aesthetically pertinent·properties. But to the degree that historical value is connected to science and research and the accumulation of knowledge of the past, and to the degree that it calls such investigative sensibilities into play, it may be conceived as an extrinsic value, though no less important than intrinsic features. On the other hand, historicity is often a notable element in the appearance of an object, so this placement is disputable.[23]

Riegl asserts that unlike historical value, age value is always inseparable from the sensible and affective impact that an object has on the viewer. And these, of course, are just the features that lend age value aesthetic weight. As quoted earlier, "Age value manifests itself immediately, through visual perception and appeals directly to our emotions."[24] What he claims is true about visual perception I argue also obtains for touch. Indeed, the point is made even more profoundly by appeal to this proximal sense, which conveys the palpable impression of being in contact with the past. As Leon Rosenstein—joining the two senses—remarks of antiques, "It is one thing to *know* the age of the work . . . but another to *see* and *feel* its palpable presence."[25] To these remarks we can add an impassioned declaration of John Ruskin:

> Let it not be for present delight, nor for present use alone;
> let it be such work as our descendants will thank us for, and
> let us think, as we lay stone on stone, that a time is to come

23. A strong case can be made that historical value also possesses an aesthetic dimension. See Rachel Zuckert, " 'The Historical' as an Aesthetic Quality," presented at the American Society for Aesthetics, Tampa, Florida, October, 2011; Erich Hatala Matthes, "Authenticity and the Aesthetic Experience of History," presented at the American Society for Aesthetics, New Orleans, Louisiana, November 17, 2017.

24. Riegl, "Modern Cult of Monuments," p. 33.

25. Rosenstein, *Antiques*, p. 33.

when those stones will be held sacred because our hands have touched them. . . . For, indeed, the greatest glory of a building is not in its stones, or in its gold. Its glory is in its Age, and in that deep sense of voicefulness, of stern watching, of mysterious sympathy, nay, even of approval or condemnation, which we feel in walls that have long been washed by the passing waves of humanity. . . . It is in that golden stain of time, that we are to look for the real light, and color, and preciousness of architecture.[26]

Age value attaches not only to cultural artifacts such as buildings, grand or humble. But also to bonzai, to tools such as flint axes, and to natural objects such as Sequoias and amber. Unlike sensory properties, being aged can never be only a property that is simply characteristic of an object and hence could be reproduced. Reproducibility is possible for descriptive properties such as being square or liquid, as well as manifest aesthetic properties such as being graceful, powerful, or lilting. But age value cannot in principle be reproduced; it is always a property *of* an object.

At this point I had better anticipate a question parallel to that addressed at the beginning regarding genuineness. Why should age be an aesthetic property and age value counted as an aesthetic virtue? Is it not better considered as a separate feature for admiration— or perhaps only curiosity—with no particular aesthetic salience? Some of the oldest living things on earth, such as 900-year-old Joshua trees, which have been called "repulsive," capture the imagination just because they have been around for so long.[27] Why saddle a simple, gawking interest with aesthetic qualifications? I answer by appealing to the phenomenal quality of touching the real thing that was elaborated in the previous chapter. While age may not always command aesthetic attention, there are surely times when it does, when one touches with awe something that has endured over time,

26. John Ruskin, *The Seven Lamps of Architecture*, Project Gutenberg, p. 177. EBook 35898. At http://www.gutenberg.org/files/35898/35898-h/35898-h.htm#Page_34 (Accessed 2.20.17).

27. John Fremont quoted on website of Mojave National Preserve: http://www.nps.gov/archive/moja/mojaanjt.htm (Accessed 7.19.2018).

or when one stands before remnants of the past. Age is often the primary determinate property of the admired object and as such is central to the encounter. This is a direct and immediate acquaintance with strong affective power, and it delivers a singular grasp of not only the significance of an object but also of its very being. This is at the heart of why discovery of error in presumed age reduces emotional impact and can even erase the experience altogether.

Age value by its very nature requires genuineness, though it is a requirement that is often satisfied only partially or spottily. Objects valued for their age are also those that are most likely to have had their original condition altered by use, deterioration, accident, or malice. This reveals that the cluster of values under discussion does not comprise a harmonious package. Age value does not resist the deterioration of objects that make time's passage manifest; in contrast, interest in historical value is more preservationist in sensibility. With careful attention to historical concerns, which often require restoration, the manifest properties that signal age are compromised. Age value may equally be at odds with the values of the aesthetic surface, and for similar reasons. A good cleaning and repair restores an object's appearance, but the presence of new paint or patches reduces the affective resonance of its agedness. On the other hand, if an ancient artifact has become so degraded that it is hardly recognizable, it has passed the point where it can be appreciated even for its age value. As Riegl puts it, the cult of age value "contributes to its own demise"[28] Age value accrues and declines, eventually disappearing altogether. One cannot resist this sequence without interfering with age value and, ironically, hastening its end.

In spite of their differences, the opposition between historical and age value should not be polarized. In practice, most attempts at conservation try in some way to sustain both. A case can be made that artifacts, including works of art, ought to be allowed to achieve the duration proper to their constitution and then be let go. But when those artifacts are especially important, such as the fragile fresco of Leonardo's *Last Supper* or a city reduced to ruins that must

28. Riegl, "Modern Cult of Monuments," p. 33.

be made habitable for thousands of people, reclaiming that which is endangered or destroyed is a compelling practical project. The artifact that results is emphatically not physically identical to the original; and of course, in cases such as a city that grows and changes over centuries, it is arbitrary to point to a true original point anyway, even if there has not been catastrophic destruction. Thus the factors that enter into genuineness are inevitably compromised and partial in many instances. To acknowledge this, however, is not to abandon its value, although it does open territory for hot disputes about identity and restoration that will be addressed in Chapter 4.

To have age value an object has to be old. Appearing old is not sufficient. But how old is old enough? How much restoration can be undertaken before it results in destruction? How much of the original construction of an artifact must be retained in order for age value to remain? At this stage of reflection, there appear to be few principles to appeal to for answers, and these are probably not situations where consistency ought to be expected. Nonetheless it is important to notice that as one proceeds along increasingly distal references, the appreciable qualities of an artifact recede to the aesthetic surface, leaving those relevant to age value behind until experience becomes directed to an intentional object so altered from what we presume it to be that it can become an occasion for aesthetic deception. Thus genuineness admits of degrees, from completely real and in its original condition, to barely like the original because of wear, restoration, or breakage. As archaeologist Chris Caple remarks, "Authenticity is perhaps the degree to which an object is or is not what it claims to be."[29]

These matters are more thoroughly addressed in Chapter 5, but to anticipate the argument: We can sketch a schematic continuum marking several gradients of change. An object from the past no longer in its original condition may be *repaired*, employing fragments of the original glued or soldered back together. While wear and damage affect its economic value, historical value might be preserved, and age value is not compromised. Or it might be

29. Chris Caple, *Objects: Reluctant Witnesses to the Past* (London and New York: Routledge, 2006) p. 209.

restored, where missing bits are replaced.[30] It might be *rebuilt*, using both old and new materials. Or it might be *reconstructed* in part or entirely. Finally, it might be *replicated*, even *reproduced* multiple times, either to preserve and record the surface qualities of the original or for market purposes if copies are to be sold. As the continuum progresses, more and more properties *of* the object become properties that are merely *characteristic of* what the object used to be. Historical value is largely preserved in at least the first stages of the process, though age value rapidly diminishes in this sequence— repair, restore, replicate, reproduce— although it need not immediately disappear, for implicit in the string is reference back to yet another "r"—the *real thing*. Replication produces multiples, though honorific reference back to the real thing implicitly recognizes the ultimately singular genuine object. In fact, reference that points to an original thing that one cannot visit, yet whose presence is known and nearby, is another practice in itself.

Replicas and reference: nearby presences

At the sites of prehistoric human habitation in Dordogne in France and the Pyrenees region of France and Spain, authorities have closed to the public many of the caves that contain the striking paintings left by people from the Paleolithic era. At the most famous, Lascaux, before the prohibitions were in put in place, carbon dioxide and moisture from human breath damaged some of the images, and destructive molds were introduced after the caves were discovered and explored. Efforts are underway to combat the decay of the ancient paintings, and some images have had to be redrawn. Some of the animals depicted on cave walls are now extinct, including the megaloceros, a huge deer with candelabra-like antlers, and the aurochs, a type of cattle whose modern descendants died out only

30. Dipert observes that a restored artifact is one "in which an artifactual feature deteriorated but whose original nature was correctly inferred by a second agent in a way causally connected to the original intention/feature and was as a consequence of this influence by the second agent intentionally reimpressed on the deteriorated object," *Artifacts, Art Works, and Agency*, p. 122.

in the seventeenth century of our own era. These ancient pictures indicate depictive customs and practices about which we can only speculate, and they bring to life entire species that are now defunct. No wonder they draw the adventurous and the curious.

Some of the painted caves remain open to the public and are popular destinations, though others, including Lascaux and Chauvet, are off limits. Replica sites have been constructed nearby so that visitors might admire copies of the wonders that remain sealed and hidden from sight only a short distance away. Some of these replications are marvelously exact, having been constructed with the aid of digital scans so that the images and their surfaces are precisely like the originals. One cannot object to providing replicas in place of originals in these cases, for the importance of protecting paintings made tens of thousands of years ago surely overrides the enjoyment of contemporary tourists. Nonetheless, it is enlightening to ask the question: What kind of encounter do these replications permit? Great pains have been taken to provide visitors with as close an encounter with the real thing as possible, and I surmise that the experience is intensified by the fact that one is in the vicinity of the real caves. Still, considering the inevitable difference between encountering a replica cave and visiting an actual one reveals another aspect of the use of touch.

Several caves are still open to the public, including Niaux in the Pyrenees. Visitors to Niaux are permitted entry only to the closest zone of paintings, the so-called Salon Noir. To get there, one must enter the mouth of the cave—a split in the steep rock wall—and traverse nearly half a mile into the mountain. It is dark; one is issued a flashlight but no other illumination is present; and the floor of the cave has been left in its natural state, pitted and uneven and in places wet and slippery; the air is cool and a bit dank. Though most of the cave is immense, from time to time one must squeeze through narrow passages. The trek is not for the claustrophobic or for those very afraid of the dark. Despite the strange atmosphere, there is a strong sense that one treads the path of others, an impression confirmed by remnants of graffiti from earlier modern visitors who left their names and dates—as early as 1609—on the nearer cave walls. By the time one reaches the first painted images of bison and ibex, the physical awareness of having made a journey to a special place is intense. You are *there*; and you have come upon the ancient past by dint of your own bodily effort and movement—striding, slipping, grabbing the occasional guide-rope for stability, your stumbles making your flashlight dance across the cave walls. The paintings are near enough to touch, although they are protected by a rope to keep visitors from doing so. But because touch is essential for awareness of proximity, movement, and physical positioning (recalling Chapter 1), that sense is vividly active in this encounter. This sort of experience dramatizes the degree to which *location* enters into encounters with the past. Remnants of history—or in this case prehistory—are not brought to you in easily available form; rather, you must go to them and stand in the very places where they were first made.

No replication, however exact, for cave walls and their images, reproduces this kind of trek into the mountain.[31] Replications permit one a glimpse of things that remain protected and therefore unseen. If a disaster were to destroy the real caves, the appeal of the replicas would doubtless change, becoming the only remaining trace of what once was. The replica would retain historical value for sure; it would preserve indispensable information for understanding painting from long ago. It would probably attain a kind of memorial status or value as a stand-in for something that once was, but the encounter with the genuine summoned by touch would vanish. I hope this intuition will never be put to the test, although it has been already with another artifact.

In October, 2015, large portions of the ancient sites of Palmyra, Syria, were destroyed by Islamic militants, including the triumphal arch of Septimus Severus. The Institute for Digital Archaeology recreated the arch with the aid of photographs and 3-D scanners, and the resurrected artifact began a world-wide tour, beginning in London's Trafalgar Square. The arch is an exact visual replica of the 1,800-year-old artifact and as such tells us what it looked like, reminding the world of what that portion of Syria was like before this willful destruction. Although the replicated arch refers to the

---

31. Unless one were to follow the scruples outlined in Jorge Luis Borges's story, "On Exactitude in Science," trans. Andrew Hurley, in *Collected Fictions*, (New York: Penguin, 1998) p. 325 in which a map must achieve the exact dimension of the territory mapped.

old one, the real thing was reduced to fragments, and the reconstruction only affords the look of the old artifact; the possibility of touching the past has vanished. (The fate of the arch will be a subject of further discussion later in this study.)

Replicated Paleolithic painted caves were built for practical purposes because of the fragility of the real ones; the recreated Palmyra Arch was constructed because the real one was destroyed. Neither pretends to be the real thing. But there is yet another role for replication that does actually qualify as a variety of genuineness. Reproduction is a practice that has long been adopted with other types of special objects that for one reason or another must not receive public display. For example, an object that is believed to be the Ark of the Covenant, containing the stone tablets on which the original Ten Commandments were presented to Moses, rests in an ancient rock church in Aksum in the mountains of Ethiopia. It is guarded by a monk at the Treasury of the Church of St. Mary of Zion, and he is one of a sequence of individuals who have kept vigil for centuries and who are the only ones who can testify to the existence of the real ark. For religious celebrations, a replica ark is carried in processions through the streets. This replica is itself accorded the status of holy relic, as it stands in for the real ark and is revered as such.[32] The reference to the original is more intimate than with the Lascaux cave because it is treated in venerable practice as the surrogate for the real thing, and thus the aura that surrounds it is perhaps closer to Benjamin's connotation than some of my other examples. I raise this case to point out that there are times when the passage of time itself produces an object that has its own claims to be genuine, even though at its point of origin it might not have been. In other words, even if there were no original Ark of the Covenant, the surrogate ark is extremely old and has achieved a place in culture and religion for a very long time. Long enough, perhaps, to be honored for its own genuine self. Of course, one will ask, a genuine *what*? And the answer will be extremely complicated. At the very least, the Ark represents what can happen when an object persists long enough

---

32. Similarly, it was a replica of the painting of the Black Madonna of Częstachowa that was carried into battle to protect the armies of Poland, as the replica was believed to carry the protective powers of the original, which remained in its home monastery.

to have become unique and emblematic of a time long ago, and to embody that time in virtue of still being around at all.

The true identity of the object that lies in the Church of St. Mary is beyond my powers of assessment, but this example dramatizes yet more of the confounding delicacies of determining what makes for an encounter with something from the past. Since I argue that a genuine experience requires a genuine object, if no true Ark lies within, is the ceremonial encounter deceptive? The phenomenon of age value makes that a hasty and superficial conclusion. As so many religious rituals are, the practice itself is very old, and can be seen itself as an ancient "artifact."[33] It takes time to accrue this sort of standing, but cultural practices themselves and the artifacts they utilize have a place in establishing the condition of genuineness.

As already noted, a skeptic about my attachment to things will argue that it is "merely sentiment" that endows this or that object with aura. Stated like this, "sentiment" sounds like whimsy and the idiosyncrasy of feeling is foregrounded. But if we think of the communal attachments and emotions that are involved with cultural practices, idiosyncrasy vanishes. When objects are venerated as part of a community or religious practice, they enter a world where they are treated certain ways, and this can be the case with a relic from antiquity that is preserved intact or with an artifact that has been replaced, when that replacement is part of established custom. In the latter case, the "something new" might be so much a part of ancient practice that it is only new if one considers the materials in use; insofar as it participates in old rituals, it also manifests age value.

A venerable example of this is the Ise Jingu Shinto Shrine in Japan, which is torn down and rebuilt about every two decades—a practice that has been undertaken for some 1,300 years. There are multiple purposes to this custom, including both deep-seated religious observances and also the practical sustenance of traditional

33. A similar claim might be made about other relics whose provenance is doubtful but which have achieved considerable cultural standing, such as the Shroud of Turin. Andrew Casper, *The Shroud of Turin as Art, Icon, and Relic in Early Modern Italy*, manuscript. I thank Professor Casper for sharing his ongoing research with me.

skills of building.[34] It is relevant to this study in being an example of something whose physical presence is rebuilt in such a way that the activity of so doing is more than simple replication but is an ancient artifactual practice. The shrine is periodically reconstructed, but each instance of it does not count as a replica in the sense of being a copy of an original. As such, its age value is measured quite differently from reference to the persistence of its material parts.[35] The importance of historical practice in determining an artifact's standing cannot be overestimated, as it contributes a great deal to deciding whether or not a thing is taken to be an authentic artifact or a replica. Indeed, other ways of staying in touch with the past, such as ritual meals that have been prepared on special occasions for centuries, depend on just such practices.

Assessment: genuine objects

The array of examples assembled here does not easily yield criteria for genuineness, though a few hints have emerged. Each of these hints, however, operates on a pendulum: on the one hand, and on the other. Sentiment toward an object contributes to its being valued, but sentiment alone does not make an object worthy of affection. With some cases, withdrawal of sentiment utterly expunges value, as is the case with Harriet Smith's little relics. On the other hand, there can be valuable objects that no one notices—things that *should* be held in higher regard than they are. So the absence of sentiment does not signal that an object is not valuably genuine. The value of old things is sometimes only apprehended retrospectively by means of regret when a person or a community notices that they neglected to care for an old building or an artifact that is treasured after the fact.

34. http://www.smithsonianmag.com/smart-news/this-japanese-shrine-has-been-torn-down-and-rebuilt-every-20-years-for-the-past-millennium-575558/?no-ist (Accessed 8.14.16).
35. Dominic McIver Lopes argues that architecture like the Ise Jingu shrine requires a different ontology from the theories that are usually put forth for buildings and other material artifacts. "Buildings in one strand of architectural practice in Japan are neither types nor material objects: they are all token events. . . . In the case of Ise Jingu, the event is rule governed and ritualized." "*Shikinen Sengu* and the Ontology of Architecture in Japan," *Journal of Aesthetics and Art Criticism* 65 (2007): 77–84, on p. 82.

Then there are cases where the standing as treasurable seems more than a little manufactured. The commerce involving relics from the *Titanic* raises this suspicion, as do new items advertised as "future heirlooms." And there are certainly cases where saving an object is just plain weird, and that includes the current market for oddities such as Napoleon's teeth or David Bowie's hair or Truman Capote's ashes. (These sorts of examples are discussed in the next chapter).

The cases with the most complexity involve old things that require repair or restoration, a topic that is treated in greater detail in Chapter 4. Approaches to restoration occupy the most contested terrain with regard to the concept of the genuine or authentic, including one approach that advises that an object not be interfered with at all and another that points out that without intervention something treasured will decay beyond recognition. The emphasis I have placed on touch and proximity may seem undermined by admitting restorations into the zone of aesthetic encounters, and it seems actually endangered if we consider replicas. At the same time, without relaxing the standards for genuine things to persist over time, we would end up with a very small set of objects that qualify for encounters with the real thing.

This chapter has raised more questions than it has answered, but the examples of questionable auras and perceptual deceptions have not been advanced merely to compile a catalogue of errors. They demonstrate the variability of what matters about an object whose presence is cherished. My purpose at this stage has been to increase the complexity of issues concerning encounters with the genuine, for it would do no good to develop a theory of encounters with the past without attending to the fact that very few can be free from compromise. When touch is given its due, those complexities become even fiercer, since that sense stands guard over the real in the physical universe. The next chapter will pursue a zone of genuineness that is rather less prone to the need for compromise about identity, namely consideration of imposture and the identity of persons. Despite notable differences, the comparison between artifacts of value and persons of value will serve to underscore the moral, historical, and aesthetic values of objects saved from the past.

3

Mistaken Identities

Skeptics about the thrill experienced when encountering the genuine are suspicious about the fact that aura can fade merely with the discovery that an object was misidentified, which makes it seem as if a perceptual experience alters with no change in anything perceptible. Likewise, there are those who believe that a replica can deliver an experience that is just as satisfying as the Real Thing and who would agree that "most people not only cannot tell original from replicas, they are just as pleased with the latter. The copy reflects 'the past' no less than the original."[1] I have already taken issue with such views, noting reasons why changed understanding might alter not only the regard but also even the very way that an object is perceived. We can add to the reasons why this is so, for a similar phenomenon is commonly recognized when the "object" in question is a person; moreover, when this occurs the skeptic is silent. Philosophers sometimes compare works of art to human beings, and this comparison will serve two purposes in this

---

1. David Lowenthal, *The Past is a Foreign Country* (Cambridge UK: Cambridge University Press, 1985), p. 295. This is an empirical claim, and the many testimonies to the thrill of the real that are gathered here belie the assertion.

chapter.[2] First of all, it will vindicate further the importance of correct understanding of the objects we value, and second, it will amplify our understanding of the experience of the genuine by noting parallels with emotional responses to persons.[3] The comparison also foregrounds the mingling of aesthetic and ethical dimensions of genuineness, a topic pursued further in the next chapter.

Joseph Margolis theorizes that there is a shared ontological structure between persons and works of art, for both are, in his words, physically embodied, culturally emergent entities.[4] Because of their cultural embeddedness, both artworks and persons overflow their material being with an accrual of meaning, historical position, and value. Thus when one speaks of George Washington as "the father of his country" or notes that Picasso's *Les Demoiselles d'Avignon* was an initiator of Cubism, one is referring to complex objects whose very being is inseparable from culture and history, and in much the same way.

Many others have insisted that accurate identification of both artworks and individual persons is necessary in order for their proper evaluation to be possible. This approach lines up forgery and imposture and examines the importance of the distinction between real and fake, even when it is difficult to tell the difference. Mark Sagoff defends the importance of authenticity with this comparison:

> One cannot appreciate a work of art simply for the sake of
> its appearance or for the feelings it induces: the identity of
> the object is crucial to its value; one must appreciate the
> work itself. There is an analogy with love. Love attaches
> to individuals and not simply to their qualities or to the

---

2. For a succinct discussion of these comparisons from a number of philosophers see Brian Soucek, "Personification of Art," *Encyclopedia of Aesthetics*, 2nd ed., ed. Michael Kelly (New York: Oxford University Press, 2014) vol. 5: 116–119.

3. In addition, there are psychological studies that show the frequency with which subjects group artworks and persons when considering persistence of identity over time. See George E. Newman, Daniel M. Bartels, and Rosanna K. Smith, "Are Artworks More Like People Than Artifacts? Individual Concepts and Their Extensions," *Topics in Cognitive Science* 6 (2014): 647–662. DOI 10.1111/tops.12111.

4. Joseph Margolis, "Works of Art as Physically Embodied and Culturally Emergent Entities," *British Journal of Aesthetics* 14:3 (1974): 187–196. See also Margolis, *On Aesthetics: An Unforgiving Introduction* (Belmont, CA: Wadsworth, 2009) Ch. 3.

pleasures they give. People are not interchangeable; we stand by old friends. Why? You love a particular man or woman—not just anyone who fills the bill. You cannot love a person by pretending he or she is somebody else.[5]

Jean Baudrillard, in a decidedly less appreciative observation about the fanaticism of the collector, remarks:

Pleasure springs from the fact that possession relies, on the one hand, upon the absolute singularity of each item— which means that it is equivalent to a human being, and eventually the subject himself—and, on the other, upon the possibility of envisaging a set or series of like items, in which is implied a prospect of limitless substitution and play.[6]

Many have also noted that when love is at stake, the issue of irreplaceable objects and singular attachments achieves dramatic specificity. Psychologist Paul Bloom maintains that at least in the case of romantic love, the attachment to a single individual is universal. We love whom we love because of who he or she is, and while if we are lucky they also have lovable traits, it is the person with the traits and not just the traits themselves that is the object of love. Love and sexual desire are "calibrated to individuals, not to their properties."[7] Bloom, too, extends this liking for the real individual thing to works of art:

We focus on individuals for *everything* that is valuable to us. This is how we reason about artwork, consumer products, and sentimental objects. If I owned a painting by Chagall, I would not be pleased if someone switched it with a

5. Mark Sagoff, "On Restoring and Reproducing Art," *The Journal of Philosophy* 75:9 (September 1978): 453–470; on p. 453.

6. Jean Baudrillard, "The System of Collecting," in *Cultures of Collecting*, ed. John Elsner and Roger Cardinal (London: Reaction Books, 1994) p. 10.

7. Paul Bloom, *How Pleasure Works* (New York: W.W. Norton, 2010) p. 88.

duplicate, even if I couldn't tell the difference. I want *that painting*, not merely something that looks just like it.[8]

According to Bloom, this feature of some emotions, love in particular, appears to be pancultural, despite demonstrable differences in marriage customs and family arrangements. The organization of social groups may adjust the way that this emotion functions, but it remains a feature of romantic love and it is especially insistent with regard to sexual attachments. (The cynical and cold-hearted among us will note that feelings of possessiveness and power circulate here too.)

Legal philosopher Joseph Raz also notes that uniqueness characterizes the objects of certain forms of attachment. In the case of persons, what he calls "logical uniqueness" is insured by common histories together. He, too, compares the attachment to a person who is irreplaceable in one's life to the attachment that might be held for works of art. Not only replicas but also human beings can substantially resemble one another such that they are hard to tell apart. It is unsettling, to say the least, when misidentification is discovered and duplicitous when it is not.

> Cases where the perceptual features of a person or object are at the core of the attachment represent a special case. Two elements mark them. First, it is normally important to people to be able perceptually to identify those they are attached to. Second, perceptual properties are not unique. Different people may look the same, etc. The combination of the two means that some attachments persist and thrive because as a matter of fact the object of attachment is unique in the experience of the person who is attached to it. Such attachments will be shattered or transformed if a perceptually indistinguishable object appears. Discovering that the object of one's affection has a perceptually indistinguishable identical twin, can put a great strain on a relationship. The discovery that one's favourite painting is

8. Bloom, *How Pleasure Works*, p. 87.

visually indistinguishable from a replica can also have an unsettling effect.[9]

Raz sums up the sentiments and attachments one has toward an object requiring logical uniqueness by stipulating that:

> The object of an attachment is unique if one of its properties, essential to the value it in fact has, and which is responsible for at least part of the value of the attachment to it, is such that it can only be instantiated once.[10]

Being instantiated only once means that attachments, including those manifest in emotions, are directed to the particular objects themselves and not just to the features they possess. This is not typical of all emotions, for many are attuned to the characteristics of their objects—to dangerousness in the case of fear, for instance—and not specifically to the individual objects themselves. With attachments that require unique objects, the characteristics of an object may have prompted the original attraction, but the emotional attachment has fixed on the thing itself.

One of the aspects of these specific "things" is the history that they and only they possess. The shared histories between two people make attachment to one person in a specific relationship logically unique. No matter how similar another can be, the double will not share the same history, even if by some science-fiction twist of plot he or she shares the same memories, since the memories would not have been accumulated in the right way.[11] This is yet another aspect of the shared cultural and temporal embeddedness of persons and artifacts, illuminating further why the particular history of an

---

9. Joseph Raz, *Value, Respect, and Attachment* (Cambridge: Cambridge University Press, 2001) p. 29.

10. Raz, *Value*, pp. 27–28.

11. Shared memories are unreliable grounds for shared histories anyhow; think of how many times in a long relationship people have recollections that are unrecognizable to the other. Simone de Beauvoir notes the discrepancies between her memories and Sartre's in *Coming of Age*, trans. Patrick O'Brian (New York: G.P. Putnam/Warner, 1973) pp. 539–540.

object bestows a valued quality, which is the phenomenon that, as we saw in the first chapter, underwrites the transitivity of touch.

These opening statements about unique attachments to particular objects and persons parallel my claim that affective responses to the genuine are prime cases of sentiments that require that their objects *really are* just what they are *taken to be*. The cases most pertinent to compare with genuineness of artifacts involve persons and the sentiments they arouse before and after the discovery of imposture. In each case, a substitute or a replica cannot sustain the attachment that the real one can. Mistaking the object of an emotion demonstrably changes that emotion—and without prejudice in the case of persons. Despite several points where similarities break down, the comparisons frequently drawn between persons and artifacts invite exploration of emotions that are directed to individuals and to physical objects.

The rest of this chapter explores various kinds of emotional change that follow upon discovery that a valued object or a person is not what or whom one believed. It is a continuation of the defense of the alteration of experience even when there is nothing directly presented in experience that alters. My goal is to confirm that appreciating one and only one thing because of what it simply is has several affective companions and therefore cannot be considered a peculiarly groundless sentiment when it comes to valuing encounters with the Real Thing.

Emotions and their objects

Emotions are a notoriously heterogeneous lot, and they display so much variation that some theorists argue that the term does not designate a unified class of mental or experiential phenomena at all.[12] Such general issues will not concern me here, for I only need to sketch the briefest of emotion-scapes in order to locate the zone

---

12. For example, Amélie Rorty, "Explaining Emotions," in *Explaining Emotions*, ed. Amélie Rorty (Berkeley: University of California Press, 1980): 103–126; Paul Griffiths, "Is Emotion a Natural Kind?," in *Thinking about Feeling: Contemporary Philosophers on Emotions*, ed. Robert Solomon (New York: Oxford University Press, 2004): 233–249.

where affective responses to the genuine best fit. There are numerous ways to analyze emotions and to group them into types that are more or less similar. Some emotions appear to be "basic." They prompt pancultural displays, appear to be shared with nonhuman animals, and present distinctive neurological and behavioral profiles. These emotions also have reactive varieties that respond quickly to stimuli with little or no thought or deliberation beforehand, utilizing their own modular paths in the nervous system. For example, fear may be aroused quickly, so quickly that one's blood pressure and pulse rise even before one realizes that the stimulating object is nothing that is really fearsome. While the category of basic emotions is contentious, those who subscribe to it are inclined to place fear, anger, disgust, sadness, surprise, and joy in this group.[13] Basic emotions can be exploited for dramatic artistic purposes, as with the pulse-pounding effects of horror or the arousal of sorrow by tear-jerker dramas. But especially in their quick, reactive modes, these are not the sorts of emotions that provide the soundest comparisons with appreciative aesthetic responses to the genuine.

Other emotions, such as hope, worry, grief, indignation, and nostalgia require a more complex context of cognition—propositional attitudes, beliefs, memories, and so forth. They are more prone to social variation than are basic emotions, and their appropriate arousal depends more heavily upon cultural fluency. A sense of home and childhood, for instance, contributes to nostalgia, and this is an emotion that seems to have historical moments when it is more noticed and cultivated than at other times. Awe, admiration, and reverence are emotions that recognize something especially grand about their objects, and while sometimes simple magnitude can inspire them (such as being overwhelmed at the first sight of the Grand Canyon or Victoria Falls) as a rule they require a good deal of understanding about their objects and surrounding events (such as being awestruck by the images from outer space captured by the Hubble telescope). Affective encounters with the genuine will fit someplace among this set of emotions, for they

13. Some of the best-known work on basic emotions has been conducted by Paul Ekman. See, e.g., "Facial Expressions of Emotion: An Old Controversy and New Findings," *Philosophical Transactions: Biological Sciences* 335:1273 (1992): 63–69.

require a fairly robust sense of history and of the passage of time in order for artifacts valued for the past they embody to prompt their characteristic thrill.

Most important in this survey of emotions is the distinction between emotions that are appropriately aroused by objects of a certain type, and those that are only aroused by singular objects, one of a kind. This distinction separates so-called fungible from nonfungible emotions. Emotions that can take any object so long as it is of an appropriate kind are fungible. The ones called "nonfungible" require exactness with regard to their particular objects.[14]

Emotions in general are designed to pick out features of the world around us that are especially important for our well-being, both individually and collectively. Fear is directed to things and circumstances that are dangerous, for example. With fear, any and all dangerous objects appropriately arouse the emotion; because fear is typically targeted to *features* of objects, and many objects share similar fearsome characteristics such as being poisonous, threatening, or precarious. Fungible emotions thus take a multitude of objects, any of which might arouse the feeling. If one fears a cobra, the fear distributes to poisonous snakes in general. It would not make sense to fear only one cobra (unless you had reason to believe that one in particular had taken a dislike to you).[15] Similarly, disgust is directed to the property of being foul, which might be manifest by all sorts of decaying organic matter, whether garbage, roadkill, or pustulous tissue. Anger is appropriate for anyone who offends one; regret for opportunities lost; and so forth.

Nonfungible emotions, by contrast, are by nature more selective and respond chiefly or only to singular objects. Love comes in many forms, and while one may love general features of things and people, there are varieties of love that hone in on very specific individuals. Parental love is for one's own children, filial love for one's own parents. Such affections can be transferred to other

14. I adopt this terminology from Ronald de Sousa, *The Rationality of Emotions* (Cambridge, MA: MIT Press, 1987).

15. Highly unlikely with snakes, but John Vaillant recounts the story of a tiger that apparently sought revenge against a particular group of people in southeastern Siberia: *The Tiger: A True Story of Vengeance and Survival* (New York: Vintage Books, 2010).

children, to other adults, but those circumstances are not paradigmatic, and they usually occur when others assume the roles of children or parents. Romantic love is a prime example of an emotion that requires it be directed to one particular person (or at least one at a time), a point so widely acknowledged that it has become a near-universal theme in storytelling, as we shall see shortly.

When it comes to emotions such as love, questions arise about the proper object of this emotion. Is the appropriate target just the properties of a person? If so, then anyone possessing the same properties deserves and receives love. Or is it in addition the person himself or herself? This might seem an odd question, because as a rule one would not love someone who did not possess at least some appealing qualities, though it is surely possible. But the claim that love of certain sorts—romantic, maternal, filial—is nonfungible means that this emotion is directed only to the particular individuals who manifest those properties. The contrast with other kinds of affections is clear: if you like chocolate, then it is the taste properties of candy that trigger the liking. If someone takes a particular chocolate-covered caramel, you just take the next one in the box. Any particular thing having the same properties inspires the same liking. But love for human beings does not operate that way; it is entangled with a more inflexible attachment directed to specific individuals.

The uniqueness of certain emotional attachments suggests that the objects of nonfungible emotions might be irreplaceable, and that irreplaceability might serve as a criterion for being significant enough to count as genuine—an elusive standard pursued in the previous chapter.[16] While there are times when valued objects, like loved persons, are irreplaceable, this criterion is too strong to serve as a requirement for being genuine in every case. Attachment to the genuine comes in forms that can be more or less fungible and utterly nonfungible. For example, a lover of violin music won't like just any piece, but might well appreciate equally performances by Joshua Bell or Itzak Perlman. A person choosing William Morris–style wallpaper

---

16. For an extensive critical examination of irreplaceability see Erich Hatala Matthes, "History," Value, and Irreplaceability," *Ethics* 124 (October 2013): 1–30.

for a room won't care just which roll is delivered. Even encounters with things sought out because they are the real thing have a place among fungible affects when it is the *type* of object that needs to be genuine rather than the individual one. Being a genuine mourning brooch of the sort discussed in the previous chapter, for instance, requires only that a certain kind of object be made during a particular historical period and under particular circumstances. Collectors of such jewelry are usually only interested in genuineness of kind. They do not need to be sure that the hair in the jewelry came from one particular head. It is sufficient that the brooch contain real human hair and that it was made under an artistic or craft practice that recognized such jewelry. However, genuineness of kind is insufficient for the object that serves as a memorial for the person for whom a mourning brooch was made. A woman who wore this jewelry in memory of her late husband cherished the brooch because it embodied him and him alone. Not just any mourning brooch would do; it must have contained his and only his hair. Uniqueness, absolute singularity is required, so this sort of affective attachment is utterly nonfungible. In the case of the jewelry collector, genuineness requires the right type of object; in the case of the mourner, it requires the right particular object, the right token of the type. The latter object is truly irreplaceable. Neither collector nor widow would value a reproduction, but the former would accept an object of the right kind as a substitute for another of the same kind. Thus we can see that, while irreplaceability can have a crucial role in determining singular objects of value, there will be qualifications for what counts as relevantly genuine for the thrill of an encounter to occur.

Let us explore irreplaceability further with the aid of a few narrative excursions. Because things can *be* different but *look* the same, it is easy to direct a nonfungible emotion to the wrong thing. The mistake can involve both persons and objects, and it is featured in tales throughout the globe.

Taking one for another

It used to be a lot easier to disappear. To take advantage of the upheavals of war, the emptiness of frontiers, and the slipperiness of memories and to assume a new identity—to become, for all outward intents and purposes, a different person. This world of possibility has dramatically shrunk with the current ease with which others can track our digital trails and with the images we leave behind in surveillance cameras, not to mention the definitive proof of identity provided by the DNA we profligately distribute. For better or for worse, with this gain in certainty comes a certain loss of freedom and mystery. Also diminished is the possibility of conducting a life along the lines of stories that have fed the imagination for millennia. Myth, legend, and literature are full of tales where certainty of identity is tenuous. Changelings occupy cradles, impostors claim inheritances, would-be lovers sneak into beds under cover of night, and gods assume the appearance of mortals to seduce their human spouses. Skillful duplicates wrongly evoke affection, and if the deception is discovered, it arouses bewilderment, horror, and anger. The hearer of such tales may also feel a terrible uncertainty: is the person I love really the person I believe him to be?

Stories about mistaken identities and imposture pervade narrative traditions throughout history. Wendy Doniger has compiled stories about "bedtricks," the sneaky substitution of one lover for another, that range from the Bible through Indian myth, Asian and European folklore and literature, and oral traditions from the Arctic to the South Pacific. Bedtrick stories are decidedly pertinent to this study because the role of *touch* is central; it is also quite specific, since at issue is sexual contact and marital fidelity. There are thousands of versions of this story, but I have chosen just a few for their similarity to the problem of detecting genuineness of artifacts and—most importantly—the change of response that occurs when deception is unveiled.[17] It is the phenomenon of that change, which occurs with no alteration of the appearance of the person, that

---

17. For a summary and analysis of numerous stories from different cultural traditions, see Wendy Doniger, *The Bedtrick: Tales of Sex and Masquerade* (Chicago: University of Chicago Press, 2000). For the ambiguities of recognition and acceptance of replacement in a famous historical case, see Natalie Zemon Davis, *The Return of Martin Guerre* (Cambridge: Cambridge University Press, 1983). A movie of the same name directed by Daniel Vigne was released in 1982. For a fictional story where a substitute wife is accepted, see Kurt Vonnegut, *Mother Night* (New York: Random House, 1961).

these narratives underscore. In this respect they are exactly comparable to the change of response to an object that is discovered to be misattributed or fake.

Shakespeare was fond of mistaken identities, a common motif in farce and comedy, especially when there is the choice of the proper sexual partner at stake. Deceptions intentional and accidental are occasioned by disguise, darkness, locked doors, and the appearance of twins who have been separated so long that each no longer knows the other exists. One tangled set of such relationships drives *The Comedy of Errors,* in which a long-separated husband and wife, whose twin sons and their twin servants had been dispersed by a shipwreck, all land one day in Ephesus. Just to keep the bewilderment at a maximum, Shakespeare also gives the twins the same names: Antipholus of Ephesus and Antipholus of Syracuse in the case of the higher-born men, and Dromio of Ephesus and Dromio of Syracuse in the case of the servants. So alike are the two sets of twins that confusion reigns to the point where magic is suspected.

Because of the complications of sex in bedtrick plots, the chief concerns of characters are directed to matters of fidelity and morality. The role of touch and its "magical" contagion has an incidental confirmation in this speech of Adriana, wife of Antipholus of Ephesus, when she first encounters Antipholus of Syracuse. She smarts from the fact that, not recognizing this strange woman, he rejects her. Wrongly believing him to be her husband, she accuses him of adultery, an illicit contact that has polluted her as well:

> How comes it now, my husband, O, how comes it,
> That thou are then estranged from thyself? . . .
> My blood is mingled with the crime of lust;
> For if we two be one and thou play false,
> I do digest the poison of thy flesh,
> Being strumpeted by thy contagion. (II:2) [18]

---

18. William Shakespeare, *The Comedy of Errors* (1591–92), in *The Complete Plays and Poems of William Shakespeare,* William Allan Neilson and Charles Jarvis Hill, eds. (Cambridge MA: Houghton Mifflin, 1942). All my quotations from Shakespeare come from this edition, though I note Act and Scene numbers rather than page numbers.

So powerful is the response of those they meet that the Syracusan twins—master and servant—begin to doubt their own identities and to wonder if they are themselves possessed. As Antipholus muses to himself: "Am I in earth, in heaven, or in hell? / Sleeping or waking? Mad or well-advis'd? / Known unto these, and to myself disguis'd!" (II:2). In desperation and in fear of his sanity, he takes refuge in an abbey, superintended by an abbess, Amelia, who conveniently happens to be his long-lost mother. Adriana, though furious at her husband and still pursuing the wrong man, nonetheless clings to him and only him in their marital bond. She demands that the abbess hand him over in acknowledgement of their unique attachment:

> I will attend my husband, be his nurse,
> Diet his sickness, for it is my office,
> And will have no agent but myself. . . .
> I will not hence and leave my husband here;
> And ill it doth beseem your holiness
> To separate the husband and the wife. (V:1)

When the long-dispersed kin finally lay eyes on one another, the resemblances disturb. Says Adriana, "I see two husbands, or mine eyes deceive me." Even after the story of the shipwreck is happily straightened out, one of the Dromios regards his twin oddly: "Methinks you are my glass, and not my brother" (V:1). The inability to tell two people apart is so unsettling that Freud marks it as "uncanny."[19] But, all's well that ends well, so to speak, and as the play closes the reunited twins walk together hand in hand.

Although the opportunity for sexual union complicates the deceptions of romantic love in these stories, it underscores nonfungibility. Despite his frequent use of mistaken identity and imposture, Shakespeare himself never permits consummation between lovers unless they are actually the "right" partners, those sanctioned by marriage or promise, not even in the vicious story of *Measure for Measure*, which involves rape and a capital crime. In the

---

19. "One face, one voice, one habit, and two persons," marvels the duke in *Twelfth Night* V:1. In this case the indiscernibility of the twins is complicated by the fact that they are of two sexes. Doniger notes this as a special theme in the tales from India and Japan in *Bedtrick*.

case of many other stories, however, propriety is less accommodated, and deception invites infidelity, adultery, and all manner of inappropriate coupling. If there is a god involved, the deception may be so complete that there would be no way for the deceived spouse to tell that she is not lying in bed with her own husband.

Consider the ancient Greek tale of Alcmene, the loyal wife of Amphitryon. Zeus, the arch seducer, falls for Alcmene, but she is too steadfast in her love of Amphitryon to succumb to his attentions. Only after he transforms himself into the living image of Amphitryon by assuming all of his perceivable qualities does she sleep with him, believing her partner to be her beloved husband. (The result of this union was Heracles.) She learns of the deception after the fact when the god reveals himself by showing off with an impressive thunderbolt—a piece of evidence quite at odds with her original perception of him. Did she reassess the emotion she felt to the man she had loved the previous night? Did her affection retroactively diminish? She did, it did, and justly so.

The story of Alcmene and Amphitryon has been the subject of drama for centuries, most famously by Plautus in antiquity and in modern times in plays by Molière and by Heinrich von Kleist (in whose plays the god is named Jupiter rather than Zeus). I choose a few passages from the latter just to add to the evidence of the consternation that arises when one mistakes the object of love.

As with *The Comedy of Errors*, this play features a second deception as well, for Mercury is serving Jupiter, having taken on the appearance of Amphitryon's servant Sosias. Both Sosias and Alcmene are dismayed at the failure of their senses to confirm the identity of the doubles. The illusion is so thorough and unsettling that when Sosias sees Mercury-as-Sosias, the former decides he is not himself. For much of the play, Alcmene is without doubt that the man with her is her husband, just returned from battle. She clings to this belief as long as she can. But her conviction is undone when she finds that the diadem on a belt he had given her is marked with the letter "J" rather than "A." To her serving woman Charis she insists that she would always know the object of her love:

If you would take away my eye, I'd hear him still;
Without my ear, I'd feel him; would I not feel,

> I still should breathe him; and if you take
> My eye, my ear, my touch, my sense of smell,
> Leave me my heart; it is the bell I need
> To find him in the whole wide world.[20]

Jupiter offers false assurance, insisting that Alcmene would know her own husband. But he also introduces an interesting observation: Because Alcmene believed Amphitryon was in her bed, it was to him that she offered her love, not to an imposter, though he himself denies deception at this stage of the game and accuses the real husband of imposture. To the distressed Alcmene he declares that the object of her love was the object in her mind, regardless of the actual identity of the man.

> Your feeling is infallible. If he vainly
> Imagined you were lying in *his* arms, *you* lay in fact
> With your true love, Amphitryon; and if *he*
> Dreamed of your kisses, *you* were kissing Amphitryon's
>   beloved lips.[21]

There is harm in the deception, and there is harm in the unveiling of the deception, and different narratives pick and choose which deception is the more grievous. When the deceived never discovers the truth, the plot leaves the possibility that no injury has been really done. The deceived person is never dismayed, and the deceiver is left only with a pang of regret that the deception was necessary. Such is the implication of the joint affections of twins Nora and Dora in Angela Carter's novel, *Wise Children*. The twins are performers, a song and dance team, and from time to time they participate in Shakespearean productions, the comic plots of which seem ready-made for their own bedtricks. A young tenor falls deeply in love with Nora, and he is loved even more deeply back by Dora, who one evening swaps perfumes with her sister—for many can tell them apart only by their scent—and enjoys her first sexual encounter with him.

20. Heinrich von Kleist, *Amphitryon*, trans. Marion Sonnenfeld (New York: Frederick Ungar, 1962) II:4, p. 41.
21. Kleist, *Amphitryon*, II:5, p. 45.

Off he went, smelling of Shalimar and sex, and I lay on the sofa and breathed in the smells of him and me that were really the smells of him and Nora and I kept a little sentimental tryst with silence and the night and the moon over Croydon and he never would have done it if he'd known I wasn't Nora. He was the faithful type.

Did we betray the innocence of the boy with our deception? Of course we did. Does it matter? Let the one without sin cast the first stone. He really thought I was the one he loved so he was not deceived. And I got the birthday present that I wanted and then I gave him back to Nora.[22]

"He really thought I was the one he loved so he was not deceived." A desperate sentiment from a girl who knows her love is hopeless, for his relationship with her was only sustained for as long as the deception lasted (which in this particular story is forever). Because, of course, he *was* deceived, albeit happy in the event. However, like Jupiter's consolation to Alcmene, pointing out that one *thought* one was with the right person at best only exonerates the intentions of the deceived; it does not right the action. Emotions, after all, are not just mental events; they are, as one philosopher puts it, "engagements with the world."[23] Therefore, their appropriate operation presumes that the world has been properly understood.

Wise Children also features another deception, this time of an artifact: The twins go on tour in the United States with their (unacknowledged) father's Shakespearean troupe, which is working in a studio where he will produce *A Midsummer Night's Dream*. To bestow some authenticity on this New World venue, he requests that they dig some earth from Stratford-on-Avon to sprinkle around in California. They do so, but during the long journey a traveling cat decides the bard's native soil would make a good litter box, and the container of earth reeks by the time it reaches its destination. The

22. Angela Carter, *Wise Children* (New York: Farrar, Straus, and Giroux, 1991) pp. 85–86.

23. Robert C. Solomon, "Emotions, Thoughts, and Feelings: Emotions as Engagements with the World," in *Thinking about Feeling: Contemporary Philosophers on Emotions*, ed. Robert Solomon (New York: Oxford University Press, 2004): 76–89.

twins hastily dispose of it and substitute some local dirt, which is ritually scattered around the set with no one the wiser.

The entanglements of sexual liaisons add a layer of complication to these stories of mistaken identity that does not pertain to deception with regard to artifacts. In these cases, there has been an act—sexual intercourse by means of seduction, rape, or deception under the cover of darkness—that cannot be undone, and that in some circumstances therefore changes the value not only of the deceiver but also of the life of the deceived. The various versions of the tale of Alcmene and Amphitryon often focus on whether Alcmene remains a faithful wife; the virtue of the woman is made central to the questions explored by the narrative. Certainly, as Jupiter counsels, her love did not vary in its direction to her husband, and she was by no means complicit in the deception. Therefore, it is hard to call her an adulteress. (In his version of the play, Molière actually keeps Alcmene in the dark about her encounter with a god. Her conscience is kept clear and uncomplicated, but it is also ignorant. Would it be folly for her to become wise to the situation?) However, the point regarding virtue is by no means the most interesting philosophical puzzle raised by the story. The more pertinent question is the one that Ronald de Sousa poses. He refers to "Alcmene's problem" as a paradigm of a puzzle about nonfungible romantic love:

> We should assume that Zeus, being after all the king of the gods, put on an entirely convincing show. He took on—though only temporarily, of course, and in some strict sense remaining Zeus all the while—all the properties of Amphitryon. . . . Here is the logicomoral problem it raises: When Alcmene finds out, ought she to mind? The man she loved that night was, by hypothesis, qualitatively the same as her husband, though not the same numerically. But wasn't it for his qualities that she loved her husband? . . . For any reason she has for loving Amphitryon, however tenuous, must relate to some of his properties. And by hypothesis Zeus has them all.[24]

24. De Sousa, *Rationality of Emotions*, pp. 8–9.

De Sousa uses the story of Alcmene to dramatize the question of just what occasions a nonfungible emotion. Once Alcmene discovers the deception, her retrospective emotive reaction to her encounter changes. But why? What accounts for the fact that she in effect disavows the emotion that she previously experienced? Explaining this furthers the parallel explanation of an evaluation of a particular object as genuine and a reevaluation when a mistake is disclosed.

Emotions, as intentional states, have "objects," the thing, event, or state of affairs that a particular emotion is directed to, that is, what it is *about*. In the optimum case, one has sufficient understanding of the facts of a situation that an emotion is appropriately directed at its intentional object.[25] However, it is easy to make a mistake about the objects of emotions, to be angry at someone who did you no harm, sad about an event that really did not take place, and so forth. Causal factors that contribute to emotional arousal can be mistaken or misunderstood, with the result that emotions are directed at the wrong things.[26] Deception is high on the list of things that can detach intentional object from cause. Jupiter is right when he tells Alcmene that her thoughts of her husband keep her faithful, since her love remains directed to Amphitryon. This is scant comfort, however. She still *thinks* of her husband, but the object of her love *in action* is not a thought, it is a person—or a god appearing as a person. And the person who ought to match the thought does not. An object is not the appropriate focus of evaluative affection unless it is also causally responsible, at least in part, for the affective experience.[27] When one is deceived about the object of an experience, one is also deceived in how one feels.

While the justified belief that she was with her husband absolves Alcmene from the taint of infidelity, the fact that she was intimate with someone other than Amphitryon arouses distress and perhaps a sense of pollution despite her pure thoughts. For while a bedtrick

25. "Appropriateness" is the favored term for when an emotion is the right one to have in a situation. See Peter Goldie, *The Emotions* (New York: Oxford University Press, 2000).

26. Some of these remarks follow De Sousa's discussion in *Rationality of Emotion*, pp. 130–139. See also Rorty, "Explaining Emotions," pp. 103–126.

27. See again Goldman, "Experiential Account," p. 340; see also my discussion of this point in Chapter 1.

is often the occasion for comic confusions (the subtitle of Kleist's play is "A Comedy"), it can equally well contribute to tragedy. When Jocasta discovers that she has unknowingly married her own son and borne two children from an incestuous coupling, she hangs herself. Oedipus blinds himself and goes into exile. Neither is guilty of intentional wrongdoing, but the abomination of their relationship mandates punishment. The same self-punishment occurs in the tale of Secundus, who, having been absent for years, seduced his own mother. Even though he refrained from consummating their relationship, when his mother discovered that she had desired to sleep with her own son, in her overpowering shame she hangs herself.[28] In none of these cases was the deceived person aware of wrongdoing; intentions were pure or at least not sinful, and in the moment, their experiences seemed right—that is, with the appropriate person. But they were not, which is further proof that the notion of a so-called genuine experience independent of a genuine object of experience is always problematic, sometimes deeply and disturbingly so.

As with persons, so too with experiences of objects that are sought because of the particular histories they are taken to possess. One can be in error about the identity of the object before one, in which case discovery of error brings about a change in affect. By now I hope it is clear that this is by no means a symptom of an overactive imagination; it is a common characteristic of nonfungible intentional states. The alteration of response when misattribution of an object is discovered is very like the alteration of response in cases of mistaken identity. If some aura appears to dim, it is not because an object was previously endowed with a projected fantasy, but because the discovery of error reveals that the encounter was with the wrong object. In short: aesthetic sentiment, like appropriately directed emotion, does not merely *bestow* qualities on its objects; it also *recognizes* them.

De Sousa again:

> The case of Alcmene poses the question, If it was Zeus in her bed in the guise of Amphitryon, why should she mind?

---

28. This is a Greek tale that was popularly retold for centuries and was translated into Latin, Syrian, Armenian, and Arabic. See Doniger, *Bedtrick*, p. 387.

In summary, the discussion of fungibility has led us to a partial answer in terms of logical form: she should mind, because not to would be a category mistake. But underlying this grammatical consideration are some natural metaphysical and psychological ones. . . . Our attachments are to particulars, and if there are no particulars, or if we have the wrong one, then something has gone wrong with the ontological correlate of our emotion. The psychological answer, in brief, is that we are so wired as to acquire attachments in the course of our causal interaction with such individuals as are posited in our metaphysics. The fabric of our social and emotional life depends on our ability to transcend the original fungibility of all reactivity and transform it into nonfungible emotions.[29]

De Sousa's speculation that the "fabric of our social and emotional life" is woven together with the relationships built from taking individuals and not types as objects, seems to fit love, loyalty, and reverence directed to persons—all emotions important for social cohesion. I posit that there is a similar function for appreciation of the genuine artifact. Affective ties to objects from the past honor that past and those who went before us, and they register the fact that time engulfs us all. Perhaps that sensibility is an aspect of social cohesion, perhaps it deepens individual reflection. Simon James has argued that failure to respect old things signals a lack of humility.[30] This observation pertains not only to individuals but to whole societies. An absence of humility is evident in the short-sighted placement of contemporary economies above longer-term consequences. Communities that permit heedless destruction of historic neighborhoods, felling trees that have grown for centuries, and building strip malls, which themselves have a short life-span and give way to cycles of yet more development—these enterprises certainly appear to lack humility. The accumulations of history are slow; their destruction is quick. What seems to build for the future may often

29. De Sousa, *Rationality of Emotions*, p. 134.
30. See Simon James, "Why Old Things Matter," *Journal of Moral Philosophy* (2013): 313–329. DOI 10.1163/17455243-4681038.

just remove awareness of what is lost from the past. My tastes here are obvious and doubtless invite rejoinder, but whatever one's assessment of urban development, we can learn an important lesson from considering the comparison of artifacts with persons. Valuing things from the past holds the real thing in a kind of regard that parallels the affections we feel for persons meaningful to our lives.

Part and whole

At the beginning of Act III of Kleist's play, Amphitryon, in agony over the fact that his wife could not detect her false lover, rails at the failure of the senses to distinguish true lover from impostor:

> In rooms lit up by candlelight, a normal person
> Has never been mistaken in his friends;
> Eyes, liberated from their sockets, even
> Limbs that have been severed from the body,
> Ears, fingers, wrapped in boxes, should suffice
> To recognize one's husband.[31]

This passage serves as a slightly grisly segue to another link between persons and artifacts, one that occurs when a part of a person, either an entire corpse or a body part, is saved as a relic. Preserved parts of bodies serve various functions, the purpose of which varies greatly with different cultural practices. Probably the most-well-known cases, at least in western culture, are the relics of Roman Catholicism—the bones, blood, and possessions of saints and martyrs. Religious relics both confirm and confuse my study of genuineness. They confirm the transitivity of touch because in so many cases a relic is believed to have healing power or to act as an intercessor with the divine.[32] They confuse because, while being a relic from the "right" saint or martyr is important, the value of relics mainly resides in their

---

31. Kleist, *Amphitryon*, III:1, p. 57.
32. The Roman Catholic Church recognizes three degrees of relics. First degree: a body part of a saint, such as a bone; second degree: something that was owned by a saint or an instrument used against a martyred saint; third degree: something that was touched by a first- or second-degree relic. www.catholicdoors.com/faq/qu86.htm (Accessed 5.24.13). Erik Seeman pointed out the relevance of degrees of relics to me.

ability to accomplish such ends. Moreover, religious relics have an extraordinarily complicated history of controversy, including within the Catholic Church, regarding their authentication, their purposes, and their uses in worship.[33] While I will not ignore these kinds of objects altogether, they will not take center stage in this discussion. Consider, instead, the following examples of secular relics.

In 1666, seventeen years after his death, the bones of René Descartes were exhumed. His skeleton, and especially his skull, has been kept ever since and now resides at the Musée de l'Homme in Paris.[34]

In 1793, in the midst of the Terror, Molière's jawbone was sent for safekeeping to the Comédie Française theater in Paris, where it remains to this day.

In 1945, Robert Brasillach was executed by firing squad for treason. His lawyer collected a drop of his blood on a handkerchief to give to his loved ones.[35]

In 2000, the brain of Ishi, the last Native American known to have lived in isolated, traditional ways, was repatriated from the Smithsonian Institution to descendants of the Yana tribe in California.[36]

In 2003, an urn containing ashes from the funeral pyre of the Buddha drew crowds when it was put on display in Santiago, Chile.[37]

---

33. Dramatic controversies over the resuscitation of relics during the Counter Reformation, as well as the decoration and revering of dubious skeletons purported to be those of early martyrs, can be found in Paul Koudounaris, *Heavenly Bodies: Cult Treasures and Spectacular Saints from the Catacombs* (New York: Thames and Hudson, 2013).

34. The complicated and sometimes controversial history of Descartes' remains is examined in Russell Shorto, *Descartes' Bones: A Skeletal History of the Conflict between Faith and Reason* (New York: Doubleday, 2008).

35. Alice Kaplan, *The Collaborator: the Trial and Execution of Robert Brasillach* (Chicago: University of Chicago Press, 2000) p. 210.

36. Orin Starn, *Ishi's Brain: In Search of America's Last "Wild" Indian* (New York: W.W. Norton, 2004). See also the Smithsonian's statement at http://anthropology.si.edu/repatriation/projects/ishi.htm (Accessed 10.26.17). Thanks to a reviewer for the press who brought this case to my attention.

37. *Chicago Tribune*, June 29, 2003. At http://articles.chicagotribune.com/2003-06-29/news/0306290267_1_buddha-buddhism-buddhist-monks (Accessed 3.6.13).

In 2005, one of Napoleon's teeth sold at auction for 20,000 euros.[38]

In 2012, a burglar stole jewelry and other objects from a home, including—apparently by accident—an urn of cremated ashes. Several months later, the urn was quietly returned in a paper bag left on the front porch.[39]

In 2013, tests conducted on bones exhumed from beneath a Leicester parking lot confirmed the identity of the skeleton to be King Richard III of England, who died in battle in 1485. A ceremonial burial was conducted two years later at Leicester cathedral.[40]

In 2016, locks of David Bowie's hair were auctioned on e-Bay, and Truman Capote's ashes were put up for sale.

This list could extend indefinitely and would include multiple cultures and historical periods when bits of the bodies of persons have been saved for posterity for one reason or another. The reasons why the remains of particular people are kept vary, and the contexts for this practice are by no means all the same. Some are presumably saved to remember and to honor persons of renown, such as Descartes' skull. Some are keepsakes harboring the memory of a loved one now departed. Some are doubtless best classified as mere curiosities—poignant, gruesome, weird, or goofy. But the point is, in every such case, it is crucial that the relics be *of the right person*. If they were mingled with others of their kind (bones, ashes), no one could tell just by looking which belong to whom, except in unusual cases such as King Richard's distinctively twisted spine. But just as love for persons requires that they be accurately identified, so does retaining their bodily parts when bones, hair, blood, and ashes become lasting artifacts.

An obverse observation is pertinent, for there are cultures for which keeping, let alone circulating or displaying, bits of persons

---

38. The accounts of Molière and Napoleon, along with many other similar stories, are found in Clémentine Portier-Kaltenbach, "The Eternal Life of Bones," *Medicographia* (May 2011) at http://www.medicographia.com/2011/05/a-touch-of-france-the-eternal-life-of-bones (Accessed 2.19.13).

39. "Stolen Urn with Remains Finds Way to Pomfret Widow," *Buffalo News*, Sunday, February 10, 2013.

40. John F. Burns, "Richard III Gets a Kingly Burial, on Second Try," *New York Times*, March 26, 2015. http://www.nytimes.com/2015/03/27/world/europe/king-richard-iii-burial-leicester.html?_r=0 (Accessed 2.16.17).

after their deaths is regarded as a desecration. This is the case with many First Nation and Native American communities, as is evident with the numerous instances where remains taken from burial grounds have been the subject of dispute and legal adjudication.[41] Ishi's brain, for instance, which was sent in 1916 to the Smithsonian for study, was ceremonially cleansed and buried along with his ashes rather than kept for science or as a memento. But note that in these instances it still matters *whose* remains are returned to ancestral grounds and reburied. Nonfungibility obtains here as well.

Again, mistakes are often made. And when they are discovered, the sentiments the objects originally inspired might change accordingly. However, the regard for questionable objects, including the remains of persons, does not always change in the way that Alcmene's affections did for the man—the god—she wrongly took to be her husband. Even after an artifact is shown to have been misidentified, there are still some who continue to revere it under the former description. In some cases this is simply stubbornness, but in others, persistent regard for wrongly identified objects reveals something more complex.

Many artifacts that were once part of living human bodies are very old and have spotty provenances. Some are clearly not what they purport to be. Though there are eleven relics that have claims to be Saint Matthew's leg, he surely had only two. Descartes' thoughts only issued from one head, but there is a second skull in Sweden that might be his. So some of the encounters with this kind of item must be deceptions. Can we leave it at that? Is it sufficient to declare that some people marveling at relics have targeted the right things, while others are deceived; and though the latter might never find out, they are still in error? This diagnosis surely describes some circumstances, but as a generalization it yields a more simplistic answer than I would prefer to endorse.

41. James [Sa'ke'j] Youngblood Henderson, "The Appropriation of Human Remains: A First Nations Legal and Ethical Perspective," and Geoffrey Scarre, "The Repatriation of Human Remains," both in *The Ethics of Cultural Appropriation*, ed. James O. Young and Conrad Brunk (Malden, MA: Wiley-Blackwell, 2009): 55–71 and 72–92.

Honoring relics can be regarded as a social institution, representing cultural, historical, or religious practices that endow those things with enduring status, a surmise that was fielded at the end of the last chapter. It is hard to clear the fog from this phenomenon, but I would countenance the idea that just as the Ark of the Covenant in Aksum is a venerable object of worship regardless of whether it houses the tablets brought down the mountain by Moses, so can relics of various sorts accrue a history that endows them with a kind of specialness. They may not be the genuine bone of a saint, religious or secular, but they have assumed that role for so long that their own historical position commands attention. In other words, the standing of an object honored just for being itself is bestowed by time and history and also by practice. And practice— over sufficient time—can create a precedent for the object, even if it was misidentified in the first place. This is very messy territory, for the distinction between genuine and deceptive, original and fake, real and double must not be abrogated. And opening the door for the "wrong" things to become considered genuine if enough time passes appears to do just that. But history and culture are complex, and with complexity comes ambiguity, misunderstanding, and shifts of identification (different from shifts of identity), all of which enter into the contexts of understanding within which we savor things that embody the past.

Compare the thrill of unearthing an artifact that has lain buried for thousands of years in an undisturbed tomb, with a ceremony that has been performed in regular cycles for centuries using as a ritual object something that was wrongly identified several hundred years ago. The one is unquestionably real, but it has emerged into the present from the past, leaving a gap between its time and ours. The other wasn't properly identified at first, but it has accrued a history of sustained reverential practice. Though the original identity of the second object is contestable, both qualify as things that afford encounters with the past. The point to bear in mind is that unless we subscribe to a principle of parsimony that cannot fail to be arbitrary and therefore will not accommodate the complications involved with actual cases, any analysis of genuineness is bound to be heavily encumbered with uncertain and murky cases.

Emotions and aesthetic responses

The excursion into emotion theory pursued in this chapter also helps to amplify the aesthetic aspect of encounters with the genuine. Philosophers of art now commonly regard emotions as being essential to full understanding and appreciation of works, especially those with a narrative dimension.[42] It is not just that a reader or an audience member recognizes that characters in novels or plays are experiencing some sort of emotion, but that an emotion is actually aroused in the appreciative reader (or audience) as well. It might be an emotion similar to that of a character (apprehension that an attack is imminent) or different (pity for Tess Darbyfield). Emotions, or more generally strong affective episodes, are hardly limited to understanding narrative moments, of course. Music can arouse floods of feelings without any obvious narrative line at all.

In the first chapter I argued that an encounter with an object of some historical momentousness satisfies some of the traditional qualifications of the aesthetic, including a characteristic feeling, a thrill, shiver, or moment of wonder. We can pursue this claim in terms of its distinctive affective arousal. An encounter with an object that summons the past before us is not like the tasteful discernment of grace or delicacy, qualities that supervene upon perceptual properties such as thinness or hue. Nor is it a sensuous experience like eating chocolate. It is more like Wow. Or more articulately, it is akin to emotions such as love, reverence, respect, awe, or wonder—those directed at the very being of an object. While an object of awe may capture attention for what it is *like* (grand, majestic, powerful) it also commands wonder at its very *existence and presence*.[43] Both

---

42. For example, Susan L. Feagin, *Reading with Feeling: The Aesthetics of Appreciation* (Ithaca, NY: Cornell University Press, 1996); Derek Matravers, *Art and Emotion* (Oxford: Oxford University Press, 1998); Jenefer Robinson (*Deeper than Reason: Emotion and Its Role in Literature, Music, and Art* (Oxford: Oxford University Press, 2005). For some considerations of problems understanding how emotion is aroused by fictions, see Kendall Walton, *Mimesis as Make-Believe: On the Foundations of the Representational Arts* (Cambridge, MA: Harvard University Press, 1990); Mette Hjort and Sue Laver, eds., *Emotion and the Arts* (New York: Oxford University Press, 1997).

43. This approach is congenial to what Peter de Bolla calls the "materiality" of aesthetic experience—the affective dimension of experience that he argues induces the sense that an artwork is a "way of knowing." See "Toward the Materiality of Aesthetic Experience," *Diacritics* 32:1 (2002): 19–37. See also Hans Ulrich Gumbrecht's suggestive

zones of appreciation are aspects of aesthetic encounters—savoring the manifest qualities before one and also contemplating the very fact that the object that possesses them is here before us.

One of the chief functions of emotions is to prompt important behavior, to protect, safeguard, or enjoin social cohesion for example. A strong case can be made for such outcomes being the very reason that emotions evolved in the first place. Fear keeps us alert for things that would endanger us and our communities, disgust averts us from toxic substances, love prompts us to safeguard our children, and so forth. But in addition to these rather obvious functions, there are aspects of emotions for which pragmatic explanations are less plausible. Indeed, there are some emotions for which it is hard to find a clear functional role, such as nostalgia, that fugitive sense of longing for something in the past that may well have been imaginary in the first place. Nostalgia, while melancholy, also has a pleasant, contemplative aspect that may be savored as poignant and bittersweet. That savoring may be explored in a work of art or relished in the moment when it is aroused. Indeed, quite a few emotions possess an aesthetic dimension, meaning that the affective state not only prompts characteristic behavior, it also invites the subject to pause and dwell upon, relish, or ponder the qualities of intentional objects and the feelings they arouse.[44] A thunderstorm not only encourages one to get out of the wet, it also rivets attention with its power and grandeur. The very qualities of the storm that arouse fear can also be the object of admiration that prompts one to fight the urge to flee, because the fearsome object is also magnificent. (This aspect of fear gives rise to classic theories of the sublime, a whole aesthetic category in itself.) Not only the qualities of an object but also its very presence capture aesthetic attention, and it is the latter that is particularly significant to illuminate what I am calling aura. Thus emotions provide parallels that help

remarks about aesthetic experience oscillating between "presence effects" and "meaning effects," in *The Production of Presence: What Meaning Cannot Convey* (Stanford, CA: Stanford University Press, 2004).

44. Compare Aurel Kolnai's observation that disgust has a built-in aesthetic aspect that invites one to dwell upon the repulsive qualities of its object. "Disgust," in *Aurel Kolnai On Disgust*, ed. Barry Smith and Carolyn Korsmeyer (Chicago: Open Court, 2004 [1929]).

remove some of the obscurity from this contested concept. On the other hand, it would be too bad if all of its mystery were to disappear, since part of an encounter with the past is a sense of wonder and marvel at what we cannot fully know.

One more aspect of the comparison between emotions and aura is significant. Emotions are not just reactions with feeling qualities attached. They are also in their own ways modes of cognition. Without fear, we do not recognize danger, without sympathy we don't notice when another person needs our help. The range of cognition that different emotions realize is enormous and diverse, for each emotion episode takes some quality from its object. Thereby emotions achieve even more heterogeneity than the diversity of their types already represents. The experience of aura also possesses a cognitive element, for being moved by an object that brings the past to life is not just enjoyment, it is also insight. A particular moment when we understand something quite different from us and from our times—a moment of awe and wonder. But again, if background knowledge changes with information that one is mistaken about the identity or nature of an object, both awe and aura vanish.

Summing up

This chapter has ranged over territories diverse and strange, all of which sustain the importance of the correct identification of objects that warrant our attachments. I have pursued two sets of comparisons; the first is between works of art—herein extended to artifacts noteworthy for rarity or age—and persons. The second is between encounters with the genuine and nonfungible emotions. Some of this analysis is uncontroversial, for it is generally acknowledged that emotions register salient properties of objects, typically properties with axiological significance. It is also widely recognized that some emotions have proper targets that are restricted to particular individuals, in which case they are nonfungible. I have made the case that the thrills and shivers occasioned by encounters with the genuine are illuminated by considering them alongside nonfungible emotions. The parallels between persons and artifacts confirm that an experience of value—aesthetic, romantic, affectionate—presupposes that the relationship with the object of that experience be one that is correctly understood. Genuine things are comparable to persons in that they inspire affective responses that are nonfungible, such that substitutes and replicas do not possess the same standing as the real thing. Because authenticity is not a manifest property, the focus of this encounter is the very being of the object. It stands to reason, therefore, that when the mistaken identity of an object is discovered, its specialness fades. Whatever mysteries the idea of aura retains, it is not unique in its dependence on correct identification of its intentional object.

The comparison of artifacts and persons also illuminates something else about historically and culturally important objects: When they are destroyed, their loss is often regarded as very like the loss of human life.[45] The next chapter will explore the kinds of harm that artifacts suffer, the efforts undertaken to palliate or redress those harms, the ethics of how things are treated, and consequences for the notion of genuineness that all of these matters entail.

45. This was literally the case with the destruction of the Golden Spruce, a giant Sitka spruce in the Queen Charlotte Islands that was sacred to the Haida. This tree was apparently the only one of its kind, bearing golden rather than green needles. Its uniqueness protected it even from logging companies, but in 1997 a demented logger cut deeply into its trunk and brought it down. The death of the Golden Spruce was treated in much the same way as the death of a person: its loss was considered murder, it was mourned, and its remains were claimed by the Haida community much as relatives claim the bodies of loved ones. John Vaillant recounts the story of this tree and its destruction in *The Golden Spruce: A True Story of Myth, Madness, and Greed* (New York: W.W. Norton, 2005). The parallels between destruction of artifacts and murder was made explicit in 1917 with the exhibit of "Assassinated Art" held at the Petit Palais in Paris as a protest against the destruction of German bombs during World War I.

4

Loss and Rescue, Help and Harm

In the final chapter I intend to sum up the fruits of these labors by presenting a general picture of what it means to be genuine—an ontological account of sorts. I have been making a case for the complexity of the concept and for the need to recognize that genuineness comes in degrees. To a large extent, those degrees pertain to the amount of "original" physical material remaining in an artifact, though the fact that I have had to put scare quotes around *original* already indicates that measuring physical persistence is not easy. This is not just a metaphysical point but a practical one as well, for among the objects that furnish encounters with the past are works of architecture and engineering, and it is the nature of those artifacts to undergo repairs and other alterations that introduce changes into their physical components, sometimes from the very beginning of their making. Although material things can outlast the measly human three score years and ten, not even the sturdiest edifice remains unchanged forever. Renovations are part of the natural life, as it were, of such artifacts. If we are to understand the nature of genuineness, it is necessary that we not wed that concept to a static notion of "original condition." Just how much of the original material state of a thing needs to be retained before an artifact loses its identity varies with the kind of thing it is. Hence the importance of considering actual examples, a tactic that also propels this chapter.

These variations and complexities are pertinent to real-world concerns regarding the way that artifacts should be treated. If we grant that objects of rarity, cultural significance, or great age furnish encounters with the past and as such possess value, questions arise that are both theoretical and practical. How ought we to treat these things? What or who is harmed when an artifact is damaged? Should important things from the past be restored when they deteriorate or even reconstructed after they are destroyed? When do present exigencies justify obliterating past treasures? Questions about the proper treatment of material objects and the harm that can be done them blend aesthetic, ethical, and ontological considerations.[1] There are numerous ways in which artifacts are harmed, some intentional, some accidental, some preventable, some inevitable. Damage can come about through development and the expansion of cities, through warfare when cultural treasures are destroyed by accident or design, and from sheer vandalism. Sometimes harm comes about inadvertently from benignant but ill-judged actions to preserve or restore things to former glory. The latter cases prompt questions about just *what* has been preserved, restored, and kept from harm. Are there times when the old object should be mourned and recognized as lost because the restored object now in its place is not the real thing at all? Or should repairs be considered revivals that bring a thing back to life, despite the need for substantial substitution of new materials to regain its former characteristics? If one is intent only to sustain the perceptual appearance of an object—the way it looks—then there is considerable impetus to restore whatever is possible. Since I have stressed the role of touch, however, and have argued that an important value is submerged beneath the perceptual surface of objects, it will be more difficult for me

---

1. Peter Lamarque, "Reflections on the Ethics and Aesthetics of Restoration and Conservation," *British Journal of Aesthetics* 56:3 (July 2016): 281–299.

to countenance techniques that restore appearance by substituting new parts. Formulating general principles to guide such decisions is additionally difficult because restoration and reconstruction do not represent actions that can be evaluated entirely apart from the kind of harm an object has suffered. Since the causes of destruction can affect the motives to repair, a survey of types of harm is a useful preview for thinking about the varieties of the genuine that remain after disaster, neglect, and the ravages of time have taken their toll.

Harming things

Looting—a practice probably as old as burials—is an obvious hindrance to historical understanding. Looting separates artifacts from their places and contexts of origin, from their temporal companions, from the history of their making. These are what one might term epistemic offenses because they interfere with historical understanding, and they quickly blend with offences against cultures. Culture and tradition reside in hearts, minds, and practices, but also in material things that accrue with the passage of time. So looting becomes an offense against a people. If it is a tomb or a grave that is looted, there is also offence against the dead, against families, against religions, and sometimes against whole cultures. All of these actions have moral aspects, being wrongs done to persons to large or small degree. As such, offences against history and science are also ethical affronts to individuals, groups, and societies. Recognizing such offences shores up the significance of the development of nonfungible attachments and their role in what De Sousa refers to as the "fabric of our social and emotional life," mentioned in the last chapter. When harm is done to artifacts, the triple values of the genuine—cognitive, ethical, and aesthetic— converge. As Ivan Gaskell puts it, "To accord an object historical and aesthetic standing is to respect it, and, by extension, its makers and first users."[2] Even more generally, as Erich Hatala Matthes observes,

---

2. Ivan Gaskell, "Ethical Judgments in Museums," *Art and Ethical Criticism*, ed. Garry Hagberg (Malden, MA: Blackwell, 2008): 229–242, on p. 235. A case can also be made that harming things of aesthetic value amounts to ethical harms as well, reducing as

"How we relate to the past is an important dimension of our ethical lives and relationships more broadly."[3]

As a rule looters do not seek to destroy or damage the artifacts they take, though they often do so in the process of removal and transport. Willful damage does occur if an object is stolen in order to extract precious metals or gems; but unless they are simply bent on vandalism, the goal of looters is not destruction but profit. Their offence is matched by participants in the market for antiquities and rarities as transporters, middlemen, and buyers. The wrongs perpetrated by looting are huge and often irreparable. However, apart from the injury caused by being wrenched out of the context that gives it historical and scientific meaning, an object successfully stolen is not deliberately damaged, for its monetary value drops if it is.

All of that changes with war. War provides occasions for looting, but it also demonstrates ways in which peoples, cultures, and nations are attacked by means of destroying their artifacts. The importance of objects is recognized in a tragically backhanded way by the fact that they can become targets in armed conflict. This has occurred numerous times throughout history when artifacts are so connected with a people that conquerors visit wholesale destruction upon them, as did Cortés, who in 1521 razed to the ground Tenochtitlán, the capitol city of the Aztecs. The examples of this kind of colonizing destruction are too numerous to catalogue here, as are acts of vengeful and wanton wreckage against enemies real or imagined. Destruction also can be directed internally during times when portions of a culture's own past are rejected with violence, as with the period of Byzantine iconoclasm of the eighth and ninth centuries, the French Revolution of the late eighteenth century, and China's Cultural Revolution of the 1960s.[4]

it does the overall goodness that humans might experience in their lifetimes. This thesis is considered with regard to aesthetic foundations for environmental ethics in Robert Elliott, *Faking Nature: The Ethics of Environmental Restoration* (London: Routledge, 1997).

3. Erich Hatala Matthes, "The Ethics of Historic Preservation," *Philosophy Compass* (August 2016): 1–9, on p. 2. DOI 10.1111/phc3.12379.

4. Dario Gamboni, *The Destruction of Art: Iconoclasm and Vandalism since the French Revolution* (New Haven, CT: Yale University Press, 1997). This book contains a wealth of information about the varieties of motives, reasons, and outcomes of the destruction of artifacts.

Acts of war against artifacts continue unabated. To mention just a few: In 1993 artillery fire brought down the 400-year-old bridge of Mostar in Bosnia and Herzegovina. Among the charges of war crimes facing the Croatian commander during the siege was the destruction of the ancient bridge, a unique product of Ottoman architecture and engineering. In 2001, members of the Taliban publically dynamited the sixth-century giant statues of Buddha carved into rock at Bamiyan in Afghanistan. Debate continues over whether and how these antiquities might be restored or rebuilt. In 2003 after the United States invaded Iraq, the Baghdad Museum that housed Mesopotamian antiquities came under fire. Little protection was afforded the site, and the US military was sharply criticized for failing to guard the museum and thereby prevent what was widely labeled a crime against humanity. In October of 2015 members of ISIS destroyed Syrian archaeological sites in and around Palmyra, including the famous triumphal arch of the Roman emperor Septimus Severus and the Temple of Ba'al. Several of these destroyed artifacts will guide my discussion here, though, sadly, many more could be invoked. Although they are all examples of objects targeted in acts of war, their subsequent histories raise different issues regarding the value of the genuine and how to preserve and sustain it.

Artifacts are also, and very commonly, harmed through neglect when economic value falters and buildings are left to deteriorate, or when development overwhelms awareness of history and deliberately destroys the old in favor of the new. That development may result from the gradual outward creep of urban environments or the dramatic destruction that occurs when large projects such as dams are built that flood older settlements or archaeological sites, as with the high dam at Aswan in Egypt or the Alqueva Dam in Portugal. In many such cases, the importance of an artifact is recognized too late to preserve it, and only belatedly are efforts mounted to redress the earlier error. Sometimes portions of original structures remain while lost components are replicated, reattached, rebuilt. In such cases, fragments of the old anchor the new, retaining some evidence of the continuities of history.

Damage and repair in all forms can result in objects that exhibit what I have labeled "degrees" of genuineness, in large part because only a certain portion of their early structures remain. Countenancing degrees of genuineness lands us in some very controversial territory regarding the preservation, restoration, relocation, and reconstruction of artifacts. Some of these debates are considered later in this chapter. There are many cases where repair and even removal are the only ways to sustain an object of value, as with public statuary endangered by air pollution or old buildings that have lost structural integrity. On the other hand, there are circumstances where alteration compromises worth entirely. Among the latter are artifacts that have become memorials. I begin with some examples of memorials, more specifically memorial sites, where the ethical demands of the genuine are particularly evident. Moreover, they demonstrate an aspect of the real thing that requires greater consideration: location, reminding us again of the role of proximity in the experience of the real thing.

Memorial sites bring into focus the convergence of values when genuineness underlies other sorts of worth and where the distinction between aesthetic and ethical considerations blurs. This observation is not a brief for bringing together aesthetic and ethical properties when they appear to be at odds with each other (as they frequently do). Rather, I claim that genuineness is at heart a quality that in itself possesses multiple values, including historical and scientific (since real things provide information about the past); aesthetic (insofar as the encounter with the genuine invites its own zone of savoring an object that embodies its history); and ethical— when objects and sites require that we honor or remember people and events from the past. While often one or another of those interests predominates, certain sorts of things summon notice of all three at once. As Marcia Eaton notes, "There may be assessments that require *both* aesthetic and ethical reflection simultaneously."[5] Memorial sites and artifacts number among the things that demand this sort of combined regard.

5. Marcia Eaton, "Aesthetics: The Mother of Ethics?" *Journal of Aesthetics and Art Criticism* 55:4 (Fall 1997): 355–364, on p. 356. See also Carolyn Korsmeyer, "Staying in Touch," in *Ethical Criticism and the Arts*, ed. Garry L. Hagberg (Malden Ma: Blackwell, 2008): 187–210. In this article I first explored several of the examples discussed in this chapter.

Memorial sites

In early July of 1863, Confederate and Union soldiers fought in an area of farms and woods in eastern Pennsylvania near the little town of Gettysburg. After three days of combat there were close to 51,000 casualties and over 7,000 men lay dead in the mud of the devastated fields. Plans to dedicate the area as a memorial to the fallen began as early as 1864, and eventually in 1933 it was taken over by the National Park Service. The site has been accorded landmark status, which now protects it from neglect and destruction. The Gettysburg Battlefield commemorates those fallen in a conflict that divided a nation and a people; visiting the site prompts consideration of the rival values of that war, the blunders and brilliance of its leaders, and its horrendous casualties—all ethical elements of the awareness enjoined by the place.[6]

The perimeter of the area where the fighting took place is not exactly the same as that marked out today as the edges of the Military Park, and because the land is no longer farmed, the terrain looks different from the way it did at the time of the Civil War. Over the years the outlines of the battleground altered as land was purchased and buildings erected; trees have grown where once there was pasture. Long-term rehabilitation projects aim to return the Gettysburg landscape as close as possible to its appearance in 1863 and to keep it that way in years to come. These efforts are considered necessary in order to present the area as it served as a battlefield, which requires removing newer growth, felling trees that interfere with older sightlines, and many other reversals of what both nature and human use have wrought over the years.[7]

This renovation has proven a sensitive point of contention in the area. In order to accomplish their goal, the Park Service must

6. Arthur Danto has pointed out some ways in which battlefields are like works of art. His moving essay "Gettysburg" is indispensable reading for understanding the complexity of the experiences this battlefield affords. See *Philosophizing Art* (Berkeley: University of California Press, 1999): 233–250.

7. The website of the Gettysburg National Military Park (https://www.nps.gov/gett/index.htm) contains much information about landscape rehabilitation. See especially "Battlefield Landscape" in the Foundation Document available there. (Accessed 7.19.18)

remove trees that have grown up for more than a century. Trying to return terrain to conditions that obtained so much earlier may seem to obviate the realities of nature and even in some respect to deny history by erasing signs of the passage of time. I am sympathetic to this objection, but resolving the issues to everyone's satisfaction is impossible because of the different reasons to visit the battlefield. Civil War buffs, for example, want to envision the battle itself, the strategies of its commanders, and its terrible stages of carnage, an imaginative exercise that is made easier by having the terrain and flora similar to the way they were in 1863.

Thus certain features of the battlefield that are like the area in 1863 have been deemed indispensable for a full and proper experience of Gettysburg. Note, however, that I have just said "like the original," not "original." While the location of things that happened, if known, will remain exactly marked, the grass that now grows is not the same as grew before, nor are replanted trees or replaced fences identical to those from long ago. That may seem an obvious and trivial point, for it would be fruitless to insist that the grass be identical to that which grew more than a century ago. Grass just isn't that kind of thing; in fact, grass in 1863 wouldn't have been identical to grass in 1862 or 1864 either. No one expects individual blades of grass to persist like marble statuary. But the observation is not trivial, for it indicates that restoration presumes more than the simple *look* of the field as it was long ago. Real grass must grow where grass did; real trees must grow, real water must run in the streams. The Park is not being outfitted with Astroturf and the replanted trees are not plastic shrubbery. This is not because plastic doesn't look sufficiently like nature, because in fact it can do so. Rather, it is appropriate that what once was farmland remain land that could be farmed.

In other words, returning a place to its appearance at an earlier time actually goes further than simple appearance; it requires appearance of the right kinds of replacement objects to substitute for those that are irretrievable in principle. Restoration of a battlefield cannot glue together original materials. But while it cannot aim at identity of condition, it can approximate kind of condition. The point to take away here is that there are aspects of artifacts that by their very nature grow and change and are replaced with things of their kind—in this case grass. It is nature's mandate that this be the case. Other kinds of replacement will arise shortly.

Locations

Whatever controversies circulate about maintenance of this site, there is one point of complete agreement: No one disputes that its geographic location is crucial. When one visits Gettysburg, one must be *at* Gettysburg. Being *there* is indispensable, for the location itself is an aspect of what one desires to encounter. Squabbles about perimeters aside, the central elements of the battle took place where the fallen are now remembered. The many instances of sites where historical events occurred represent evidence of the importance of accurate location, perhaps most dramatically with locations that become memorials. The importance of location is assumed by both rehabilitationists and those who prefer that nature be permitted to change the terrain in its own way. This tacit agreement acknowledges that the battlefield is still there even if natural growth and its changes now pervade the precincts.

A much more recent memorial further testifies to the crucial necessity of location: the Memorial to United Flight 93 in Shanksville, Pennsylvania, also maintained now by the US National Park Service (and about a hundred miles west of Gettysburg). This is the crash site of the aircraft that was brought down by passengers and crew in their attempt to regain control of the plane from hijackers who apparently intended to complete the terrorist attacks of September 11, 2001, by hitting Washington's Capitol building. Much of the site traces the trajectory of the plane just before it went down; the invisible flight path is marked by a granite walkway placed below.[8] Nothing here can be moved. It is the place itself that one encounters. Trees may grow and fall, weather may erode the terrain, the memorial walkway itself could be destroyed. Oddly, the site where the plane flew, the flight path, will remain—there and only there. The

---

8. Similarly, the reflecting pools of the Nine-Eleven Memorial in New York City describe the footprints of the Twin Towers in their exact location.

path itself is not the sort of thing that can be either preserved or restored, though our knowledge of where it was can be kept or lost. Though obliterating the granite walk that marks the path could be considered a desecration of the memorial, what precisely would be erased is orientation—knowledge of where one is in relation to the event commemorated.

In other words, some signal is required to mark a site: a statue, a plaque or historic marker. Often remnants of the past are simply gone, and location is the *only* factor available to notice by way of the label testifying to a past event. Because such sites populate places where daily practical life still takes place, historical markers are easy to ignore. So much has happened before our times that no one can keep it all in mind and stay sane. The effort would be paralyzing. Yet there are times when the smallest of markers can capture attention and stun us into recognition of something long gone. Once when, tired and hungry, I trudged up a large staircase at the University of Vienna, I glanced down at my feet and discovered that I was stepping on the very spot where in 1936 Moritz Schlick was murdered. The sudden awareness of just where I was drove away my fatigue, but the students flooding up and down the stairs merely found my dumbstruck pause an inconvenience. It takes either dramatic discoveries or particular attentiveness to make a label command attention. Highway stops on the New York State Thruway are pocked with historical markers noting events from the French and Indian Wars. A traveler might pause to read the signs while finishing an ice cream or looking for a trash can, though they are usually ignored. But the point is that the signs could not be moved to a more convenient or reverent site because they mark the *real* (location of) an event.

The invisibility of what one pays homage to and the need for a marker to orient position affords an important insight: a memorial site invites a distinctive sort of physical participation: visitors place themselves *where* something of moment occurred.[9] Mere outlines of past places can provide not only information about what once

9. See Jennifer Judkins, "On Things that Aren't There Anymore," *Journal of Aesthetics and Art Criticism* 72:4 (Fall 2014): 441–445.

stood there but even a sense of stepping back in time, of standing in history. Such is the case with the outlined frame of Benjamin Franklin's house, where one can walk in and out of invisible rooms tracing footsteps of colonial Philadelphia.[10] Bodily position and movement, as noted earlier, are registered strongly by the sense of touch, and wandering amid this kind of site puts the visitor in proximity to that which is called to mind. This is a profoundly *situated* experience—which is another aspect of things that embody the past; they engage our own physical participation. There is no such thing as a traveling exhibit of a memorial site; regardless of what is built or what grows upon it, the real site is not portable and admits no change of location.

The desire to visit sites where important events occurred has some odd variations that demand especially keen imaginative engagement. Among the strangest is the veneration held for an oak tree in Ohio that was the locus of a scene in the 1994 movie *The Shawshank Redemption*. The movie recounts the friendship that develops between two men who serve long prison sentences together, and it garnered a large admiring audience. Many traveled to visit that tree in order to "be at" the movie's climactic scene, when Red (played by Morgan Freeman) reads a letter from his friend and unburies money left by Andy (Tim Robbins). In addition to the fact that Red and Andy are fictional, the plot of the movie situates the tree not in Ohio but in Maine. The tree was fictionally in Maine while literally in Ohio, so *Shawshank* fans had to visit Ohio, suspending their knowledge of place in favor of proximity with the object. (In 2011 when a violent windstorm damaged the oak, thousands worried that it would die. It survived, although another storm brought it down in 2016.) In this case, the reality of the tree overtook the fictionality of the place. The *Shawshank* tree indicates the power that a thing can exert over the imagination, and the object that is the focus of attention must be the real thing—albeit oddly understood in this instance. This tale provides a touchingly goofy confirmation of my thesis.

(On the other hand, perhaps it seems odd mainly because of the absence of traditions for visiting fictional sites in the United States. In contrast consider Iceland, an old culture where little of the antique built environment survives since dwellings were commonly made of sod and thatch. The famous sagas that present tales of heroes, warriors, and ordinary folk trace the terrain that still defines the island. Citizens and tourists alike may go to stand in the places of warfare, revenge, loss, and triumph that are detailed in the sagas.[11])

Moving places

Fictional sites aside, location represents an almost unchangeable aspect of the real thing with artifacts such as memorial sites. Almost. Already, however, I have to let the pendulum swing back a little, for there is a sense in which *sites* can be distinguished from the physical *places* that they inhabit. Sites are identified by a particular set of coordinates that describe where an event occurred. As a rule, site and place are co-located, the terms even more or less synonymous. But more loosely speaking, place also connotes the physical terrains that sites occupy. Earth and stone are composed of materials, and parts of them can be removed and taken elsewhere. Exiles, immigrants, and refugees who must flee to alien lands might carry with them a handful of native soil. Those who want to be buried in a particular country might settle for having some earth from the desired resting place sprinkled in their grave. (Christian crusaders sometimes returned home with soil from the Holy Land for that purpose.) If one cannot go to a place, a bit of that place may be transported.

This custom also confirms the importance of the real physical thing, and it is not only an antique or even particularly rare practice. The now-familiar ritual of scattering the ashes of the dead over a favorite spot of land or water might be considered a version. Here is a more elaborate example. The first president of Miami University in

---

11. For a map of the Icelandic Sagas, see http://sagamap.hi.is/is/ (Accessed 9.30.16).

FIGURE 4.1 Circle of Remembrance, Miami University, Ohio, 2015. Photo by author.

FIGURE 4.2 Stones from Broughty, Angus, Pitlochry, and Muirhead, 2015. Photo by author.

Ohio was Robert Hamilton Bishop (1777–1855), a native of Scotland. He and his wife are buried on campus near a Circle of Remembrance in which are embedded stones from various parts of Scotland (Figures 4.1–4.2). Location is important again, but now it is the location of origin of the stones which have been moved thousands of miles away. A tiny part of a place can be moved, carrying its home with it when situated in a context where that origin is accorded importance.

In short, even with something as intuitively immovable as location, there is some wiggle room for the conditions that validate that the real thing is present—if that is, by "location" one refers to the materials that come from a special place. No amount of wiggling, however, establishes the possibility of moving a site.

These first examples include memorial sites that require sameness of location and are immovable, as well as physical portions of places that absolutely must be from a particular location but can be noted as such and moved elsewhere. Visitors who travel to memorials frequently have tribute or vigil as a purpose for their journeys; and for those charged with maintaining memorials the moral weight of such places can be hard to overlook. Here is a relatively recent statement about the preservation of the notorious death camp at Auschwitz-Birkenau:

> Since its creation in 2009, the foundation that raises money to maintain the site of Auschwitz-Birkenau has had a guiding philosophy: "To preserve authenticity." The idea is to keep the place intact, exactly as it was when the Nazis retreated before the Soviet Army arrived in January 1945 to liberate the camp . . .
>
> It is a moral stance with specific curatorial challenges. It means restoring the crumbling brick barracks where Jews and some others were interned without rebuilding those barracks, lest they take on the appearance of a historical replica. . . .
>
> And it means deploying conservators to preserve an inventory that includes more than a ton of human hair; 110,000 shoes; 3,800 suitcases; 470 prostheses and orthopedic braces; more than 88 pounds of eyeglasses; hundreds of empty canisters of Zyklon B poison pellets;

patented metal piping and showerheads for the gas chambers; hundreds of hairbrushes and toothbrushes . . .[12]

An example such as this one demonstrates especially dramatically how encounters with memorial sites are freighted with moral import among their other values. As such, they invite not only aesthetic responses of the sort already described but also reflection, honor, remembrance of tragedy or heroism, pity for victims, condemnation of perpetrators. Thoughts of some or all of these things converge, and they all contribute to the impact of the encounter. This is also the case with much smaller artifacts that become objects of remembrance.

Memorial objects

Part of the Historical Museum of the City of Krakow, Poland, the branch known as "Silesian House," occupies a set of buildings that in 1939 was taken over by the Gestapo. In one group of small rooms located half-underground, Poles who were arrested on suspicion of anti-Nazi activities were detained, interrogated, tortured, and sometimes executed. On the cement walls of these cells are more than six hundred inscriptions scratched by prisoners who left their names, their prayers, their protests, and their final messages to family and friends. Over time those marks have faded, and the caretakers of the museum have redrawn some of them so that they are still readable. On portions of the walls that have not been so kept up, one can discern only faint traces.[13]

These messages are personal farewells, laments, prayers, historical records—and now they are also memorials. That the wall-inscriptions are the exact marks made by prisoners is part of their impact. Stepping close to the wall, close to those scratches,

---

12. Rachel Donadio, "Preserving the Ghastly Inventory of Auschwitz," *New York Times*, April 15, 2015, https://www.nytimes.com/2015/04/16/arts/international/at-auschwitz-birkenau-preserving-a-site-and-a-ghastlyinventory.html?hp&action=click&pgtype=Homepage&module=second-column-region&region=top-news&WT.nav=top-news&_r=o.

13. This description matches the museum when I visited it in 2004.

the visitor is moved to retrace the marks with her own fingers—to touch that which was first inscribed under circumstances one painfully struggles to imagine. There is a sense of continuity in touching what others have touched. In this place touch provides, or at least seems to provide, intimate contact with those who were there imprisoned.

I say "seems to provide" because while the deceivability of vision is familiar, touch is often thought to be less prone to illusion. It is the outstretched hand that determines if a hallucination is real or not. But we can be just as mistaken or misled about the authenticity of the object of touch as we are about anything else, and here lies one nexus of the aesthetic and the ethical value of the real thing. Touch, including proximity (as defended in the first chapter), imparts a sense of being in the presence of something unusual, special, or unique. Being deceived or mistaken about such an object, and therefore of the value of the experience, is not trivial. Does the renewal of the messages by hands other than the prisoners' themselves lessen their genuineness and dilute the profundity of the encounter?

In one sense we could say it does, because intervening marks have accrued between the original moment of inscription and the present, building up a layer, albeit a very thin one, between the past and the present state of the walls. One's contact is to that degree mediated. But in a more important sense it does not. Not only are the inscriptions renewed so that they continue to be visible, but there is a continuity of renewals, a continuity that perpetuates the transitivity of touch. And they are not redrawn at another place. The fact that the marks are kept visible so that future visitors will remember what happened there is a significant factor in this continuity, as well as a means to keep the place functioning effectively as a memorial. The marks are not replicas of the last messages; they remain the very messages once left, fully retaining their power to provide encounters with the real thing. Actions that serve to preserve an object in good shape are not necessarily interruptions to the transitivity of touch.

Another display at the Silesian House dramatizes even more momentously the importance of being before the real thing. Upstairs there is a large room with vitrines full of objects from the Nazi occupation. One of them holds a collection of grisly detritus from the camps, including a set of dice made by a prisoner from lumps of bread and a gold-embossed cigarette case made from human skin. One cannot tell that the case is made from skin just by looking. It could be any thin, pale leather. But it is crucial to the experience of this item that one believe that one is in the presence of the real thing—a frivolous object made from a fragment of what once was a living person.

When face to face with a horror such as that cigarette case, there is no doubt of the moral resonance of the object. Only the genuine object can bear witness to itself. This is yet another example where the real thing demands an attitude of respect and a measure of moral sensibility. Another similarity between objects and persons might be registered here, though in this case the similarity is horridly intimate. I have been arguing throughout that despite perceptual indiscernibility, there is an aesthetic difference between experiences of objects that are what they are believed to be and those that are not. I hope that this claim will be even more convincing with the addition of moral aspects to encounters with things preserved from the past, experiences that register both what an object is and the human loss it signals.

The difference between renewal and replication is illustrated by another personal example. Not long ago I stood before Durham

Cathedral reading a plaque by the door. For centuries, it stated, people needing sanctuary had only to seize the heavy iron knocker above my head and strike loudly to seek admittance. Feeling a kind of archaic sympathy with that gesture, I raised my hand to add my own knock to the tally. But reading further, I learned that the original object had been removed to the cathedral museum and the iron knocker now in place was a replica (Figure 4.3).[14] My hand fell away.

FIGURE 4.3 Sanctuary Knocker from the North Door of Durham Cathedral, 12th century. Photo credit: HIP/Art Resource, NY.

14. There are numerous instances where an important part of a site has been substituted with a replica, either to preserve a fragile object or to forestall theft. In 2009 the insignia over the entrance to Auschwitz that famously proclaims "Arbeit macht frei"

Had the knocker been polished, remounted, cleaned, or repaired, the impulse to touch would have been sustained. It was only discovery that the object before me only looked like the original but was a replica that halted the gesture.

The viewing public is usually not in a position to judge the authenticity of an article on display and must trust to interpretive labels. For that matter, even experts, unless they are engaged at the moment in professional analysis, may not be sure about matters of restoration, repair, and replication. One purpose of skillful restoration is to render objects such that the apparent continuity with their past seems to resist the more destructive changes that time brings about. Some advocates for restoration deem it successful if restored artifacts avail a full affective experience, including the insight made possible by presenting an object that appears to be in its original condition. If this is the only criterion of success, this view implicitly endorses the theoretical position that locates the aesthetic value of artworks entirely in the experience they prompt. Previous discussion, I hope, has established that one cannot isolate an experience from what that experience is *of*, and when its object is a replica, the experience it occasions is different from what it would be if the object were genuine. This is especially dramatic with cases where the ethical aspect of genuineness is in play. With the addition of moral value to the equation, the shallowness of the view that "genuine" modifies experience alone should be even more persuasively evident. Of course, one can be fooled, as with any perceptual encounter. But being fooled constitutes a flaw in the experience itself—albeit the flaw is not always recognized. Matthew Kieran makes a similar observation when he discusses the compromised aesthetic value of both forgeries and non-deceptive simulacra of works of art, a point stressed in the first chapter that is worth repeating here:

> The crucial point is, even if we did have perfect copies, we
> would still have reason to value the originals more than the

---

was stolen. Though later recovered, the genuine object was not reinstalled but a replica put in its place. The original is now in the Auschwitz-Birkenau State Museum. (In this case the original was sequestered because of indications that the camp signs were being retrieved by neo-Nazi groups.)

perfect copies. It is neither irrational nor sentimental to do so, since the reason runs very deep indeed.

What is the reason then? It concerns the essentiality of origin. What this opaque phrase picks out is the idea that what matters regarding our attitudes to something is not just a function of what its inherent qualities are, but also a matter of the relations in which the object stands to us.[15]

Can one, however, consistently maintain all of the claims I have been defending: (1) that genuineness admits of degrees; (2) that the status of being genuine need not exclude repairs and restorative additions to damaged objects; and (3) that the only really legitimate experience must be of the real thing? Has the notion of *real thing* become too compromised by the second statement to distinguish veridical experience from encounters with a misunderstood object? These questions merge with ongoing disputes over restoration and the techniques of that complicated enterprise. Much of this debate concerns works of fine art, though the reasons advanced for one side or another can be extended to artifacts of all sorts.

Restoring versus destroying

Artifacts can be vandalized, broken, smashed, or looted, and in addition to those obvious forms of harm, they can be treated in well-intentioned ways that inadvertently damage them, sometimes gravely. Hence ongoing arguments about how best to preserve things of value, whether to restore them, and whether to rebuild them if they reach a point where restoration is no longer possible. A great deal has been written on this subject, much of it by practitioners who also address the technical complexities involved in preservation and repair. I shall engage only some of the argument that has been contributed by philosophers.

The very concept of restoration makes a number of assumptions about the artifact in need of treatment. Only something considered valuable would merit restoration, but that value resides in different

---

15. Matthew Kieran, *Revealing Art* (London: Routledge, 2005) p. 14.

aspects of a thing and may not present clear options. Especially if age value is in question, one could argue that any tampering with the effects of time will compromise the worth of the object. But in addition, to what point in its past should something ideally be restored? In the case of recent destruction, as with warfare or vandalism, restoration to the immediately past condition is probably mandated, although the recent injuries might present an opportunity for improvement of older damage as well. When it is time and slow deterioration that caused an artifact to decay or fade, it is less clear what points in its history should be approximated. The answer to this will depend heavily on what kind of thing it is: a painting, a building, a section of a city, an archeological site. Especially with the latter two, it is clear that a choice has to be made about what point in the past should be aimed at in order to restore an artifact to a former condition; sometimes only stabilization of what remains is mandated. But even when dealing with smaller objects, those that might not have changed in the course of normal use, such as paintings or sculptures, turning back the clock requires dicey decisions. A patina may have developed on a sculpture that was actually intended by the artist, or colors may have faded or bloomed in ways that enhance appearance. If one has information about makers' intentions, they can act as a guide, but in many cases decisions will depend on old photographs, descriptions, or inferences.

Inferences about how an artifact used to be are important in Randall Dipert's account of the nature of restoration. He stresses that an artifact is the result of intentional action, and hence the intentions of the original makers determine the direction of restoration. Sometimes those intentions can be divined; other times they cannot. Dipert notes that some

> deterioration . . . leaves the originally intended feature inferable with some degree of probability from the present observable features of the object (or its remains). Thus, a building may no longer be standing, but we can recover its intended design from the ruins. In other cases, the intended features may be inferable from other than the object (e.g., diary entries). Finally, in many cases of deterioration,

artifactual features are not now inferable at all (at least not with any reasonable likelihood).[16]

Some of the most controversial restorations are those that guess at an original feature of an artifact with insufficient evidence, as was the now notorious case when Sir Arthur Evans rebuilt a portion of the ruins of Knossos.[17] Even when a maker's intention is inferable, complex as that may be in the case of a city, where many builders would have been working, there is still the question of restoration that introduces new material in order to recreate the older appearance of an object. This is where the look of an object can separate from its continued identity. If the arms of the famous Venus de Milo were to be discovered and reattached, one could confidently say that Venus has regained *her* arms; but if a restorer were to infer their size and position and attach newly-sculpted marble arms, even if the result happened to match the appearance of Venus at her first making, one could object that those arms are not truly hers. (Compare the various attempts to figure out the exact disposition of the arms of the Laocoön sculpture.)

This aspect of debates over restoration is particularly pertinent to consider with the thesis that old things offer encounters with the past, because here again we have a separation of the objects of the senses with which we approach artifacts. Even if a restored artifact looks just like it did when it was first made, the material that makes up the renewed portions is new and therefore does not sustain the impression of the transitivity of touch.[18] The discrepancy between vision and touch mirrors arguments about "appearance" versus "reality" in some vigorous debates about restoration.

The terms of use in this debate pit "purist" restoration against "integrationist" techniques. The latter seek to restore the look of an

---

16. Randall R. Dipert, *Artifacts, Artworks, and Agency* (Philadelphia: Temple University Press, 1993) p. 122.

17. For a detailed analysis of this reconstruction and the social values and styles that informed it, see Cathy Gere, *Knossos and the Prophets of Modernism* (Chicago: University of Chicago Press, 2009). Thanks to a reviewer for informing me of this study.

18. What is more, an object might have been so cleaned up that it no longer manifests the age that it has accrued, a factor that sometimes prompts restoration only to appearance at a relatively recent point of history. As far as I know, restorers of Greek statuary almost always resist painting marble in the way the ancient Greeks favored; those iconic sculptures and their Roman copies have a place in history without their paint.

artifact by filling in missing parts with other materials, thus making the finished product "impure" in the sense that alien substances now adhere to the original. Probably the most famous example of this sort of restoration is Michelangelo's *Pietà*, which was damaged in 1972 by a madman wielding a hammer. The director of the Vatican Museum, Redig de Campos, oversaw a restoration that reattached the fallen parts of the sculpture and filled in missing fragments with a material that to the unassisted eye produced a repaired sculpture that was indistinguishable from the original. Only under an ultraviolet light is the filler visible; moreover, it is removable in case a future repair is necessary. This is considered a masterful example of integrationist restoration that presents to the viewing public the look of the undamaged *Pietà*; does not deceive because information about the repair is public and because the repairs can be discerned under certain viewing conditions; and is reversible should circumstances arise that make that advisable.

So what is there to complain about? Mark Sagoff, who was quoted in the previous chapter comparing artworks and persons, presents a principled objection to the technique and a well-known argument on behalf of purism, the view that absolutely no material addition is justified in restoration. The reasons he advances against incorporating foreign materials into a damaged art work are very like the reasons I have presented on behalf of the special aesthetic standing of genuineness. In brief, he insists that when a valued experience is directed to a mistaken object, it is inappropriate and the result of deception. This is another way to stress that aesthetic properties are not just surface perceptual qualities but also properly belong to an object under correct identification. Sagoff places himself among those

who value a work of art in itself: they recognize the goodness of art as inhering in it rather than as arising in an experience produced in them; they admire the work then, as being the particular subject of *these* characteristics, not the characteristics, as it were, detached or detachable from their subject; they respect the painting or the sculpture as the object of *this* experience, but not that sort of experience in the absence of its particular object; they are rewarded in their perception, of course, because the work is good, but they do not regard it as good because it rewards them, nor something else as equally good, from which they can obtain a similar response. They value the particular, substantial, actual thing.[19]

I agree wholeheartedly with almost everything that Sagoff says, which is substantially what I have been stressing throughout this study: experience is not self-validating but must be appropriate to its object; that object must be correctly understood to avert deception; encounters with the genuine are with singular or rare objects whose replicas do not sustain all their values; aesthetic properties are not limited to the perceptual surface but include implicit or submerged properties, including histories of making. Whereas one can replicate properties that are *characteristic of* an artifact, genuineness is not of this sort; it can only be a property *of* an object and as such cannot be reproduced. What is more, my claim that touch is among the senses at work in encounters with the genuine seems to make my position even more deeply wedded to retention of the physical materials of objects from the past, for even if a repaired object looks just as it did, what we touch cannot be the same. However, I do not object to integrationist restoration, which I believe has achieved some remarkable and thrilling results.

Sagoff focuses on works of what we now term fine art. Purist arguments are most compelling when one has objects like sculptures and paintings in mind. What is more, his discussion targets not just any artworks but those that stand as icons of culture. (Think not only of the *Pietà* but also of the controversies that swirled around the restoration of the Sistine Chapel ceiling or Leonardo da Vinci's fresco of *The Last Supper*). However, many of the artifacts that invite an encounter with the past are not stand-alone works of fine art. They are homes, temples, churches, canals, streets, alters, utensils, clothing—or fragments of any of these. The list is enormous, and

19. Mark Sagoff, "On Restoring and Reproducing Art," *Journal of Philosophy* 75:9 (Sept. 1978): 453–470, on p. 463. Sagoff's article has come in for a great deal of discussion. For arguments against his views see Michael Wreen, "The Restoration and Reproduction of Works of Art," *Dialogue* 24 (1985): 91–100; Rafael de Clercq, "The Metaphysics of Art Restoration," *British Journal of Aesthetics* 53:3 (2013): 261–275; Richard Stopford, "Preserving the Restoration of the *Pietà*," *British Journal of Aesthetics* 56:3 (2016): 301–315.

many of the objects on it are things that did not have a definite completion date even in their own times of greatest function. They probably would have undergone physical alteration while they were whole and in use. Canals are extended and widened, buildings are repaired, broken windows replaced, knives sharpened, new blades inserted into old handles; walls are repainted or replastered; garments are altered to fit; steeples torn down and rebuilt, and on and on. At what point in the lives of any of those things do we say *this* is the original? While one might accede to a directive not to touch up a painting from the hand of a Raphael or a Titian, it would be less sensible not to repair a roof, replace a drainpipe, or sharpen a knife. The concept of fine art just might permit a purist view of what counts as a "work," but objects that fall outside that category are less prone to such scruples.

The above list notes changes such as repairs, patches, and mends that involve additions to restore the character of an artifact and that are relatively continuous with the history of a thing. But artifacts are also subject to disasters, and if they are sufficiently meaningful they may demand reconstruction, as with St. Paul's Cathedral after the Great Fire of London in 1666, as were most of the churches of Krakow, subject to fires until rebuilt in stone. Earthquakes in historic cities of Italy, Nepal, Japan, and elsewhere have required massive reconstruction in their aftermath. With or without a history of catastrophe, most old cities have a building or two that is valued for its past but is only standing now because of numerous repairs. Changes may be gradual and routine, in which case genuineness may not even come into question; but they may also be repairs of a more dramatic sort where it is by no means irrelevant to worry about whether restoration really reclaims the damaged object or produces something entirely new that cannot retain the values of the original. There are cases where we can chart distance from the real thing by noting partial replacement with components that only resemble it, resulting in genuineness by degree.

Restoration, replication, reconstruction

Here is a relatively recent example where remnants, replications, and reconstruction not only illustrate the complexity of genuineness but also foreground location again. To see all of these aspects requires going into some detail. Frank Lloyd Wright built his most elaborate prairie-style home for Darwin D. Martin and his family in Buffalo, New York, between 1903 and 1905 (Figure 4.4).

It comprised five adjoining and connected buildings, including the main residence, a secondary residence (the Barton House) for Martin's sister and her husband, a carriage house, conservatory, and long pergola. After the family left the house in the 1930s, portions of the complex were sold, and the remaining buildings stood empty for years. In 1960 a developer demolished the pergola, conservatory, and carriage house and erected three apartment buildings on their site. Belatedly, the value of Wright's works for the history of architecture was recognized. Preservation efforts began in the 1990s, and now the apartments are gone and the missing parts of the entire complex have been rebuilt. The exterior of the structure and some of the interior have been restored to appear as they were in 1907, the designated "year of significance" for restoration.[20] Efforts are underway to plant the grounds in the way that Wright mandated too. Note that those in charge of restoration had to stipulate a year to match. Not only is 1907 a year when the house was complete and

FIGURE 4.4 Frank Lloyd Wright, Darwin Martin House. Built 1903. 2017. Photo by author.

20. See website of the Darwin Martin House: http://www.darwinmartinhouse.org/restoration.cfm (Accessed 4.2.16).

FIGURE 4.5 Darwin Martin House panorama, 1906. University Archives, University at Buffalo, State University of New York.

occupied, but also there are extensive photographs of the building as it was at that time (Figure 4.5) and Wright's original plans are still available to consult and follow. Luckily, in the case of this building complex, there are solid grounds for inference about the maker's intentions and little guesswork is required.

Wright designed not only his houses but also furniture, fixtures, tiles, carpets, and utensils; and he paid particular attention to windows. There were nine primary vertical window patterns in the main house alone and sixteen patterns throughout the complex, totaling 394 windows in all in the form of exterior windows, laylights, and glass panels on elements of the interior (Figures 4.6–4.7) . Many of these were removed before portions of the house were demolished, but quite a few fell victim to the wrecking ball. There are still some originals in the house, but other surviving windows are now in the possession of museums, including the Corning Museum of Glass and the Art Institute of Chicago, that display them as stand-alone works of art.[21]

Since windows are fragile, they represent aspects of architecture that often require repair or replacement. And since repairs are routine changes to houses over time, it is not unreasonable to ask: does

21. Some original objects that were removed from the house have been returned by the institutions and individuals that acquired them, including several of the windows. (Conversation with Martin House Executive Director Mary Roberts and Curator Susana Tejada, March 21, 2016). In October 2017, seven more windows were repatriated from the Museum of the University of Victoria, British Columbia. http://www.uvic.ca/home/about/campus-news/2017+legacy-galleries-wright+media-release (Accessed 11.22.2017).

FIGURE 4.6 Darwin Martin House, Dining Room, 1907. Photo by Henry Fuermann. University Archives, University at Buffalo, State University of New York.

FIGURE 4.7 Darwin Martin House, Tree of Life window, University Archives, University at Buffalo, State University of New York.

it matter if these windows are the very ones that Wright had installed in the house?

Those that are replicated will be visually indistinguishable from the originals. We won't be able to tell, so does it matter? If you are inclined to say "No" because windows are routinely replaced, then consider that for the long period of restoration, delicate plastic films mimicking the so-called Tree of Life windows have been designed to cover the clear glass panes presently in place. These, too, are visually indistinguishable from Wright's originals. But these are not leaded glass windows at all but illusions of leaded-glass windows. The reproduced windows will be true windows—not *Wright's* windows strictly speaking, though one could say they are Wright windows, where the name of the architect serves as a style-adjective. But glass is the right *sort* of replica. The plastic screens are rather like the imagined Astroturf battlefield, though an important difference is that the windows could have been preserved, whereas the grass that grew in 1863 could not have.[22]

22. For comparison with a very different kind of window, see Lamarque's discussion of the Great East Window of York Minster. Lamarque, Peter. "Reflections on the Ethics and Aesthetics," 281–299.

Reproduction presents another sort of perplexity when we consider the pergola and conservatory. The pergola is a hundred feet long, and it terminates in a conservatory densely full of leafy and flowering plants. Looking from the main house down the long stretch of open corridor, one gazes towards what has been called the "jewel" at the heart of the whole architectural composition: a life-sized replica of the Nike of Samothrace (Figure 4.8).[23] The destruction of the conservatory took Victory with it, and now the statue on site is another replica. Since Wright's "original"

FIGURE 4.8 Darwin Martin House Conservatory, 1907. Photo by Henry Fuermann, University Archives, University at Buffalo, State University of New York.

was itself a replica, does this one matter as much as the windows? Does it clarify the answer to know that the company that made the original Martin House Nike had not destroyed the mold, and the replacement was cast from the same one? Or that the first Nike was one of several that Wright planted in his houses and so could not have been considered unique to the Martin House even if it had survived?

The questions that arise with even this one example demonstrate the complexity of estimating what is to count as original material and the degree to which other factors are in play with genuineness. Continuity of material structure is supplied by the central living quarters and the adjacent Barton House. The rest has had to be reconstructed using the original plans, but the structure is still on the exact footprint of the first dwelling. Therefore, one

23. Theodore Lownie, "Introduction," in *Windows of the Darwin Martin House*, ed. Jack Quinan (Buffalo: Burchfield-Penney Art Center, 1999): p. 8.

stands in the right place amid some original and some replicated sections. Moreover, the newer materials both match the first ones in appearance and are manufactured using the same production processes that were in use the early twentieth century (at least as nearly as possible). Given that this is a work of architecture, manufacture and replacement of parts—albeit as a rule of a much more piecemeal sort—is consistent with the usual treatment of such artifacts. Except where current building codes demand otherwise, the right *sort* of materials were used for the needed replications. The virtually undetectable plastic films standing in for the art glass windows are merely a stop-gap measure until reproduction glass windows can be completed. Recognition that simple appearance is insufficient is implicit in the requirement that replicated materials, such as windows, bricks, and tiles, be manufactured or crafted as the first ones were. However, certain updates were mandated. Being a building that people frequently visit, the house was brought up to code, although the former curator insisted that a portion of the original asbestos insulation be preserved behind a transparent panel. This may seem a quirky decision without much consequence, but in fact, it points to a tricky issue. If we decide to leave the old materials in place, we not only violate improved safety regulations, but we also do not acknowledge that it is in the nature of buildings to be repaired and updated from time to time. We treat them as a kind of thing that they are not. On the other hand, if we decide that the innards don't matter because they are hidden, then we might be implying that only "surface" appearance matters, which overlooks the real tangible thing and does not differentiate the values of replica and original. This is an example of the kinds of choices that sometimes must be made between appearance and original structure.

Unless we consider works of architecture like musical performances, each structure equally qualified as instances of the work (the architect's plans being comparable to scores), a restored building differs from the first one, no matter how closely it duplicates it.[24] With drawings, buildings are in principle multiply realizable, as

24. Robert Wicks, "Architectural Restoration: Resurrection or Replication?" *British Journal of Aesthetics* 34:2 (1994): 163–170.

are performances. But that is only in principle; in practice they are either one of a kind or a run of a kind—as with housing developments. Idealist views about artifacts abrogate the importance of physical experience of them, including the role of touch, physical movement and location. This point will be amplified in the next chapter.

Resurrection

When time and neglect have taken their toll, restoration requires a certain amount of reconstruction, which often occurs in such incremental stages that the existence of the artifact is uninterrupted. But when an artifact has been completely destroyed, reconstruction is so discontinuous that it might be considered a type of resurrection. Just what is resurrected and why the effort is worthwhile are questions that need to be addressed together. While trying to hold onto the past in every circumstance and at all costs is an ill-judged refusal of progress, rebuilding artifacts demolished by acts of hostility can be regarded as an act of defiance as well as a redemption of cultural heritage.

The possibilities for wholesale reconstruction of lost artifacts confront several types of decisions that James Janowski has summarized into six options. He is speaking of the Bamiyan Buddhas destroyed by the Taliban in 2001, but his remarks pertain generally to large artifacts that have been wholly or partially destroyed.

> There seem to be (at least) the following possibilities. The sculptures might be resurrected: 1) on the same site using the same (numerically identical) materials; 2) on the same site using the same type of materials; 3) on a different (presumably proximate) site using the same (numerically identical) materials; 4) on a different (presumably proximate) site using the same type of materials; 5) on the same site using completely different type of materials; 6) on a different site using completely different type of materials.[25]

25. James Janowski, "Bringing Back Bamiyan's Buddhas," *Journal of Applied Philosophy* 28:1 (2011): 44–64, on p. 46.

To illustrate: the Darwin Martin House was restored by combining choices (1) (where identical materials were reclaimable) and (2) (where they were replicable using similar techniques), with occasional departures to (5) (as with the insulation materials). Thereby an iconic work that had fallen into disrepair and partial dismantlement was restored.

The Mostar Bridge mentioned earlier is an artifact that suffered complete destruction when it was deliberately targeted in an act of war. The sixteenth-century structure was a product of Ottoman architecture whose techniques of building were no longer completely understood. Over time it had become a symbolic anchor of the town, and therefore its devastation in 1993 was more than just the loss of a piece of useful property. With the help of an international team led by a group of Spanish architects, the bridge was rebuilt in the early 2000s (Figure 4.9). The reconstructed bridge comprises entirely new materials though it looks almost exactly like the original one. What is more, it spans the same part of the river and has resumed the function of the original bridge. The physical thing is different and continuity of touch with the old artifact is forever interrupted. But the location is the same, so physical presence remains in the right place. That is to say, those who cross the bridge trace the same path as earlier travelers, although the materials beneath their feet were replaced in a wholesale manner rather than by means of the renewal of infrastructure that occurs periodically and routinely to roads and bridges. Since the bridge occupies the same site as the earlier one, and since sites themselves are indestructible, there is some continuity between the old and the new with this artifact.

FIGURE 4.9 Mostar Bridge, built 1557–1566, destroyed 1993, rebuilt 2001–2004. Photo by Manuel Cohen/Art Resource, NY.

The examples thus far illustrate different possibilities

for restoration and reconstruction. These kinds of repairs and rebuilding projects represent long practices undertaken by necessity throughout the histories of our built environments. They thus participate in a familiar kind of continuity over time, though how best to account for this claim is an issue to be addressed in more detail in the next chapter. But now another—hitherto unimaginable—kind of reconstruction has risen above the horizon of possibility: remaking historical artifacts by means of digital technology and 3-D printing. These techniques are now capable of rendering exact copies of things by amalgamating data from photographs, scans, and measurements and using them to create a precise replica of a lost original. The process is eerily close to what previously were merely possible-world thought experiments about exact reproduction and the properties that may or may not be retained from original to copy. The technology is so new and my imagination so sluggish that the comments about the following example, which was alluded to in the last chapter, must remain tentative.

The city of Palmyra grew from an ancient trading center that linked Greece, Rome, Persia, India, and China. So significant are its remains that it was designated a Syrian national monument and in 1980 it was declared a UNESCO World Heritage site. Reasons advanced for this designation are indicated in the following description:

> The splendour of the ruins of Palmyra, rising out of the Syrian desert north-east of Damascus, is testament to the unique aesthetic achievement of a wealthy caravan oasis intermittently under the rule of Rome from the 1st to the 3rd century AD. The grand colonnade constitutes a characteristic example of a type of structure which represents a major artistic development.
>
> The grand monumental colonnaded street, open in the centre with covered side passages, and subsidiary cross streets of similar design together with the major public buildings, form an outstanding illustration of architecture and urban layout at the peak of Rome's

expansion in and engagement with the East. The great temple of Ba'al is considered one of the most important religious buildings of the 1st century AD in the East and of unique design. The carved sculptural treatment of the monumental archway through which the city is approached from the great temple is an outstanding example of Palmyrene art.[26]

Nor is the site of merely antiquarian interest. The director-general of UNESCO, Irina Bokova, has asserted that "Palmyra is a pillar of Syrian identity, and a source of dignity for all Syrians."[27]

A terrible confirmation of the importance of the site to modern Syrians was supplied by its selection as a target by ISIS (ISL/Daesh), which in October of 2015 began a campaign of massive destruction of the archaeological artifacts in and around Palmyra. The extensive area was heavily damaged and its grandest and most important structures smashed. What is more, the site was chosen as a place of public execution of those who resisted ISIS and who tried to protect the artifacts slated for destruction.[28]

The state of affairs at Palmyra represented fresh losses of material heritage and brutal treatments of those who valued it, and the question immediately arose: how to address the damage? The area is immense and contains some artifacts that might be repaired to their precedent condition, as well as others that were smashed to pieces, including the Temple of Ba'al. Another heavily damaged artifact was the triumphal arch of Emperor Septimus Severus that opened part of the ancient city to the long colonnade described above (Figure 4.10).

26. http://whc.unesco.org/en/list/23 (Accessed 9.27.16). This website includes an extensive gallery of photographs of the ruins of ancient Palmyra before the area was damaged in 2015.

27. http://whc.unesco.org/en/news/1488 (Accessed 9.27.16).

28. Several months earlier, members of ISIS executed a senior archaeologist, Khaled al-Asaad, reportedly for heroically refusing to disclose the location of ancient artifacts that had been removed from Palmyra for safekeeping. This event was reported widely, including in The Slate: http://www.slate.com/blogs/the_slatest/2015/08/19/isis_kills_81_year_old_syrian_archaeologist_palmyra_expert_executed.html   (Accessed 8.29.16).

Portions of this artifact have had a remarkable rebirth, for as it happened, a great deal of information about its design was available to aid in its resurrection. Anticipating the need to preserve important artifacts from the past, the Institute for Digital Archaeology, based in London, has amassed vast

FIGURE 4.10 Monumental Arch built under the reign of Septimus Severus, Palmyra, Syria (193–211 AD) prior to 2015 destruction. Photo by Manuel Cohen/Art Resource, NY.

amounts of data recording artifacts and archaeological sites, including the Palmyra Arch. Information about its appearance, including exact measurements, proportions, and surface features, was coded into programs that then instructed drilling machinery to re-sculpt the arch from another piece of marble. The resulting artifact replicates precisely the look of the one that was destroyed in 2015, including the cracks and marks of deterioration that time had etched into the stone (Figure 4.11). There was no attempt to replicate the arch as it had been when it was first built but rather as it existed in 2015, making the model an exact replica of the one that was deliberately destroyed. The result is a remarkable reconstruction. It cannot be called a restoration because it was wholly remade. On the other hand, it would be hard to say that it was made from scratch because the characteristics of the original were captured in digitized form.

The replication is weirdly like reenactment in new material of the qualities the first arch endowed upon the programs used for its resurrection. This technological wizardry is remarkable both in the accuracy of the products it can produce and in the very fact that such feats have become possible. Pondering the outcome prompts some questions that open new debates, and the central one is: Just what is the status of the new arch? Miraculous as it is, is this really a

FIGURE 4.11 Palmyra Arch Replica in London, Trafalgar Square, April 2016. Photo by Richard Pohle.

resurrection of the old artifact? Or just a copy made with a new technique, stunning in its accuracy but possessing the same standing as any replica made by more familiar means?

Referring to the six options for reconstruction mentioned above, it is not clear whether the arch is described by (4) on a different site using the same type of materials or by (6) on a different site using completely different type of materials. The new arch is also marble, a fact that weighs on the side of (4), qualifying the materials as the same type. On the other hand, its method of making is incomparably different. Of great significance for pondering these issues is location, for the new Palmyra arch is now treated less like a piece of architecture rooted in place and more like a very large sculpture. After completion, the arch began a tour of London, New York, and Dubai, though its ultimate destination is to be returned to Syria to be placed near the site where its progenitor stood.

Worries have been expressed that the capacity to recreate ancient things might eventuate in a flattening of the distinction between archaeological sites and theme parks, making something ancient and rare as accessible as a carnival ride. Sheer cost and practically probably forestall that outcome, but it is not irrelevant to think about conditions that make devaluation a consequence of duplication. More important for my purposes are the implications for what counts as genuine when we consider the loss of touch in encounters with the past that such artifacts yield. Any replica diminishes what

I labeled the transitivity of touch, but not everyone cares about that loss. Consider these comments from Roger Michel, director of the Institute for Digital Archaeology. In defense of reported concerns that replicas will blunt our sense of history, Michel replied:

> Part of it is a culture clash. In the West, we are very fetishistic about originality. We want to touch the object that the master touched. This goes back to the days of reliquaries when people had bits and pieces of saints that they carried around with them. . . .
>
> For people in other parts of the world, the role of objects is not to somehow through the object itself bring you close to history. It is a visual cue that provides memories of history. The history and heritage resides in the mind.[29]

Michel goes on to observe that many other archaeological sites have been reconstructed over the years—stabilized, partially rebuilt—implying that the new 3-D technology should be regarded as just the most recent stage in the preservation of ancient places.

Granting that this technology is marvelous, I would observe that several of the above claims require challenge. First of all, history is not memory and heritage withers unless it continues to be recognized in practice. One may remember recent historical events, but no one remembers ancient Palmyra or anything else that takes place before one's birth. Seeing a replica certainly can remind us that Palmyra once was, and for those who have been there it might prompt a memory of having visited. However, although the event of being reminded may possess its own charm, reminding is not an adequate analysis of the nature of encounters with the past by means of proximity with the genuine (a point that was argued in Chapter 2). Moreover, memory is dependent upon past experience that is summoned to recollection, but encounters with material

29. Scott Simon, "Upon Reclaiming Palmyra, The Controversial Side of Digital Reproduction," interview between Scott Simon and Roger Michel, NPR Weekend Edition, April 2, 2016. http://www.npr.org/programs/weekend-edition-saturday/2016/04/02/472784684/weekend-edition-saturday-for-april-2-2016?showDate=2016-04-02 (Accessed 7.19.18).

artifacts can be thrilling for what they bring to mind that we did not know before. With the loss of the real thing and with monuments both real and duplicated uprooted from their locations and sent around the world, inevitably what is known and familiar about history and cultural heritage will diminish. To an extent this is inevitable with the passage of time and the changes it brings, but one should not moot the loss by folding history into what one can be reminded of.

Second, and more centrally important for this study, the above comment cedes the perceptual experience of artifacts entirely to vision at the expense of other modes of acquaintance. In fact, artifacts invite multisensory engagement, particularly when they are works of great size. As Jenefer Robinson puts it, "To appreciate a work of architecture fully requires not only grasping the structure of a building with the eyes and mind, but also *interacting* with it, moving through and around it, feeling what it is like to live or work or act in it. . . . One has to engage one's whole body in the process of understanding and appreciation."[30] Bodily engagement involves all the senses as well as physical movement. Artifacts that are also ruins similarly invite moving amid them and marveling that one stands where others lived so long ago.[31] No matter how stunning the traveling replica, it has lost the capability of the original to invite such encounters, in large part because one lacks the sense of being there, proximate to the aged artifact, near enough to touch. Situated experience is no longer possible.

Third, the slighting comparison with handling relics provocatively implies that there is a little papist homunculus lurking in the cultural DNA of the west. But this assumption errs by reversing the direction of importance of the sense of touch. Insofar as religious and other relics are the objects of the desire to touch, it is because of the power of touch itself. It happens that there are religious traditions that promote the efficacy of material relics by

30. Jenefer Robinson, "On Being Moved Through Architecture," *Journal of Aesthetics and Art Criticism* 70:4 (2012): 337–353, on p. 340.

31. Carolyn Korsmeyer, "The Triumph of Time: Romanticism Redux," symposium on The Aesthetics of Absence and Ruins, *Journal of Aesthetics and Art Criticism*, 72:4 (Fall 2014): 429–435.

means of contact, but touch did not thereby become regarded as an especially powerful sense. Rather the reverse: the sense of touch has capacities that invite such religious practices in the first place. As we have seen from numerous examples, proximal acquaintance is desired for all sorts of things—keepsakes and meteorites as well as antique treasures. The resurrected Palmyra arch does possess many of the properties that are characteristic of the arch before destruction, though it is detached from the larger structure in which it functioned. But one can no longer stand before the arch where the legions of Septimus Severus paraded. No replica is the real thing, and this one can only refer to the old one now destroyed. On the other hand, it has other virtues: informative, beautiful, and marvelous as an achievement. Moreover, insofar as its recreation gives hope and sustenance to those whose material past was destroyed, it stands defiant and resilient.[32]

The pendulum continues to swing. Because the new Palmyra arch can travel, integrity of location is not sustained. On the other hand, unlike a bridge, this archaeological treasure no longer had a working role in its community, so continuity of function would not have obtained anyway. It is also the case that many gigantic structures from one civilization have been relocated to other places, there to take up a new role, perhaps as a mark of empire. Napoleon's transfer of ancient monuments from Egypt to Paris is one such example. Indeed, museums frequently—and sometimes notoriously—uproot artifacts from their home territory. Portions of medieval churches are now in New York, a huge gate from Babylon is in Berlin, a massive Chinese tomb is in Toronto, and bits of the Parthenon are in London. Both change of location and the process of dismantling an artifact from its home and reassembling it elsewhere are major factors to reckon with in laying out a full picture of genuineness and the persistence of artifacts over time. Site, material persistence, continuity of function, recognizable appearance—all

---

32. This view is disputable. Janowski asserts that wholesale reconstruction actually amplifies loss rather than redressing it. Janowski, "Bringing Back," p. 56. For an appreciative assessment of the replicated Arch, see Erich Hatala Matthes, "Palmyra's ruins can rebuild our relationship with history," *Aeon* (March 2017) https://aeon.co/ideas/palmyras-ruins-can-rebuild-our-relationship-with-history (Accessed 11.25.17).

crisscross in the objects that furnish encounters with the past, sometimes competing with and sometimes reinforcing one another. The next chapter will try to bring these elements into order.

Perhaps the most important aspect of the new Palmyra arch is its function in another role: that of memorial. The replicated arch is a talisman of what was lost, a reminder to those who visit it of the conflict that has destroyed so many lives, so many homes and communities, and so many treasured remnants from the past. The arch is not the real thing, but it is a moving tribute to the one now gone and to everything else that went with it.

5

Relics, Remnants, and Scrap

This chapter addresses more fully a question that has been raised already in passing: what are the conditions that sustain the persistence of an object over time such that it still qualifies as genuine in the present? More specifically, such that the encounter that summons the impression of being in touch with the past—including what I have called the transitivity of touch—is warranted to strong or weak degree? The heterogeneous examples that have been discussed thus far indicate that there are diverse and shifting ways to answer that question. Moreover, the whole topic is complicated by competing values and time-worn puzzles that involve matters ranging from practical urgency to the details of metaphysics. Although the discourses are usually conducted separately, metaphysical views are implicit in pragmatic discussions about how best to treat artifacts of value. This is particularly notable with controversies reviewed earlier over restoration where arguments involve the identity of what is restored. Attending to touch and its various forms mandates certain ontological positions, as I shall argue; and it also opens several different paths to understanding encounters with the past. This chapter will tease out a few of the intersections between metaphysics and real-world practice that arise with reflection upon the value of old things.

It must be borne in mind that "genuine" is both a descriptive and an evaluative term. As noted briefly earlier, there are lots of things that are what they seem to be, but they are too insignificant to label them with a term of value. One easily speaks of a genuine pre-Columbian pot but, as a rule, not of a brick left over from any old torn-down structure. Only things with some kind of presumptive importance merit being called "genuine," and the zone of value examined here has to do with their inviting aesthetic encounters with the past. Things that are valuable enough to keep are things that matter, for as Peter Railton observes, "Valuing enters the picture when mattering does."[1]

Does it matter to a family if a wedding dress is kept? Does it matter to a neighborhood or community if an old house is preserved or a burial ground remains undisturbed? Does it matter more to a region or a nation if an historic site is protected rather than a dam constructed? Obviously, there will be conflict over what matters sufficiently to save and which competing value ought to prevail. The array of examples discussed heretofore indicates that the circumstances under which things matter vary so radically that there are too many factors shaping this choice to make general criteria for mattering a sensible goal. This is not because decisions about preservation lack justification but rather because the values that attach to things that matter are rooted in so many traditions, interests, and contexts that they resist distillation into a formula. Approaching the task of "measuring what matters," Marcia Eaton remarks that "values are systems or networks of desires and preferences and purposes."[2] When aesthetic, ethical, scientific, and historical values mingle, those systems are multiply complex.

---

1. Peter Railton, "Aesthetic Value, Moral Value, and Naturalism," in *Aesthetics and Ethics: Essays at the Intersection*, ed. Jerrold Levinson (Cambridge: Cambridge University Press, 1998): 59–105, on p. 62.
2. Marcia Muelder Eaton, *Aesthetics and the Good Life* (Cranbury, NJ: Associated University Presses, 1989) p. 94.

While historical significance is an aspect of the evaluative element of the genuine, particularly with things that can claim general cultural importance, the actual conditions that determine sufficient significance to merit preservation cannot be formulated with either accuracy or adequate latitude. This has proven to be the case, in part, because I do not limit the scope of Real Things only to artifacts that can claim global cultural standing. Treasuring an object for the past it embodies also characterizes relationships with small, domestic items cherished only by individuals. But "mattering" pertains here too. As a consequence, I make no attempt to lay out conditions that make old things in general worth being called genuine. In setting out the conditions under which the ascription of genuineness is well-grounded, I simply presume that the object in question matters enough to merit the term—at least prima facie, for there are many times when mattering is withdrawn.

The disadvantage of this conclusion is probably obvious: it leaves decisions about individual artifacts leaning on a radically particularist foundation. However, to detail the qualities that make an artifact sufficiently important to be protected and preserved because it is genuine simply relocates the question about what matters, it does not answer it. For whatever criteria one formulates, there will an enormous zone of indeterminacy between things that obviously count as genuine and those that are obviously discardable as scrap. Therefore, bearing in mind both the tombs and castles of kings and the left-behind tools and shoes of their unknown builders, I prefer to acknowledge that the circumstances that make an artifact worthy of the label "genuine" are unpredictable.

The argument of this book has proceeded in stages that culminate in a case for degrees of genuineness as well as for different gauges of what is to count as the real thing. The result is not particularly neat, and it has left a number of loose ends to tie up. To review the preceding claims briefly: "Genuine" is a term that names a property of objects pertaining to the history of their making and use, and that also possesses values—cognitive, ethical, and aesthetic. Among those values is the capability of old things to bring the past into presence, providing an aesthetic encounter of a particular charm or thrill. With such encounters, the sense of touch plays a vital role in that it summons awareness of proximity or even contact with an object that embodies a special history. Because of the emphasis on the past, most of the examples I have discussed are objects of considerable age, but genuineness pertains to new things as well, and there is no requirement of antiquity to make this point. The "hand" of the artist is equally important in valuing contemporary works; hence the outrage of forgery extends beyond monetary concerns. The same phenomenon occurs not only with very old but also with singular or rare artifacts or with those that were used (and touched) by certain people and under special circumstances, such as the paper on which Lincoln wrote the Gettysburg address or a violin, now silent, once played by Paganini. Because of the emphasis on touch, this claim entails attention to the persistent physical existence of an object—that which is, at least in principle, palpable.

Tangibility

A consequence of this view deserves mention right away, for claiming genuineness as an aesthetic property challenges some reigning views about the ontological status of entities that possess aesthetic properties, including works of art. While most of this study has not invoked objects of fine art as examples to ponder, artworks are obviously among the artifacts that can put us in touch with the past—sculptures made by hands long gone, paintings still discernible on the walls of tombs, tapestries woven by fingers whose deft work bridges centuries. A good deal of philosophical work has examined the status of the kind of artifact we call art, and my brief on behalf of real things needs to be situated within these conversations.

Artworks, especially those in the fine art tradition, are particularly assessed for their aesthetic attributes, their power, delicacy, expressiveness, and so forth. Properties such as *fierce, airy, poignant, mournful, lilting,* and *dynamic* are standard examples of aesthetic attributes.[3] Such adjectives, however, do not seem

---

3. This sort of aesthetic property is influentially discussed by Frank Sibley, "Aesthetic Concepts," *Philosophical Review* 58 (1959): 421–450.

properly to describe physical matter as such, according to many philosophical approaches. This is one factor (of several) that has displaced the materiality of artworks from many accounts of their ontological standing. Consider, for example, Brancusi's famous bronze sculpture titled *Bird in Space* (Figure 5.1). Regarded as a *physical* object it can be described as being made from material containing a certain proportion of copper and tin, as weighing so many pounds, and as being approximately 54 inches high. The *aesthetic* features that describe it include being *light* and *soaring*, properties implicit in the following description:

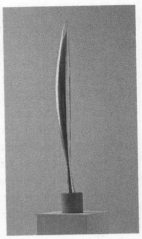

FIGURE 5.1 Constantin Brancusi (1876–1957) © ARS, NY. *Bird in Space*, 1928. Bronze. 54 x 8 ½ x 6 ½." Museum of Modern Art/Digital image © The Museum of Modern Art/Licensed by SCALA / Art Resource, NY. Succession Brancusi—All rights reserved (ARS) 2017.

> It offers not just the image of a bird, but of a bird in flight, the form of the piece charting the trajectory of its skyward movement. Positioned directly below a skylight, the gleaming bronze surface dissolves in the light from overhead in a manner the artist would have loved.[4]

Strictly speaking, properties such as *soaring* or *dissolving in the light* or *having skyward movement* do not seem to describe the object as a mere physical thing. The literal meaning of such terms, in other words, is stymied, for light cannot dissolve bronze and nothing that large and heavy could soar—at least without an engine. What, therefore, is the object that is so aptly described with this feathery language? Because of the apparent incompatibility between aesthetic properties and descriptive physical properties,

---

4. Roni Feinstein, "Brancusi and the Space of Modern Sculpture," http://visual. uclaextension.edu/brancusi-and-the-space-of-modern-sculpture/ (Accessed 11.8.16). The comment refers to the cast of the sculpture at the Norton Simon Museum in Pasadena, California.

many philosophers argue that another account of the ontology of artworks is required. The bearer of aesthetic properties is perhaps better described not as a mere physical thing but as an ideal object, an abstract object, as a perceptual object regarded under certain strictures, or as a performance—or some alternate way to single out an "aesthetic object" that is related to but not identical with the brute, material thing.[5]

We need not review those options in detail, however, for granting genuineness aesthetic standing does not mandate that one abandon reference to the physical object. In fact, the opposite is the case. Not only awareness of the history and origin of an object but also attention to what one can touch, including to the phenomenon of the transitivity of touch, fastens genuineness to the material thing itself. This fairly obvious fact makes me more than a little sympathetic to what is termed the physical object hypothesis regarding the ontology of artworks, which maintains that at least some kinds of art (not all; certainly not music and poetry) are properly identified as physical things, albeit described in terms more expansive than a geologist or a chemist would select.[6] Thus we may take one step in the direction of an ontological account of real things that provide encounters with the past and that have occupied this study. They are things with a physical presence: things that we can touch or draw near to (recalling from Chapter 1 that often proximity is the best one can do). With genuineness there is little temptation to resort to a nonphysical aesthetic object to which to attach the property.

Although I will not pursue the point here, this observation could be expanded beyond genuineness to more standard aesthetic properties as well. As Jerrold Levinson observes, aesthetic properties pertain to physical objects that have entered culture through having

---

5. Sherri Irvin reviews several such ontologies in "Artworks, Objects, and Structures," in *The Bloomsbury Companion to Aesthetics*, ed. Anna Cristina Ribeiro (London: Bloomsbury, 2015): 55–73.

6. The physical object hypothesis is presented by Richard Wollheim, *Art and Its Objects*, 2nd ed. (Cambridge UK: Cambridge University Press, 1980) p. 233. Interestingly, his discussion of the Bamiyan Buddhas (see previous chapter) also leads James Janowski to similar sympathies with the physical object hypothesis. James Janowski, "Bringing Back Bamiyan's Buddhas," *Journal of Applied Philosophy* 28:1 (2011): 44–64, on p. 48.

been intentionally crafted to have certain meanings and roles, and as such descriptors attach to them without requiring a more ethereal ontology. In his words, "though the identity of such an object is . . . culturally given and determined, there is little reason to think of the object itself as occupying an ontological *plane* different from that which rocks and chairs inhabit."[7] This perspective removes "mere" from qualifying "physical object" by emphasizing the importance of the historical and social standing that surrounds cultural artifacts. I would add that attention to what can be touched underscores the physical nature of the object in experience, for what we touch requires material presence.

In short, thesis #1: Aesthetic encounters with Real Things, those that bring the past into the present, require the presence of a tangible, material object. (A qualification of this assertion and a variation on this theme regarding place is acknowledged below.)

Nonetheless, the qualification of objects as genuine does not depend solely on the degree of original physical material left to them. To reiterate the obvious: we almost never have objects from the past that are both whole and in their original condition, a fact that underlies the distinction between historical and age value. What even counts as original with objects that took years to build, sometimes in fits and starts, such as China's Great Wall or York Minster or the streets of Kathmandu? Or with an object that was altered in the course of its history in order to enlarge its use, such as the Erie Canal, which was widened and repaired many times before portions of it were buried? And once unburied and restored, how significant are new patches of concrete or rearrangement of the blocks of limestone on its sides? These will not make much of a visible difference, so visitors probably won't notice; but I have argued that authenticity is a presumptive quality even though it is not perceptually manifest and that its absence induces aesthetic deception. Therefore, the invisibility of such changes cannot simply be dismissed as unimportant. What is more, if part of the charm of touch is what I called its transitivity, such that an encounter with

---

7. Jerrold Levinson, "The Work of Visual Art," in *The Pleasures of Aesthetics: Philosophical Essays* (Ithaca, NY: Cornell University Press, 1996): 129–137, on p. 136.

the past summons a sense of being in contact with what others have touched and standing where others have stood, then this too seems to require that the actual old physical thing remains to be (possibly if not actually) touched. And yet the object is likely to have changed, sometimes quite a lot. Fragments of the famous Ishtar Gate, once a portal to Babylon, anchor a reconstruction that has made the giant gate whole, but in Berlin. Only a small portion of this artifact actually resided in the ancient city. Not only its partialness but also its relocation interferes with the genuineness of the present gate. Neither this object nor thousands of others in similar states of repair or fragmentation can claim to be exactly what and where they once were. They may all call to mind the time of their prime, and some of them embody it, at least in part. There are cases, however, where that embodiment may have become so attenuated as to be nearly insignificant.

When these observations were first offered, I suggested a rough and ready continuum to describe physical integrity, a continuum that suggests the most intuitively obvious gauge of genuineness by focusing on what remains of original, or at least early, physical composition. To repeat: A real thing from the past no longer in its original condition may be *repaired* when fragments of the original are glued or soldered back together. Or an object might be *restored*, where missing pieces are replaced with un- or barely-detectable new ones. It might be *rebuilt*, using both old and new materials. Rebuilding might require that it be *replicated* in part or entirely, on the original site or elsewhere, perhaps even *replacing* the original. These stages are obviously not discrete but overlap and blend. When replication is entire, the object is *reconstructed*. One could wonder if the latter amounts to *resurrection* of something otherwise lost. If size permits, it might be *reproduced*, ideally retaining the original's aesthetic surface qualities. Reproductions may also be multiplied and distributed, as with sculptures available at museum shops, although many reproductions reduce the scale of the original object. Age value diminishes in this sequence—repair, restore, reconstruct, replicate, reproduce—although it may not always disappear altogether, for implicit in the string is *reference* back to another R: the *Real* thing. (Bearing in mind that what makes it real, and just at what time that reality is assessed, is part of the problem under discussion.) For example, the Mostar Bridge currently spanning the Neretva River is not old, but it was built in the location of the original with the intention of replacing something of great value that was deliberately destroyed. The conditions under which it was rebuilt and the intentions that lay behind that project are relevant to the standing of this object. The compositional materials are not the same, but it draws our attention to something that *was* genuine. The "r" here is *reference*, which is also aided by another R: close *resemblance* to the one that was destroyed. Moreover, the reference is not incidental; it is part of the history of the place and as such the new bridge resumes the position and the function of the old. This kind of replication is quite different from building an Ottoman-style bridge as part of a theme park.

As one proceeds along increasingly distal references, the appreciable qualities recede to the aesthetic surface, leaving behind age value and awareness of contact with the past, until experience becomes detached from the real thing and is focused only on the immediate impression that the present object makes. The latter stages of this process can produce objects that are interesting, enjoyable, or moving, but they do not substantially embody their pasts and are unlikely to yield an aesthetic encounter of presence that survives reflection. They may also become occasions for the kind of aesthetic deception that, once discovered, deflates or even erases the initial experience.

This continuum pertains to physical persistence of decreasing amounts of original material in an artifact. This, however, is not the only factor involved with a thing's ability to carry the past into the present, and acknowledging this fact softens the requirement of material persistence. We do not just reach to touch old things any more than we gawk at them in passive wonder. Contemplative awe might be aroused by vestiges of past splendors protected now in museums. But many artifacts from the past are still in use: public items such as bridges, buildings, and streets. Smaller domestic things are handled daily (tools, candlesticks, silverware) or on special occasions that span generations (holiday ornaments, dishes for special events, religious or civic artifacts), being used repeatedly in ceremonies private or public. The prevalence of such things is easily overlooked, as one is unlikely to be awestruck by an aesthetic encounter on a daily basis, which might be an interruptive and in-convenient event, although one may pause while setting a holiday table to stroke an heirloom brought out for the occasion. After all, aesthetic encounters and the moments of insight they bring can be quotidian and passing as well as rare and stunning.[8]

Artifacts in use often require replacement from time to time as they wear out, break, or are lost. If such changes are gradual, they fold into the habit and tradition of function and the object reaps a degree of realness endowed by continuity of use, of regard, of cultural role (part of being a close continuer over time). This phenom-enon prevents me from insisting that an object misidentified years ago is always an example of deception and should be abandoned when its true identity is revealed. Its function as a culturally im-portant entity bestows a certain standing, and if that goes on long enough, the originally misidentified object may become sufficiently venerable that it achieves its own status as the real thing. Objects used for centuries in religious ceremonies are examples of this kind of adventitious substitution.

This latitude may seem too generous, and it opens a difficult question, for one may reasonably ask just how long is long enough? If a week is not sufficient, a thousand years is too daunting a standard. This question is one that is rarely asked early in the life of an artifact, at which point rectification would be relatively easy. And the fact that its standing is usually recognized retroactively grants some leeway about the age an object must attain to qualify as the real thing—not being what it first purported to be but having achieved venerability of its own by dint of having been treated as if it were. This tangential observation is not intended to vindicate errors of identification, which can have pernicious consequences. Rather, I mean to underscore the fact that sustained treatment in a cultural position over time is one of the things that keeps the past alive in the present, and when an object assumes that role it becomes folded into that history of use.

The assembly of examples heretofore discussed thus indicates that genuineness is a function of several factors and does not

8. Yuriko Saito, *Everyday Aesthetics* (Oxford: Oxford University Press, 2007).

preclude certain sorts of change. But how much change can occur before the real thing slips away altogether?[9] This question engages a venerable philosophical problem in metaphysics: What conditions enable an object to persist over time while retaining its identity, including persistence through the kinds of changes that befall material objects through wear, conflict, and use? When does continuity of function suffice to mend the breaks, gaps, and substitutions in the thing that remains before us?

The metaphysics of things that matter

In what follows I revisit claims I have made about old things that might appear to run aground on metaphysical principles. I shall not attempt to formulate a complete ontology of genuine objects, a project pretty much thwarted by the indeterminacy of "mattering" noted above. However, a few of my observations regarding the damage wrought by time, the restoration of artifacts, and the fragmentary character of what remains from the past may seem to ignore some standard metaphysical challenges. Therefore, I shall address a few well-known puzzles, situate Real Things among them, and appeal to theories developed by others that are congenial to an understanding of genuineness and that help to lay to rest any nagging philosophical doubts. I begin by reviewing the problem of persistence of identity over time in its oldest and most familiar version, for there is an ancient scenario that serves as an apt model for the pursuit of the genuine: the story of the ship of Theseus.

After slaying the Minotaur, the Greek hero Theseus sailed home, and his ship was preserved in Athens for years. Over time it was repaired, plank by plank, occasioning a question that long ago went philosophically viral: If all the planks of the ship are eventually replaced, is it still the same ship, the real ship of Theseus?

9. It is worth noting that many works of contemporary art make deliberate use of ephemeral materials or biological substances that change on their own. Objects of such "active matter" present additional zones of challenges to conservation. See "Cultures of Conservation" located at Bard Graduate Center: http://cultures-of-conservation.wikis. bgc.bard.edu/.

Aristotle is among those who said yes, arguing that the gradually restored object retains its identity since its formal cause remains the same. (The formal cause refers to the essential nature of a thing that makes it that thing and not another, that imposes form on matter.) As the original planks of the ship are replaced with new ones, the material cause changes (the stuff that takes the form), but the repaired object remains the same ship. This story dramatizes the difference between "genuine" and "original," for if identity (and thus genuineness) is retained through change of parts, the two concepts inevitably separate. However, given the emphasis I have placed on touch, one might not be satisfied with Aristotle's answer because the object of touch—the material of the ship—does gradually alter. Discomfort on this issue may occasion doubts about the admission of gradual change into the degrees of genuineness I have posited. These worries are complicated further by a twist to the puzzle added by Thomas Hobbes in the seventeenth century: Suppose all the original planks had been set aside and preserved and later used to build a second ship along the lines of the first. Now we have two ships, but which of the two counts as the real ship of Theseus?

Hobbes's question brings to the fore various options for counting something as persisting as the same thing over time. If "same" means "contains exactly the same original materials," then only the second ship is even a candidate. On the other hand, choosing that ship as the real one faces a grave problem: its history is interrupted, and the notion of persistence entails continuity of being. Interrupted existence, as we shall see shortly, poses a thorny problem for the ontology of things. But gradual change also represents one of several places in metaphysical accounts of persistence over time that rapidly depart from ordinary usage, for in fact continuous retention of exactly the same materials in their original composition is a very strict notion of sameness that obtains for few (if any) physical objects of any great age. As a rule and in practice we recognize that an object can have a part lost or replaced without losing its identity. A chipped plate is still *that plate*. It has acquired a chip, but it has not become a different plate altogether. A tree trimmed in the backyard is still the same tree that continues to grow in the same backyard. Or so a commonsense view would have it, though common sense does not always provide a stable or universally acceptable foundation for metaphysics.

The importance of sameness of identity persisting over at least some kinds of change is perhaps even clearer if we extend the question to persons. A person remains the same through inevitable physical changes, such as occur with the gradual transition from childhood to adulthood. And a person also retains identity despite sudden changes, such as before and after having a tooth pulled. Otherwise, one would owe the dentist payment for a procedure undergone by someone else. However, I shall not include debates over personal identity in this discussion, despite my earlier comparison of things and persons in the service of arguing for the importance of genuineness. Theories of the identity of persons over time must deal with the complexities of consciousness, a crucial feature of being human that is not only difficult to understand in itself but also raises terrible real-life dilemmas when consciousness is compromised. These issues do not pertain to things.

Puzzles like the ship of Theseus continue to circulate because there are several plausible ways to address it that are usually considered mutually exclusive, a scruple of logic I shall resist. The literature on this subject is immense and full of detailed and often technical debate. There are two protocols that will help to chart a course through this material. First, the language of ontological description must be sufficiently consonant with ordinary usage that it actually illuminates practice. A good deal of the philosophical literature on the subject makes use of technical language that is out of keeping with the address of this book. Therefore, I shall use as little of it as possible, considering the identity of things over time in what Roderick Chisholm, following a usage coined by Bishop Butler, would call the "loose and popular" rather than the "strict and philosophical" sense of identity.[10] Actually, however, I aim at something in between: an account of persistence of an object that is stricter than unexamined usage might accept yet still recognizably describes cultural practice. The second protocol heeds the

---

10. Roderick M. Chisholm, "The Loose and Popular and the Strict and Philosophical Senses of Identity," in *Perception and Personal Identity*, ed. Norman S. Care and Robert H. Grimm (Cleveland, OH: Case Western Reserve University Press, 1969): 82–106.

particular type of experience this book concerns: encounters with the past. Therefore, the role of touch needs to be borne in mind, along with the idea of transitivity. Both these constraints will render certain metaphysical positions more useful than others.

Another decision about how to address identity will rule out some ontologies whose target of interest diverges from the kinds of objects here under discussion. I am not interested in what one might call a metaphysics of ultimate reality. Such theories seek to discover the basic components that make up the world, whether conceived as atoms, subatomic particles, or some other kind of simple object that in combination comprises the larger composite objects we live with. Those interested in ultimate reality tend to focus on what exists regardless of the presence or absence of human consciousness, an approach that is ill-suited to deal with culture and with the realities that come into being through human activities.

It must be stressed that artifacts created by human beings are still *realities*, though not ultimate (however that may be construed). As Randall Dipert observes, artifacts are "primary elements of our lives" and are not secondary in metaphysical importance to fundamental components of nonhuman nature.[11] Ontologies that aim to illuminate the products of human endeavor and the values they accrue concern reality on a human scale. They pertain to what are sometimes called "medium-sized objects," those things that we encounter in daily life, such as chairs and buildings and spoons. It is in this range that the picture of real things needs to be sought. To this end, I agree with those who argue that ordinary, medium-sized objects are themselves "irreducibly real."[12] They come into being and are destroyed, and the persistence of whatever basic particles compose their make-up is irrelevant to their own identity as objects of their specific kind. As Amie Thomasson puts it, "Reducing ordinary objects to, or identifying them with, entities of other sorts—where these have different frame-level identity conditions, and thus

11. Randall Dipert, *Artifacts, Artworks, and Agency* (Philadelphia: Temple University Press, 1993) p. 120.
12. Lynne Rudder Baker, *The Metaphysics of Everyday Life: An Essay in Practical Realism* (Cambridge: Cambridge University Press, 2007) p. 5 and passim. I find Baker's theory among the most sensible and persuasive of those on offer, and I use it extensively in this discussion.

are of different categories—is a nonstarter."[13] It makes no sense anyway to discuss what is "really real" absent human consciousness when discussing aesthetic encounters, or the ethical attitude taken to memorial objects, or the cognitive insight old things permit, all of which involve aspects of consciousness. Human beings are part of the world, and the things we construct materially and culturally are also part of the world of real things that are here in question.[14]

That ground cleared, let us pick up the story of the ship of Theseus. Hobbes presents us with the choice between two ships: one that has undergone gradual replacement of parts but has a continuous history of use, and the other with no continuous history of use but composed of original material parts. The often-repeated positions on the question of which object counts as *the* ship of Theseus include (1) the first one, (2) the second one, and (3) that the situation is too indeterminate to answer. These disagreements contain some useful observations, including the fact that there are different standards for sameness and continuity. If the gradually repaired ship is chosen, then continuous history of use trumps sameness of material parts. If the ship reconstructed out of the saved original planks is chosen, then material identity overrides continuous usage. If one finds the situation indeterminate, this indicates that both criteria can plausibly be used and there is no gauge to determine a priori which one is more appropriate. These different standards may appear as rivals in the philosophical debate such that they cannot both obtain. In practical terms, however, both are guides in different circumstances when dealing with artifacts whose authenticity is significant or in question.

Interruptions

These variations on possible answers are not mere philosophical teasers. We can see them in actual practice, including the ones

---

13. Amie Thomasson, *Ordinary Objects* (New York: Oxford University Press, 2007) p. 190.

14. For a general thesis about continuity between biology and culture see John Searle, *The Construction of Social Reality* (New York: The Free Press, 1995).

that seem logically dubious such as those that posit so-called interrupted existence. For instance, of the two ships, the one with the same material components would seem to preserve a sense of sameness that for the purposes of this study has the advantage of supporting the sense of transitivity through touch, since the same material can be touched repeatedly over time. But should we select this ship, reconstructed from original materials, as *the* ship? Its identity as such is questionable because, as a ship, it lost structural integrity during the period when it was a pile of planks. Hence for a time it was not a ship at all. If this ship is chosen as being identical to the ship of Theseus, it underwent a period of interrupted existence, which is a problem because the very notion of persistent identity over time presumes continuity.[15] Among other difficulties, it would seem to endow the same ship with two existential starting-points, which violates the logic that we expect one and the same thing to obey.

However, interrupted existence, or something that looks quite like it, simply has to be permitted if we are to make sense of the actual treatment of certain objects of material culture. Think of the cases where whole buildings are disassembled, their bricks and stones and planks and windows and hinges carefully labeled and then painstakingly reassembled elsewhere, as is the case with any number of chapels, temples, and houses that have found their way onto new sites or into museums. If a temple is disassembled, the dispersed components are no longer a temple; the object has lost its kind-identity and hence the temple has gone out of existence.[16] After reassembly, it again counts as a temple. A huge Ming tomb in the Royal Ontario Museum in Toronto is among hundreds of examples of architectural artifacts that were taken apart and reassembled in order to be moved from their first place of use to a museum. In the

---

15. For a cogent discussion of interrupted existence and the options for solution of the ship puzzle, see E. J. Lowe, "On the Identity of Artifacts," *Journal of Philosophy* 80:1 (1983): 220–232. Difficulties of formulating standards for continuity are discussed extensively in David S. Oderberg, *The Metaphysics of Identity Over Time* (New York: St. Martin's Press, 1993).

16. This language makes use of Baker's notion that things have identity according to their "primary kinds." "A primary kind is a kind in virtue of which a thing has its persistence conditions" (*Metaphysics of Everyday Life*, p. 35).

process their locations change, and an argument can be made that there is a loss of aesthetic quality with relocation, as I indicated in the last chapter. Optimum appreciative conditions aside, however, the question of the identity of objects that have been dismantled and reassembled is still on the table.

Systematic methods undertaken for transporting large objects recognize the precariousness of disassembly and take measures to protect identity, whatever change of location they undergo and despite a period of time—sometimes lengthy—during which they were taken apart. The Ming tomb was not intact at every point in time, but denying that reassembly restored its sameness would amount to the claim that reassembly itself is a delusion. Something has to be the same as it was in order to have been *re*assembled at all. There is a lot at stake here, since unless the objects remain the same, the possibility of their providing the very kinds of encounters that have been the subject of this study disintegrates.

E. J. Lowe defends interrupted existence under conditions that exactly pertain to the reassembly of such artifacts. Lowe argues that it is not really the case that a dismantled object goes out of existence, any more than a watch taken apart while under repair goes out of existence. What sustains its existence is a reliable procedure for reassembly, and so long as such a procedure is in place, the watch (or the ship or the temple) still has only one beginning. In other words, reassembly is not a new beginning, so that paradox is skirted.[17] The problem of interrupted existence implicitly presumes the absence of such reliable procedures, but both in theory and in practice they are important components of persistence conditions for many sorts of things. In short, the existence of an object that is taken apart and put back together is not really interrupted at all, though one could say that the parts of an object are temporarily rearranged and for a

17. Lowe, "On the Identity," 222–223. Lowe is inclined, however, to opt for continuity of use over reassembly of original pieces when he selects the first ship as *the* ship of Theseus. For purposes of this discussion I am radically simplifying Lowe's argument. See also more generally Kathrin Koslicki's mereological account of identity, wherein the structural organization of the parts of an object is itself a part of that object: "The structure which dictates how the remaining parts of a whole are to be arranged is itself, literally and strictly speaking, *part* of the whole it organizes." Kathrin Koslicki, *The Structure of Objects* (Oxford: Oxford University Press, 2008) p. 5.

time its kind-identity is suspended. The outcome here should be no surprise, for this phenomenon is easily taken care of in ordinary conversation when we say things like "this tile belongs to the roof of the tomb" or "the tomb will occupy this wing when we put it back together." Reassembly entirely preserves the qualities and the identity of an artifact.

The practice of restoration also mandates this conclusion, though with an added complication. When an archaeologist puts together the shards of an ancient pot, she is not making a new pot. That is a different sort of enterprise altogether. Rather, she is reassembling and gluing together the extant pieces of the same pot. Unlike disassembly and reassembly, the result of restoration is often not qualitatively identical in all its original components, since fillers and replacement pieces may have been necessary. In all likelihood the put-together pot is not indiscernible from what the original would have been like. But it still has claims to be numerically identical in that it is the same pot, once whole, then broken, and now repaired. If there remain grounds for challenge regarding the sameness of the repaired pot, they would pertain more soundly to the amount of what has been replaced rather than to interruption of its existence during the time that it was broken. With a restored object, the degree of genuineness it possesses is a function of both the amount of original material remaining and whether it was put together with sufficient indicators of original shape and size acting as guides for reassembly or reconstruction.

There are many more examples that could further amplify and complicate this investigation. The general point is that a workable sense of genuineness of artifacts persisting over time must countenance disassembly and reassembly. Appeal to reliable procedures for reconstruction takes care of the problem of what is really better called "interrupted integrity" rather than "interrupted existence." Criteria for genuineness should not make persistent identity impossible in such cases.

In short, thesis #2: Things persist over time despite temporary derangement of their physical components; namely, they can undergo carefully managed disassembly and reassembly while retaining their identity as the same thing they were before being taken apart.

There are obvious limits to this. A building smashed to powder cannot be reassembled unless one possesses a magic wand. Even after destructive change, however, one might keep a portion of that powder as a memorial. In this case a thing has been destroyed because it no longer exists as the kind of object it once was. Nonetheless, even small fragments of that thing can sometimes retain the power of presence. In this sort of case, even unrecognizable material that once composed a thing is set apart and honored. This practice assumes that the original thing was sufficiently momentous that a memorial is appropriate, as with, say, the powdered remains from the attack that destroyed the Twin Towers of the World Trade Center. (Reportedly, there are small memorials here and there in New York where people have refused to dust a shelf since 2001.)[18]

Considerations leading to this second conclusion indicate that the ontology that suits the pursuit of the genuine must rule out metaphysical positions that would make even tiny changes alter the identity of an object. This is a place where the loose and popular and the strict and philosophical senses of identity part company dramatically. One might maintain that every one of an object's parts is essential to it, to the extent that an object does not retain identity when it suffers change—not strictly speaking, that is. Whatever logical reason supports this brand of strictness, it violates not only common sense but also the very conceptual stability that makes ordinary reference to things possible. This strictness might—just might—be warranted in a few cases when the object in question is a work of art where every property might contribute to its artistic and aesthetic value, and thus where it is marginally less absurd given the sensitivity of some artworks to even slight changes in composition.[19] However, the property of

18. "Objects and Memory," PBS Documentary: http://www.pbs.org/program/objects-and-memory. Artist Xu Bing created a work in which he wrote *And Where Does the Dust Itself Collect?* in dust collected from Lower Manhattan after 9/11. See https://mymodernmet.com/xu-bing-where-does-the-dust-itself-collect/

19. See again Mark Sagoff, "On Restoring and Reproducing Art." *Journal of Philosophy* 75:9 (1978) 453–470. For complexities of exact identity, see Nelson Goodman, *Languages of Art* (Indianapolis: Bobbs-Merrill, 1968) Part III. For a skeptical analysis of this approach see Jerrold Levinson, "Aesthetic Uniqueness," in *Music, Art, and Metaphysics: Essays in Philosophical Aesthetics* (Ithaca, NY: Cornell University Press, 1990): 107–133.

genuineness that underlies encounters with the past does not require such scruples since it is not a perceptually manifest property. Our discussion of aesthetic encounters with objects that embody their pasts need not make use of this kind of theoretical stipulation.

There are two final points that prove such restrictions unworkable: One concerns the application of theory in practice, for if we did try to countenance such strictness, there would be hardly anything genuine lingering from the past, maybe nothing at all. The second concerns the accommodation of the kinds of value that are in play with aesthetic encounters with the past. This point is especially notable with regard to age value. Age value is recognized when an object manifests the history it has undergone, the expanse of the time that it has existed. In the duration of that existence, it is likely that time has worn it away or that it has been damaged or subject to decay. Age value summons an awareness of transience. However, we can make no sense of age value whatsoever unless we countenance persistence of an object during the time that it suffers its wear and alters in appearance. If an object, strictly speaking, does not survive a change in its parts, then the object accorded age value is different from the object that would age. This is close to incoherent. An object that is worn or that has undergone repairs still remains, to borrow again a phrase from Robert Nozick, the closest continuer to the original piece and hence retains identity even though some of its properties have changed through wear, chips, or other sorts of damage.[20] In other words, a real old thing is usually an object that shows the marks of time.

---

20. "To say that something is a continuer of x is not merely to say its properties are qualitatively the same as x's, or resemble them. Rather it is to say they grow out of x's properties, are causally produced by them, are to be explained by x's earlier having had its properties, and so forth." Robert Nozick, *Philosophical Explanations* (Cambridge, MA: Harvard University Press, 1981) p. 35. Rafael de Clercq expresses a similar idea in terms of a restored object being a "successor" to the original. His account, however, proposes a more complicated thesis, namely that the restored object be considered the one that legitimately can be denoted by the same name as the original. De Clercq, "The Metaphysics of Art Restoration." *British Journal of Aesthetics* 53:3 (July 2003): 261–275.

Time

Historical value, age value, and encounters with the past all summon a sense of *time*—our time, past time, the endurance of things beyond the spans of time that our more transient human lives can witness. Time is foregrounded as a component of the identity of a thing by a metaphysical position known as four-dimensionalism. Since inserting time into the ontology of things might seem a promising approach to illuminate an object's genuineness, this perspective deserves a brief mention.

Four-dimensionalism bypasses the problem of accounting for identity when an object suffers a change of material parts by conceiving of an object not as single three-dimensional entity that undergoes change but as a succession of temporal parts.[21] The properties assigned to those parts are not the same during all the stages of the object, but because the object is conceived in terms of discrete stages or segments, the four-dimensionalist does not have to deal with altered properties of one and the same object. Building time into the very concept of a persisting object may seem an auspicious approach to the sorts of objects for which time is itself part of their aesthetic appeal, which is one way to put encounters with the past. However, four-dimensionalism is actually ill-suited to understanding the concept of the genuine and the objects that possess that property. First of all, the sacrifice to our ordinary concept of a thing is considerable. Temporal parts are not just what we might ordinarily consider periods of time when an object is in a certain condition, as for example the time before the handle is broken off a cup. The latter has measurable duration during which one might experience the cup both before and then after it was broken. But ultimately, temporal parts do not have any more duration than a point has extension.[22] There are several unfriendly upshots to this approach that defeat the concept of genuineness.

21. E.g., Theodore Sider, *Four Dimensionalism: An Ontology of Persistence and Time* (Oxford: Clarendon Press, 2001).

22. This emphasizes one aspect of the theory. Sider permits conglomerates of stages, as when he notes that while each temporal part exists only for an instant, one can also extend the concept to say things like "my today part exists for a day, my this-year temporal part lasts a year," and so forth. Sider, *Four Dimensionalism*, p. 2.

One consequence is that it is hard to understand how one experiences an object at all, for experience amounts to one's own temporal part interacting with an object's temporal part in a succession of (theoretically) discrete instants.[23] Perhaps the most significant loss for the notion of a genuine object is that it does not provide an adequate understanding of what it means for a series of temporal stages to have a history such that an object can embody its past. Here is one place where the analogy pursued between space and time breaks down, for if an object is broken, it loses a bit of its spatial identity but retains its history; in contrast, a temporal part would seem unable to accrue a history.[24] That is, the chipped plate has a history of having been chipped, of suffering damage, of being used, of manifesting that use in its sensible properties, for we can both see and feel the rough spot where the chip occurred. Thereby this object embodies its past. Valuing an object because it embodies a past requires a more robust sense of continuity of one and the same object persisting over time, not an object conceived of in terms of segments to avoid the problem of continuous existence.

So, thesis #3: Real things are to be understood as objects having a three-dimensional spatial identity that persists over certain degrees of change, an identity that is sufficiently continuous to accrue a sustained history. Without this stipulation, one cannot explain the value to be found in encounters with things from the past.

This conclusion deliberately skates over several problems that propel metaphysical theories, including how one identifies as the same an object that undergoes substantial change of material parts. I omit detailed consideration of these matters not only because they would shift attention to issues beyond the scope of this study, but also because they can be laid to rest in a wholesale way if one accepts

23. Baker objects that "An instantaneous temporal part physically cannot be experienced" in *Metaphysics of Everyday Life*, p. 9, fn. 9. According to Baker, four-dimensionalism entails that ordinary objects do not come into and go out of existence. All we have is a succession of temporal parts. But unless we reduce ordinary objects to component particles, we have to account for their inception and destruction. Since ordinary objects themselves are irreducibly real, four-dimensionalism is not a satisfactory theory. See her chapters 1–2.

24. Oderberg develops this line of objection in *Metaphysics of Identity over Time*, 135–137.

that a certain amount of indeterminacy is not only theoretically tolerable but factually reasonable. Accepting this requires that we grant that objects themselves—their boundaries, their exact edges, and the times when they come into and pass out of existence— can be simply *vague*. My use of "vagueness" probably qualifies as a more-or-less loose and popular sense of the term, but it is useful to have philosophers who endorse it at my back because it supports the (possibly eyebrow-raising) claim that genuineness can come in degrees.

Vagueness

While the embrace of vagueness appears to be a minority position among metaphysicians, those whose interests focus on ordinary material things have less difficulty countenancing it.[25] Vague objects create a logical bother because they appear to violate the law of excluded middle, the principle that maintains that something is either *p* or *not-p*. One way to address this problem is to separate the ontic and the epistemic issues and to maintain that nature itself is not vague, though our way of describing it often is. Vagueness, by this approach, is a function of partial knowledge and imprecise reference. The alternative approach, which is far more useful for this study, is to grant that nature itself contains vagueness. This perspective countenances with relative ease the ongoing processes of wear, decay, and breakage that old things undergo.

The world is full of processes during which something both comes to be and goes out of existence, and for the duration of those processes, there simply is no clear determinate point where the *thing* in question—that is, the one whose identity and persistence we are interested in—pops into being or goes out of existence. (It is apt for considering degrees of genuineness to fold together vagueness of identity and vagueness of existence.) When does an egg become a tadpole, a tadpole become a frog? This is a fairly rapid

25. Theodore Sider, "Against Vague Existence," *Philosophical Studies* 114 (2003): 135–146.

process, but it is impossible to say: *Now!* The tadpole has passed out of existence and the frog has arrived. Not only natural but also artifactual creation displays the same period of indeterminacy. When does a symphony come into being? With the first note? No. Only with the last? Surely, no again. Somewhere in the middle it begins to take shape and grow, but at no particular point is it *suddenly there*.[26] Composition is a process with gradual coming-to-be of a piece of music.

We can apply this idea readily to the problem of wear and tear on objects over time. When does your grandmother's favorite teaspoon cease to exist? When it is polished so often that the gold wash on the silver bowl begins to wear away? No. When it falls down the garbage disposal and snaps in half? Maybe, maybe not. Perhaps it can be fished out and soldered back together. It is worth going to that effort only if one values *that spoon* and conceives of it as irreplaceable, a point of view that presumes that the identity of the spoon survives even major injury. Why bother to repair a different spoon? It is the same spoon and retains its sentimental, historical, and age value, though it may lose some artistic value and it suffers a noticeable qualitative transformation in becoming *that spoon now damaged*. When damage is too major, the spoon is finally destroyed. If it is melted down and made into a silver bullet, it is the bullet that kills the werewolf, not the spoon, which has ceased to exist during the process of melting, and for a time there was only the elemental substance before the silver was poured into a bullet mold. The thing to which we refer is indeterminate during that period of time, gradually slipping away from being the kind of thing that is a spoon to being melted silver.

In her persuasive defense of vagueness in nature, Lynne Rudder Baker asserts that "medium-sized objects are typically spatially vague." She points out that the concept of *dog*, for example, is spatially vague because if it is not, in order to be precise, one would have to stipulate the exact number of hairs on a dog. (That may sound silly, but if one insists on precision with regard to major

---

26. This statement is at odds with Nelson Goodman's famous assertion that even a symphony requires that no single note be misplaced because of the compliance test provided by a score. *Languages of Art*, pp. 117–119.

physical changes, such as whether the dog loses its tail, one must carry that precision to the most detailed level.) But *dog* is vague, and in this case it is clear that "the vagueness is not exhausted by any indeterminacy in the concept *dog*. An animal that may have loose hairs is what the concept *dog* is a concept *of*."[27] Therefore, vagueness is not linguistic or epistemic, it is metaphysical—meaning it describes aspects of the world itself.[28]

So, thesis #4: Objects that persist over time are vague in that their precise parts and their exact dimensions are not so determinate that change automatically destroys identity. Rather, their being is intact within what we might term a zone of continuous or recurrent identifiability. We need to take this into account when formulating parameters for genuineness.

Fragments

So far I have borrowed from established metaphysical positions that maintain a view of objects that accommodates the value of genuineness and of age. However, there is one topic that is particular to aesthetic encounters with old artifacts that needs to be added, and that is when one treasures a mere fragment of what once was. As noted in Chapter 2, a fragment is a piece of original material that is damaged and partial, and yet it still is able to bring the past into awareness with vivid immediacy. The difference between a fragment, understood as a portion of a larger artifact that still carries

27. Baker, *Metaphysics of Everyday Life*, pp. 129–130. She boldly declares, "I do not take the law of excluded middle as an a priori constraint on reality" (p. 124). Other philosophers accept vagueness more cautiously. E.g., David Wiggins on works of art: "Note that there is vagueness here, because partial destruction, hostile to integrity but insufficient to bring the work to the point of destruction or replacement *tout court*, is an idea that makes sense in this sort of case. That, after all, is the sad condition, all too easily aggravated by mindlessly scientistic restoration, of many fine works." *Sameness and Substance Renewed* (Cambridge: Cambridge University Press, 2001) p. 137, n. 40.

28. As a reviewer for this manuscript noted, the account of vagueness that I endorse is a metaphysical view rather than one that locates vague boundaries in social or linguistic conventions. However, there are certain practices within cultures that indicate those factors operate as well, such as the concept among First Nations Pacific coast peoples to regard totem poles as living, gradually decaying, and then going out of existence.

its past with it, and just a bit of stuff that is more or less scrap, takes us back to Hobbes's variation on the ship of Theseus. One can imagine a pile of old planks as simply scrap. Only their original role as part of a famous ship gives them any value, but as individual planks they are unrecognizable as such.[29] In a general sense, the un-reassembled planks are fragments. But "fragment" also denotes a recognizable category of artifact—a piece of something that is still perceptually distinguishable as *of* that thing: a broken piece of a statue that is still obviously that statue's foot, for instance. As such, the fragment itself possesses genuineness as being of some now-lost thing, which carries with it not only thoughts of its whole but also the pathos of its damage.

Linda Nochlin describes a fragment of a statue of Louis XIV as "a single, beautifully modeled foot from this colossal sculpture . . . eloquent in its isolation, its suggestion of the passage of earthly grandeur"[30] The fragmentary nature of an artifact can add to its poignancy and to the encounter that brings loss and destruction to mind. But this is only possible if the fragment is recognizable as being part of something larger that is now gone. (In a pinch, one could rely on the testimony of an expert to guide perceptual experience.) This observation is an addendum to Baker's claim that a thing is destroyed when it is no longer a thing of its kind. With a fragment there certainly has been destruction of a thing of its kind (sculpture of a king), but not complete loss of authenticity and of possibilities for encounters with the real thing. A fragment does not possess a diminished degree of genuineness, for it is a fully genuine object that was a part of an object whose kind is destroyed but which has left behind another thing that is real even though not complete. (More on fragments below.)

29. Even the notion of recognizability admits of some vagueness, for while certain kinds of fragments are immediately recognizable as being part of some whole, others require external information to regard them as such. The above discussion focuses on fragments that retain the marks of having been part of a whole—such as a piece of a sculpture.

30. Linda Nochlin, *The Body in Pieces: The Fragment as a Metaphor of Modernity* (London: Thames and Hudson, 1994) p. 9.

Genuineness: a continuum

From the several factors that contribute to the persistence of objects over time, it is no surprise to learn that genuineness is not a crisp category, nor that precise criteria distinguishing the genuine from the non-genuine will not be forthcoming. Objects that provide encounters with the past are themselves often in partial condition— partly made from original materials, partly from old replacements, partly from new replacements—and often fragmentary. I shall now draw these observations together and summarize a working concept of the real thing whose tangible presence can bring us in touch with the past. For ease of keeping track, I have numbered these observations, though they tend to blend into one another in a continuum rather than function as discrete standards.

I start with the easiest cases, those at the real end of the spectrum from real to reproduction where the persistence of original material is most evident, and which therefore fully satisfy the requirement of tangibility for things that embody their pasts. The standard alternatives on offer for the famous ship offer two approaches, each of which suits certain kinds of artifacts: (1) An object qualifies as genuine if it is in its original condition or has undergone minimal repair or restoration. This includes having retained all or most of its material parts in their appropriate composition or arrangement. And also: (2) an object qualifies as genuine if it is in its original condition or has undergone the gradual repair and replacement of parts in the course of continuous use in the role it was made for. This second condition is important to accommodate the kinds of artifacts where repair and replacement of parts is a relatively routine and expectable aspect of their maintenance, such as buildings, ships, painted walls, plumbing fixtures, furniture, and so forth.

Bearing in mind the endemic vagueness of objects as described above, the first description applies to many objects that have remained relatively intact through the years. It does not require strict intactness and identity of all parts over time, because that requirement makes genuineness virtually impossible. This formulation is the one that most depends upon retention of materials from an artifact's original making; it describes objects that suffer wear but have not required actual replacement of parts. The second describes objects whose nature is such that their parts require occasional renewal over the time of their use. The first captures the importance of original materials; the second notes that many kinds of artifacts routinely alter material composition in the course of maintaining continuity of function. That there are two conditions here acknowledges that the nature of objects differs, it being expected in the case of buildings or engineering projects that they are the kinds of things that change from their very inception.

Condition (2) pertains to things whose nature is to require maintenance, including replacement of parts when they wear out. Such changes are different from the repair of things that are broken but for which breakage is not a routine aspect of use. In other words, such objects were broken but might and should not have been, and if they had not been they would satisfy criterion (1). Therefore, a third measure is in order: (3) An object qualifies as genuine if it was broken or otherwise importantly damaged, but has been repaired with all or most of its original parts and reassembled according to an orderly and informed procedure. This condition, which employs Lowe's language, follows from the defense of interrupted existence—rephrased as interrupted integrity—offered above. Holding the fragments of an ancient pot can ground an aesthetic encounter, as can holding the pot glued back to its original shape. It is not the pot in its entirely original condition, for there may be pieces missing, chipped glaze, or faded paint. But, following the defense provided above, it qualifies as the same pot.[31] The changes it has undergone are indicators that it doesn't just look old, it embodies its past. The wear of the pot, perhaps the wear still evident from its first users, manifests the history endured and imbues perceptible age value in the pot.

These first three conditions link genuineness with the persistence of one and the same material object over time, noting that a certain degree of damage does not compromise persistent identity.

---

31. "Artifactual identity through time does not seem to require in its ordinary understanding the preservation of all the original physical properties of the artifact." Dipert, *Artifacts*, p. 123.

The next one retains genuineness even when the object's kind identity is compromised or lost. This concerns fragments—damaged bits of things that are indisputably real since they comprise original material. But since an object is destroyed when it is no longer the kind of object it originally was, fragments invite their own account: (4) An object qualifies as genuine if it is a fragment of an object that satisfies (1) or possibly even (2) (for a caveat, see below).

A fragment of a pot is not a pot; a cornice from a building is not a building. But as already noted, fragments are *of* their objects, and this relationship persists even if those objects do not. Fragments therefore can provide encounters with the past, possessing transitivity of touch when one handles a piece of what once was whole. The size of a fragment matters, for as a rule the object must be identifiable by some means that are more ready-to-hand than would be, say, examination in a scientific laboratory (even though scientific means are often important for confirming that one has accurately identified a thing). A mite of dust that once was a part of the Parthenon is not identifiable in the required way; the head of a statue that gazed from a pediment qualifies. The importance of a fragment is both a function of the size of original—the more the better—and of the remaining properties that make the relationship to the original recognizable. For instance, a fragment of a frieze that retains details of faces or flowers has a more important standing than a pile of indistinguishable chips. The problem with indistinguishable chips is not only their size, it is the difficulty in recognizing them as fragments of anything in particular. Still, something very small that remains from something very large can be highly evocative—a carving from a temple is far smaller than the temple itself, but its detail makes that fragment significant. (The dust from the attack on the Twin Towers is an unusual case where the remains of obliterated objects might be kept as memorials. They are identifiable not by inspection but by the recorded history of when they suddenly became residue of the towers. Obviously in a case such as this, external sources identifying the dust are essential in encountering it as the remnants of the originals.)

In certain cases, a fragment might still qualify as the same kind of object as the original of which it is now a remnant. Medieval tapestries were wall-sized, and if an eight-inch square of a tapestry is all that remains, the wall-covering-object did go out of existence. Yet the fragment is still a piece of dense weaving that may picture a flower, a hare, a unicorn. Because of these tapestry-traits, this fragment is also still tapestry. Whether fragments retain the kinds of their originals depends on the determining properties that make an object a thing of a specific kind. The extant ancient tiles from the Ishtar Gate are not themselves gates but tiles that are fragments of the gate; a carving from a church pew is neither a pew nor a church. But a fragment of a tapestry is still tapestry. (One or two threads are not.) If there are enough fragments left from a larger object, they can be reassembled to make a restored object like those described in (3). They might also become an element of a replicated and rebuilt object as with (5) below. But also a fragment can remain a fragment and be the object of an aesthetic encounter on its own. A fragment is entirely genuine, even if only a small bit of what once existed.

One must be cautious about fragments, especially considering objects that fall under (2) whose nature is such that repairs are part of continuous use. The reason for such caution is that it might be possible to have a fragment of an object that happens to be only the most recent replacement part. Suppose a ship undergoing continuous renewal of parts over a thousand years catches fire. The only remaining plank not reduced to ash is the one that was nailed in yesterday. Would this fragment qualify as a genuine object that provides an encounter with the past (through presence, touch, and so forth)? I doubt it. But so much detail is required to raise this counter example that it makes articulating conditions for genuineness unduly cumbersome, so I leave this thought as a caveat rather than a prompt for a more detailed formulation.

And just to add complexity to the mix, a piece of one kind of thing can become part of an entirely different kind of thing and yet retain its identity as part of the first, as happens when a portion of an old building is retained to construct one with a new purpose (hence not falling under the description of (2) above). An ancient coin can be made into modern jewelry, its antiquity being one of the reasons it was chosen for the design; a disused train station can become part of a hotel, and so forth. There is no continuity of use here, but the histories embodied in the older parts remain both recognized as such and serve as reasons, because of the anchor they provide to the past, for those parts to have been chosen.

One more qualification needs to be attached to these observations, for as previous examples have indicated, sometimes it matters whether an object is exactly identical with an individual object with a particular history, and sometimes it only matters if an object is truly of a type that has that history. The clearest example of this distinction that was introduced earlier is the mourning brooch—a type of jewelry made from the hair of a loved one. To a relative of that person, it matters that the hair in the jewelry really be the hair of the deceased individual; to a collector of Victorian-era jewelry, it matters just that the brooch be truly one of that type of thing—that it contain real human hair and have been fashioned as a commemorative object. To accommodate this difference, one can refer to genuine individual artifacts and genuine types of artifacts, making use of a type-token distinction under circumstances where the individual thing is less important than its membership in a class of things.

With conditions (1)–(4), the grounds for genuineness are fairly solid because of the steady persistence of materials of an artifact, whether whole or not. What we touch is what was also touched years ago—or at least some of it is. But we can extend consideration of fragments to notice more ambiguous circumstances. With the next set of guidelines, genuineness becomes partial and begins to diminish. It does not disappear altogether, but it recedes from experience as replacement parts take over more and more of the palpable object that remains.

Replication, rebuilding, reuse

If enough fragments of a thing remain, they might be reassembled to restore that thing, as with as with criterion (3). But fragments might be the sole survivors of objects, and when the latter are rebuilt a fragment can become part of a new thing that replicates the old. Sometimes there is sufficient information that rebuilding can recreate the original to a high degree. Such is the case with Wright's Darwin Martin House, discussed in Chapter 4. As an architectural complex, this is an example of a very large object, and the "fragments" are the two entire remaining houses that now anchor a reconstructed whole. Thinking about this kind of example suggests a fifth gauge for being genuine: (5) An object possesses a fair degree of genuineness if a portion of it is a fragment as in (4) and the whole replicates the original from which the fragment survived.

Several qualifications emerge that distinguish things that are truly *rebuilt* from things that are built anew from old materials. In the case of Wright's house, the guidance of his drawings, floorplans, and precise descriptions meant that the complex could be reconstructed in such a way that the rebuilt complex exactly *matches* the first one. Here it is not only the incorporation of the remaining real fragments—conceiving of whole houses as fragments of complexes—that lends genuineness, but the fact that construction followed the same plans in just the way that the first one did and utilized the same kinds of materials and to the extent possible, the same manufacturing methods. It is this possibility that lends credence to the comparison of architecture (with its blueprints) to music (with its scores).[32] Equally important is the fact that this reconstruction preserved exact location. Location is significant not only for the appreciation of how a building fits into its setting, its appropriateness for surrounding landscape, and so forth. It is also a major contributor to encounters with the past—being *there*, where something important stood or still stands, or where something of note occurred, a claim that was defended in the previous chapter.[33] Condition (5) might describe a rebuilt object in a new location, but if so the encounter with the past of that object would be a diminished experience of the real thing, having sacrificed integrity of location.

There are some more ambiguous examples that need to be included in this investigation, where arguably new artifacts are fashioned out of appropriate old ones, and where the outcome is

32. Wicks, Robert. "Architecture Restoration: Resurrection or Replication?" *British Journal of Aesthetics* 34:2 (1994): 163–170.

33. For a confirmation of this claim, see Michelle McClellan, "Place-Based Epistemology: This Is Your Brain on Historic Sites," National Council on Public History, May 25, 2015. http://ncph.org/history-at-work/place-based-epistemology/ (Accessed 12.8.17).

not straightforward with regard to identity or age value. Consider the practice of reusing old materials with the purpose of making something that is like—characteristic of—old things themselves. The result is structures that have some grounds to qualify as both old and similar to something from the past, a stand-in of sorts, but they come into being at a new time. This kind of re-use can be domestic and ordinary, as with the use of old bricks from torn-down buildings to construct a patio. In this case it is probably the aged look of the bricks that appeals, for time has worn their sharp edges and imbued a pleasant warmth to their tone. But sometimes the age of materials is significant beyond the appearance of the final product. The Cloisters Museum in New York, for example, was partly assembled from portions of medieval buildings removed from Europe, making a new "medieval" structure come into existence in the 1930s. It is not just that the structure looks appropriately old; much of its composition uses materials that really are old and that retain their age value.

This example bears some comparison with the rebuilt old city of Warsaw discussed earlier, though there are many differences. The most important of these is disruption of continuity of place and history. Warsaw stands in the same place, and it was reconstructed after the devastation of war. The claims for continuity are greater there, despite the almost total replacement of parts of the city. In contrast, building a medieval European structure in twentieth-century New York lacks continuity of both place and history. And of course the goals of construction are markedly different: the one to rebuild a devastated city where people could live again, the other to provide an appropriate ambiance for the Metropolitan Museum's collection of medieval European art. (The Cloisters is designed to display to the visiting public some five hundred years of development of architectural style. As such, the complex is itself a display object.)[34] Both places invite a trip back into history; neither deliberately deceives; neither is the way it was at the time the buildings now in existence would have been first

34. See the Cloisters Museum website: http://www.metmuseum.org/about-the-museum/history-of-the-museum/the-cloisters-museum-and-gardens (Accessed 6.27.13).

constructed; neither is fully genuine; both may conjure the presence of the past.

With structures such as these, there may be some continuity of kind identity of the parts transported and rebuilt. The Cloisters contains several structures that themselves were cloisters at their place of origin and are labeled as such. Not only is some material integrity retained but reassembly was undertaken in such a way that portions retain a degree of persistence, as with (3). But even when there is no reassembly of an old object in a new place, if parts of the newly made buildings are themselves fragments of other old buildings, they were chosen not only for their appropriate appearance but also because of what they had actually once been. A degree of historical continuity represented by the use of old material is significant even in the making of a new structure. Among the materials used in Warsaw were actual remnants of artifacts and architectural structures—remnants of old buildings and their very stones, not polymer blocks or cast concrete made to look like stone. Reconstruction utilized components that had legitimate claims to be real old things, not only appropriate kinds of materials but materials that had been already parts of similar artifacts—of buildings, columns, walls, and so forth. The points of origin for materials chosen to become portions of rebuilt things are measured in terms of when they were first fashioned into artifacts—not when they came into being as stones or minerals that eventually would be regarded as possible building materials. Stones themselves are thousands or millions of years old already, but it is the buildings they compose(d) that count as the "objects" that we seek to identify as persisting (or not) over time; not the materials considered as sedimentary or igneous or composite, granite, marble, or fieldstone. This is another instance where it is clear we are dealing with a cultural ontology, not just a catalogue of items that exist without a context of human activity that makes things what they are.

This thought is presented as a sixth observation about the genuine: (6) An object possesses some degree of genuineness if a portion of it is a fragment as in (4) which composes an entire object that is in the style of some original from which the fragment survived. This kind of reconstruction is not restoration, and it is far from the gradual repair and replacement of parts that often occur with an object as it is used over time. The latter maintains continuity of use, a continuous history. Nor is this a case of reassembly of broken parts, nor is it reconstruction according to an extant detailed plan. With (6) something new and different has come into existence. Nonetheless, the fact that a portion of the old guides the new lends partial genuineness or authenticity to these sorts of objects. Here we enter territory where the real thing is receding from experience, though it has not departed entirely. But as an object possesses less and less old material and its construction is more and more reliant on imaginative reconstruction, assuming that it does not possess continuity of function, genuineness does begin to disappear.

Presence in place

Touch is the sense that especially arouses awareness of bodily position—drawing attention to *where* one stands. Location reminds us that encounters with the past are often active explorations of places; not just visiting historical objects but also getting as near as possible to where something happened. This can be a departure from normal activity (traveling to Angkor Wat) or continuous with the cycles of life. Preservation of location sometimes means replication of the objects that once stood there. Consider the copies of marble statues in cities such as Rome and Florence, which have replaced those that were being eaten away by acid rain, some of which are now removed into museums. They still look as they did some years ago, and they stand where the originals did, retaining integrity of location if not continuity of materials.

I have made the case that sites where memorable events occurred provide a thrill of presence and that visits to certain places are situated experiences that diminish or disappear if one is in the wrong place. The thrill of encounters with old things is affected not only with their physical state but also with whether or not they remain in their place of origin. However, many objects have been moved from their original homes, as virtually all things of a certain age have been when we encounter them in museums. Triptych altarpieces that once prompted worship are separated and acquired by different institutions. Broken statuary from South Asian temples has migrated all over the world and is now displayed as stand-alone sculpture. And then there is the bizarre case of London Bridge, part in London, part in Devon, and part in Arizona, where it forms the nucleus of the second most popular tourist attraction in the state (after the Grand Canyon). All of these are objects with age value, and all invite contact with their pasts, displaced though they are from their original sites. A good deal of this disruption is the outcome of the passage of time and changing societies. Museums serve to protect things that would otherwise be looted or deteriorate, and it is also the case that *appropriateness* of location need not always require *sameness* of original location.[35]

Relocating old things does not always compromise their genuineness as artifacts, though it does uproot them from the environment that gave them meaning and thereby reduces the encounters with the past that they offer. That consequence may be justified to preserve endangered artifacts or to make them available to a wider public, but it is still important to notice the resulting effects of loss of place. Our current comfort with museum venues blinds us to the role that touch plays and the engagement with bodily presence that it affords. Here is where memorial sites can be illuminating, for they are immovable. Being present at a memorial site is literally putting oneself physically in a special place, and there and only there does one encounter the past that is honored. Memorial sites, incidentally, are in some sense not material objects at all, though their presence requires some tangible markers of what is to be remembered. The distinction between site and physical place is evident in cases such as the flight path at Shanksville, though the insubstantial characteristic of what it marks is not typical. Not every old thing is a memorial, but they all were situated somewhere. And integrity of location—being there—adds a depth to encounters with the past that no museum can provide.

35. Rosa Parks's childhood home was saved from demolition by an American artist, Ryan Mendoza, and moved for some years to Berlin. Plans are underway to return it to the US, including a possible exhibition at Brown University's Center for the Study of Slavery and Justice. The founding family of Brown made their money in the slave trade. https://news.brown.edu/articles/2017/10/rosa-parks (Accessed 10.31.17).

I conclude with an account of the outcome of the example with which I opened this study: the terminus of the Erie Canal. This is not a museum piece but part of a city, and as such it has resumed its role as a site with continuous occupation and use, which will be the case with most remnants of the past that are not sequestered in protected environments. That use, however, has changed dramatically from the purpose for which the canal was designed. The terminus, Commercial Slip, was uncovered and restored, and remnants of it remain. They are called "the Ruins," and one can stroll among them and touch the very stones of the Real Thing (Figure 5.2).

This remnant of the old slip is now part of what has become Canalside, a much larger area that comprises not only partial reconstruction of old waterways but also park and recreation areas, which are adjacent to boat slips in the summer and skating rinks in the winter. Nothing of the extensive recreation area resembles the original Erie Canal, though from certain vantage points one can glimpse areas that resemble past vistas. From most perspectives, however, the contemporary built environment is evident to view (Figure 5.3). This is as it should be, for communities have both presents and pasts, and continuity between them is part of the dynamism

FIGURE 5.2 Erie Canal terminus facing west, "The Ruins," 2017. Photo by author.

FIGURE 5.3 Erie Canal terminus facing south 2017. Photo by author.

of societies that by their very nature change and grow, losing bits of older material history while moving into the future. In other words, valuing encounters with the past and preserving artifacts that embody history need not entail that we live in archives or museums. On the other hand, without protective environments, real things will gradually slip away. The pendulum continues to swing.

The palpable presence of old things is the firmest ground for the genuine, although the conclusions reached in this book are fairly generous about the status of genuine things and have attempted to accommodate both different sorts of artifacts and the contributions of historical and social practice to the standing of artifacts in contexts of use, including ceremonies, rituals, and the power of place. Repairs and restorations that attempt the greatest possible retention of old materials are therefore high on my list of recommendations, even if the look of an artifact is compromised.

With the advent of digital recording of ancient things, reconstructing the look of sites and artifacts is becoming easier. But only their look. I take touch in its various manifestations seriously as a mode of apprehension that affords encounters with the past, which means that wholesale resurrections, no matter how accurate their appearance, do not sustain the value of the real thing. Digital recreations are a wonder, and what they preserve for the unraveling future of material artifacts is invaluable. They are marvelous, but they are not things of the same kind as that to which they refer. They are as like to real things as can be imagined, but likeness is not identity, and the possibility of palpable contact with the past is forever lost. They do not carry the past into the present, though they do remind us of what has been irrevocably destroyed. For those who continue to believe that transitivity of touch is a vestige of mere primitive ways of thinking, digitally-produced artifacts might seem the welcome final nail in the coffin of premodern relics of thought. Obviously, I am not in that company.

Coda

It is probably inevitable that a rumination on encounters with the past ends on a melancholy note. This study is a philosophical exploration of tangible experiences of things that embody their pasts, and it also addresses practical concerns that arise at many levels, from individuals who must decide what to discard when moving residences, to communities considering whether to invest in a project of historical restoration, to government agencies weighing the relative costs and benefits of building dams, highways, shopping malls; or draining swamps, renewing urban neighborhoods, or permitting suburbs to expand into old farmland and forest. What is valuable enough from the past that it should be saved, preserved, restored, protected? And although most of my discussion has focused on human-made artifacts, the consequences for depredation of what remains of our natural environments are dire. Decisions over what to destroy and what to preserve and protect can be pressing, difficult, even tragic, but they are unavoidable. Mistakes are made, and when those mistakes are only recognized years later, one realizes that missing at the time of decision was a grasp of what people of the future would see as irredeemable loss uncompensated by progress. One cannot save everything nor is everything worth saving. To believe otherwise makes hoarders of individuals and renders built environments static and worn-out. So we all confront questions about how to decide what is valuable enough to save and what can be discarded; what is *worth* keeping, restoring, protecting, harboring.

Competing interests, especially economic interests, target relatively immediate benefits, often to the detriment of long-term consequences. The real problem is that one needs not only to figure out what matters most now but what will matter in the future, for decisions made now will be irrevocable. Thoughtful decisions enjoin caution and imagination to foresee consequences beyond immediate outcomes and to envision what will be praised as worthwhile progress or condemned as short-sighted expediency. A theoretical exposition such as this one cannot provide a formula for precise answers to such questions, given the diverse circumstances in which they arise. But I hope I have offered a general sense of the value and the unique encounters afforded by objects that embody the past: *genuine objects—real things*—because they possess values that no substitutes provide. Failing to keep things that matter truncates such experiences and the thrills and insights they invite, trapping us in our present concerns and dulling our awareness of all that has gone before.

Bibliography

Ambrose, Stephen. "Join Us on the Trail." *National Geographic Traveler* 19:2 (March 2002).

Aristotle. *De Anima*. In *The Complete Works of Aristotle*, ed. Jonathan Barnes. Princeton: Princeton University Press, 1984.

Austen, Jane. *Emma*. New York: New American Library, 1964.

Baker, Lynne Rudder. *The Metaphysics of Everyday Life: An Essay in Practical Realism*. Cambridge: Cambridge University Press, 2007.

Baudrillard, Jean. *Simulacra and Simulation*. Trans. Sheila Faria Glaser. Ann Arbor: University of Michigan Press, 1995.

———. "The System of Collecting." In *Cultures of Collecting*, ed. John Elsner and Roger Cardinal. London: Reaction Books, 1994: Ch. 1.

Beauvoir, Simone de. *Coming of Age*. Trans. Patrick O'Brian. New York: G.P. Putnam/Warner, 1973.

Benjamin, Andrew. *Art's Philosophical Work*. London and New York: Rowman and Littlefield, 2015.

Benjamin, Walter. "The Work of Art in the Age of Mechanical Reproduction." In *Illuminations*. Trans. Harry Zohn. New York: Harcourt, Brace, Jovanovich, 1968: 217–252.

Benthien, Claudia. *Skin: On the Cultural Border between Self and the World*. New York: Columbia University Press, 2002.

Berger, John. *Ways of Seeing*. London: BBC/Penguin Books, 1972.

Berkeley, George. *An Essay Towards a New Theory of Vision*. London: Dent, 1910 (1709).

Bloom, Paul. *How Pleasure Works: The New Science of Why We Like What We Like.* New York: W.W. Norton, 2010.

Borges, Jorge Luis. "On Exactitude in Science." In *Collected Fictions.* Trans. Andrew Hurley. New York: Penguin, 1998: 325.

Brooks, Geraldine. *The People of the Book: A Novel.* New York: Penguin, 2008.

Budd, Malcolm. "The Acquaintance Principle." *British Journal of Aesthetics* 43:4 (October 2003): 386–392.

Burleigh, Nina. *Unholy Business: A True Tale of Faith, Greed, and Forgery in the Holy Land.* New York: HarperCollins, 2008.

Burns, John F. "Richard III Gets a Kingly Burial, on Second Try." *New York Times,* March 26, 2015.

Candlin, Fiona. *Art, Museums and Touch.* Manchester: Manchester University Press, 2010.

Caple, Chris. *Objects: Reluctant Witnesses to the Past.* London and New York: Routledge, 2006.

Carroll, Noël. "Aesthetic Experience: A Question of Content." In *Contemporary Debates in Aesthetics and Philosophy of Art,* ed. Matthew Kieran. Malden, MA: Blackwell, 2007: 69–97.

———. "Art and the Domain of the Aesthetic." *British Journal of Aesthetics* 40:2 (2000): 191–208.

———. *Beyond Aesthetics: Philosophical Essays.* Cambridge: Cambridge University Press, 2001.

———. *On Criticism.* New York: Routledge, 2009.

———. "Recent Approaches to Aesthetic Experience." *Journal of Aesthetics and Art Criticism* 70:2 (Spring 2012): 165–177.

Carter, Angela. *Wise Children.* New York: Farrar, Straus, and Giroux, 1991.

Chisholm, Roderick. "The Loose and Popular and the Strict and Philosophical Senses of Identity." In *Perception and Personal Identity,* ed. Norman S. Care and Robert H. Grimm. Cleveland, OH: Case Western Reserve University Press, 1969: 82–106.

Classen, Constance, ed. *The Book of Touch.* Oxford: Berg, 2005.

———. *The Deepest Sense: A Cultural History of Touch.* Urbana: University of Illinois Press, 2012.

Cohen, G. A. "Rescuing Conservatism: A Defense of Existing Value." In *Reasons and Recognition: Essays on the Philosophy of T. M. Scanlon,* ed. R. Jay Wallace, Rahul Kumar, and Samuel Freeman. New York: Oxford University Press, 2011: 203–230.

Connor, Stephen. *The Book of Skin.* Ithaca, NY: Cornell University Press, 2004.

Crowley, David. "People's Warsaw/Popular Warsaw." *Journal of Design History* 10:2 (1997): 203–223.

Currie, Gregory. "Aesthetic Explanation and the Archaeology of Symbols." *British Journal of Aesthetics* 56:3 (July 2016): 233–246.

———. *An Ontology of Art.* London: Macmillan, 1989.

————. "Empathy for Objects." In *Empathy: Philosophical and Psychological Essays*, ed. Peter Goldie and Amy Coplan. Oxford: Oxford University Press, 2009: 82–96.

Danto, Arthur. "Gettysburg." *Philosophizing Art*. Berkeley: University of California Press, 1999: 233–250.

Davies, David. *Art as Performance*. Malden, MA: Blackwell, 2004.

Davis, Natalie Zemon. *The Return of Martin Guerre*. Cambridge: Cambridge University Press, 1983.

De Bolla, Peter. "Toward the Materiality of Aesthetic Experience." *Diacritics* 32:1 (2002): 19–37.

De Clercq, Rafael. "The Metaphysics of Art Restoration." *British Journal of Aesthetics* 53:3 (2013): 261–275.

Delk, J. L. and S. Fillenbaum. "Differences in Perceived Color as a Function of Characteristic Color." *American Journal of Psychology* 78 (1965): 290–293.

Derrida, Jacques. *On Touching—Jean-Luc Nancy*. Trans. Christine Irizarry. Stanford, CA: Stanford University Press, 2005.

De Sousa, Ronald. *The Rationality of Emotions*. Cambridge, MA: MIT Press, 1987.

De Waal, Edmund. *The Hare with Amber Eyes: A Hidden Inheritance*. New York: Farrar, Straus, and Giroux, 2010.

Dipert, Randall. *Artifacts, Art Works, and Agency*. Philadelphia: Temple University Press, 1993.

Donadio, Rachel. "Preserving the Ghastly Inventory of Auschwitz." *New York Times*, April 15, 2015. https://www.nytimes.com/2015/04/16/arts/international/at-auschwitz-birkenau-preserving-a-site-and-a-ghastly-inventory.html?hp&action=click&pgtype=Homepage&module=second-column-region&region=top-news&WT.nav=top-news&_r=0.

Doniger, Wendy. *The Bedtrick: Tales of Sex and Masquerade*. Chicago: University of Chicago Press, 2000.

Douglass, Frederick. *The Life and Times of Frederick Douglass*. New York: Dover, 2003.

Ducasse, Curt John. *The Philosophy of Art*. New York: Dover, 1966 [1929].

Dunbar, Robin. *Grooming, Gossip, and the Evolution of Language*. Cambridge, MA: Harvard University Press, 1996.

Dutton, Denis. "Artistic Crimes." *British Journal of Aesthetics* 19 (1979): 304–314.

Eaton, Marcia Muelder. *Aesthetics and the Good Life*. Cranbury, NJ: Associated University Presses, 1989.

————. "Aesthetics: The Mother of Ethics?" *Journal of Aesthetics and Art Criticism* 55:4 (Fall 1997): 355–364.

Eco, Umberto. *Faith in Fakes*. Trans. William Weaver. London: Secker and Warburg, 1986.

Ekman, Paul. "Facial Expressions of Emotion: An Old Controversy and New Findings." *Philosophical Transactions: Biological Sciences* 335:1273 (1992): 63–69.

Elliott, Robert. *Faking Nature: The Ethics of Environmental Restoration.* London: Routledge, 1997.

Feagin, Susan L. *Reading with Feeling: The Aesthetics of Appreciation.* Ithaca, NY: Cornell University Press, 1996.

Frazer, James. *The Golden Bough: A Study in Magic and Religion.* New York: Macmillan, 1951 (1890).

Fulkerson, Matthew. *The First Sense: A Philosophical Study of Human Touch.* Cambridge, MA: MIT Press, 2014.

Gamboni, Dario. *The Destruction of Art: Iconoclasm and Vandalism Since the French Revolution.* New Haven, CT: Yale University Press, 1997.

Gaskell, Ivan. "Ethical Judgments in Museums." In *Art and Ethical Criticism,* ed. Garry Hagberg. Malden, MA: Blackwell, 2008: 229–242.

Gere, Cathy. *Knossos and the Prophets of Modernism.* Chicago: University of Chicago Press, 2009.

Goldman, Alan H. "The Experiential Account of Aesthetic Value." *Journal of Aesthetics and Art Criticism* 64:3 (2006): 333–342.

Goodman, Nelson. *Languages of Art: An Approach to a Theory of Symbols.* Indianapolis: Bobbs-Merrill, 1968.

Goldie, Peter. *The Emotions.* Oxford: Oxford University Press, 2000.

Greenblatt, Stephen. "Resonance and Wonder." In *Exhibiting Cultures: The Poetics and Politics of Museum Display,* ed. Ivan Karp and Steven D. Lavine. Washington, DC: Smithsonian Institution, 1990: 42–56.

Griffiths, Paul. "Is Emotion a Natural Kind?" In *Thinking about Feeling: Contemporary Philosophers on Emotions,* ed. Robert Solomon. New York: Oxford University Press, 2004: 233–249.

Guignon, Charles. *On Being Authentic.* London and New York: Routledge, 2004.

Gumbrecht, Hans Ulrich. *The Production of Presence: What Meaning Cannot Convey.* Stanford, CA: Stanford University Press, 2004.

Hawthorne, Nathaniel. *The Marble Faun.* Forgotten Books, 2012 [1860].

Healy, Jack. "Remote Utah Enclave Becomes Battleground Over Reach of U.S." *The New York Times,* Sunday, March 12, 2016: 1, 16.

Hein, Hilde. "Museums—From Object to Experience." In *Aesthetics: The Big Questions,* ed. Carolyn Korsmeyer. Malden, MA: Blackwell, 1998: 103–115.

Henderson, James [Sa'ke'j] Youngblood. "The Appropriation of Human Remains: A First Nations Legal and Ethical Perspective." In *The Ethics of Cultural Appropriation,* ed. James O. Young and Conrad Brunk. Malden, MA: Wiley-Blackwell, 2009: 55–71.

Herder, Johann Gottfried. *Sculpture: Some Observations on Shape and Form from Pygmalion's Creative Dream.* Trans. Jason Gaiger. Chicago: University of Chicago Press, 2002.

"Historicity of the Eye." Symposium with articles by Arthur Danto, Noël Carroll, Mark Rollins, and Whitney Davis. *Journal of Aesthetics and Art Criticism* 59:1 (2001): 1–44.

Hjort, Mette and Sue Laver, eds. *Emotion and the Arts.* New York: Oxford University Press, 1997.

Hopkins, Robert. "Aesthetics, Experience, and Discrimination." *Journal of Aesthetics and Art Criticism* 63:2 (Spring 2005): 119–133.

——. "*Re*-Imagining, *Re*-Viewing, and *Re*-Touching." In *The Senses: Classic and Contemporary Philosophical Perspectives,* ed. Fiona Macpherson. Oxford: Oxford University Press, 2011: 261–283.

Hutson, Matthew. *The 7 Laws of Magical Thinking: How Irrational Beliefs Keep Us Happy, Healthy, and Sane.* New York: Plume, 2013.

Irvin, Sherri. "Artworks, Objects, and Structures." In *The Bloomsbury Companion to Aesthetics,* ed. Anna Christina Ribeiro. London: Bloomsbury, 2015: 55–73.

Iseminger, Gary. *The Aesthetic Function of Art.* Ithaca, NY: Cornell University Press, 2004.

Iyer, Pico. "Keeping it Real." *T: The New York Times Style Magazine,* November 15, 2015: 37–38.

James, Simon. "Why Old Things Matter." *Journal of Moral Philosophy* 14:4 (2013): 313–329.

Janowski, James. "Bringing Back Bamiyan's Buddhas." *Journal of Applied Philosophy* 28:1 (2011): 44–64.

Johnson, Mark. *The Body in the Mind.* Chicago: University of Chicago Press, 1987.

——. *The Meaning of the Body.* Chicago: University of Chicago Press, 2000.

Jonas, Hans. "The Nobility of Sight." *Philosophy and Phenomenological Research* 14:4 (1954): 507–519.

Judkins, Jennifer. "On Things That Aren't There Anymore." *Journal of Aesthetics and Art Criticism* 72:4 (Fall 2014): 441–445.

Jütte, Robert. *A History of the Senses from Antiquity to Cyberspace.* Trans. James Lynn. Cambridge: Polity Press, 2005.

Kant, Immanuel. *Critique of Judgment.* Trans. Werner Pluhar. Indianapolis: Hackett, 1987 [1790].

Kaplan, Alice. *The Collaborator: The Trial and Execution of Robert Brasillach.* Chicago: University of Chicago Press, 2000.

Kaufman, Robert. "Aura, Still." *October* 99 (Winter 2002): 45–80.

Kempf, Jack. "Reburying the Canal Doesn't Make Sense," "Viewpoints." *Buffalo News,* August 30, 1999: 3B.

Kieran, Matthew. *Revealing Art.* London: Routledge, 2005.

Kivy, Peter. *Authenticities: Philosophical Reflections on Musical Performance.* Ithaca, NY: Cornell University Press, 1995.

Kleist, Heinrich von. *Amphitryon.* Trans. Marion Sonnenfeld. New York: Frederick Ungar, 1962.

Kolnai, Aurel. "The Standard Modes of Aversion: Fear, Disgust, and Hatred." In *Aurel Kolnai on Disgust*, ed. Barry Smith and Carolyn Korsmeyer. Chicago: Open Court, 2004 [1929]: 93–108.

Korsmeyer, Carolyn. "Aesthetic Deception: On Encounters with the Past." *Journal of Aesthetics and Art Criticism* (Spring 2008): 117–127.

———. "Genuineness." *Material Religion* 11:3 (2015): 409–412.

———. "A Lust of the Mind: Curiosity and Aversion in Eighteenth Century British Aesthetics." In *Suffering Art Gladly: The Paradox of Negative Emotions in Art*, ed. Jerrold Levinson. Aldershot, UK: Ashgate: 2014: 45–67.

———. "Real Old Things." *British Journal of Aesthetics* 58:3 (2016): 219–231.

———. "Staying in Touch." In *Ethical Criticism and the Arts*, ed. Garry Hagberg. Malden, MA: Blackwell, 2008: 187–210.

———. "The Triumph of Time: Romanticism Redux." *Journal of Aesthetics and Art Criticism* 72:4 (Fall 2014): 429–435.

———. "Touch and the Experience of the Genuine." *British Journal of Aesthetics* 52 (2012): 365–377.

Koslicki, Kathrin. *The Structure of Objects*. Oxford: Oxford University Press, 2008.

Koudounaris, Paul. *Heavenly Bodies: Cult Treasures and Spectacular Saints from the Catacombs*. New York: Thames and Hudson, 2013.

Kubler, George. *The Shape of Time: Remarks on the History of Things*. New Haven, CT: Yale University Press, 1962.

Lamarque, Peter. "Reflections on the Ethics and Aesthetics of Restoration and Conservation." *British Journal of Aesthetics* 56:3 (July 2016): 281–299.

———. *Work and Object: Explorations in the Metaphysics of Art*. Oxford: Oxford University Press, 2010.

Langer, Suzanne. *Feeling and Form*. New York: Charles Scribner, 1953.

Leddy, Thomas. *The Extraordinary in the Ordinary: The Aesthetics of Everyday Life*. Peterborough, Ont.: Broadview Press, 2012.

Levinson, Jerrold. "Aesthetic Properties II." *Aristotelian Society Supplementary Volume* 79:1 (July 2005): 211–227.

———. "Aesthetic Uniqueness." In *Music, Art, and Metaphysics: Essays in Philosophical Aesthetics*. Ithaca, NY: Cornell University Press, 1990: 107–133.

———. "The Work of Visual Art." In *The Pleasures of Aesthetics: Philosophical Essays*. Ithaca, NY: Cornell University Press, 1996: 129–137.

Lindholm, Charles. *Culture and Authenticity*. Malden, MA: Blackwell, 2008.

Livingston, Paisley. "On an Apparent Truism in Aesthetics." *British Journal of Aesthetics* 43:3 (July 2003): 260–278.

Lopes, Dominic McIver. "*Shikinen Sengu* and the Ontology of Architecture in Japan." *Journal of Aesthetics and Art Criticism* 65 (2007): 77–84.

Lowe, E. J. "On the Identity of Artifacts." *Journal of Philosophy* 80:1 (1983): 220–232.

Lowenthal, David. *The Past Is a Foreign Country*. Cambridge: Cambridge University Press, 1985.

Lownie, Theodore. "Introduction." *Windows of the Darwin Martin House*. Buffalo: Burchfield-Penney Art Center, 1999.

Lyotard, François. *The Postmodern Condition: A Report on Knowledge*. Trans. Geoff Bennington and Brian Massumi. Minneapolis: University of Minnesota Press, 1984.

Macdonald, Helen. *H is for Hawk*. New York: Grove Press, 2014.

MacGregor, Neil. *A History of the World in 100 Objects*. New York: Viking Press, 2011.

Macpherson, Fiona. "Cognitive Penetration of Colour Experience: Rethinking the Issue in Light of an Indirect Mechanism." *Philosophy and Phenomenological Research* 84:1 (January 2012): 24–62.

Margolis, Joseph. *On Aesthetics: An Unforgiving Introduction*. Belmont, CA: Wadsworth, 2009.

———. "Works of Art as Physically Embodied and Culturally Emergent Entities." *British Journal of Aesthetics* 14:3 (1974): 187–196.

Massie, Pascal. "Touching, Thinking, Being: The Sense of Touch in Aristotle's *De Anima* and Its Implications." *Existentia* 23 (2013): 155–174.

Matravers, Derek. *Art and Emotion*. Oxford: Oxford University Press, 1998.

Matthes, Erich Hatala. "History, Value, and Irreplaceability." *Ethics* 124 (October 2013): 1–30.

———. "Palmyra's Ruins Can Rebuild Our Relationship with History." *Aeon* (March 2017). https://aeon.co/ideas/palmyras-ruins-can-rebuild-our-relationship-with-history.

———. "The Ethics of Historic Preservation." *Philosophy Compass* (August 2016): 1–9. DOI 10.1111/phc3.12379.

Mauss, Marcel. *A General Theory of Magic*. Trans. Robert Brain. London: Routledge and Kegan Paul, 1972 (1902–1903).

McClellan, Michelle. "Place-Based Epistemology: This Is Your Brain on Historic Sites." *NationalCouncil on Public History*, May, 25, 2015. http://ncph.org/history-at-work/place-based-epistemology.

Merleau-Ponty, Maurice. *The Phenomenology of Perception*. Trans. Colin Smith. London: Routledge and Kegan Paul, 1962.

Montagu, Ashley. *Touching: The Human Significance of the Skin*. New York: Harper and Row, 1986.

Nancy, Jean-Luc. *Noli me tangere: On the Raising of the Body*. Trans. Sarah Clift, Pascale-Anne Brault, and Nichael Naas. New York: Fordham University Press, 2008.

———. *The Birth to Presence*. Trans. Brian Holmes et al. Stanford, CA: Stanford University Press, 1994.

Nehamas, Alexander. *Only a Promise of Happiness: The Place of Beauty in a World of Art*. Princeton, NJ: Princeton University Press, 2007.

Newman, George E., Daniel M. Bartels, and Rosanna K. Smith, "Are Artworks More Like People Than Artifacts? Individual Concepts and

Their Extensions." *Topics in Cognitive Science* 6 (2014) 647–662. DOI 10.1111/tops.12111.

Newman, George E. and Rosanna K. Smith, "Kinds of Authenticity." *Philosophy Compass* 11:10 (2016) 609–618. DOI 10.1111/phc3.12343.

Nicholas, George P. and Alison Wylie. "Archaeological Finds: Legacies of Appropriation, Modes of Response." In *The Ethics of Cultural Appropriation*, ed. James O. Young and Conrad G. Brunk. Malden, MA: Wiley-Blackwell, 2009: 11–54.

Nochlin, Linda. *The Body in Pieces: The Fragment as a Metaphor of Modernity.* London: Thames and Hudson, 1994.

Nozick, Robert. *Philosophical Explanations.* Cambridge, MA: Harvard University Press, 1981.

"Objects and Memory." PBS documentary, August 17, 2009.

Oderberg, David S. *The Metaphysics of Identity Over Time.* New York: St. Martin's Press, 1993.

O'Shaughnessy, Brian. *Consciousness and the World.* Oxford: Clarendon Press, 2000.

Pamuk, Orhan. *The Innocence of Objects.* Trans. Ekin Oklap. New York: Abrams, 2012.

Perricone, Christopher. "The Aspiration to the Condition of Touch." *Philosophy and Literature* 30:1 (April 2006): 229–237.

Portier-Kaltenbach, Clémentine. "The Eternal Life of Bones," *Medicographia* (May 2011) at http://www.medicographia.com/2011/05/a-touch-of-france-the-eternal-life-of-bones.

Prinz, Jesse. "Emotion and Aesthetic Value." In *The Aesthetic Mind: Emotion and Psychology*, ed. Elisabeth Schellekens and Peter Goldie. Oxford: Oxford University Press, 2011: 71–88.

———. "Really Bad Taste." In *Knowing Art: Essays in Aesthetics and Epistemology*, ed. Matthew Kieran and Dominic McIver Lopes. Dordrecht: Springer, 2006: 95–107.

———. "Wonder Works: Renovating Romanticism about Art" blogpost at *Aesthetics for Birds*, August 5, 2013. http://www.aestheticsforbirds.com/2013/08/wonder-works-renovating-romanticism.html#more (Accessed 8.27.15).

Railton, Peter. "Aesthetic Value, Moral Value, and Naturalism." In *Aesthetics and Ethics: Essays at the Intersection*, ed. Jerrold Levinson. Cambridge: Cambridge University Press, 1998: 59–105.

Raz, Joseph. *Value, Respect, and Attachment.* Cambridge: Cambridge University Press, 2001.

Riegl, Alois. "The Modern Cult of Monuments: Its Character and Origin." (1928) Trans. Kurt W. Forster and Diane Ghirado. *Oppositions* (1982): 21–52.

Robinson, Jenefer. *Deeper than Reason: Emotion and Its Role in Literature, Music, and Art.* Oxford: Oxford University Press, 2005.

————. "On Being Moved Through Architecture." *Journal of Aesthetics and Art Criticism* 70:4 (2012): 337–353.

Rorty, Amélie. "Explaining Emotions." In *Explaining Emotions*, ed. Amélie Rorty. Berkeley: University of California Press, 1980: 103–126.

Rosenstein, Leon. *Antiques: The History of an Idea*. Ithaca, NY: Cornell University Press, 2009.

Rothstein, Edward. "Artifacts with a Life All Their Own." *New York Times*, May 29, 2014.

Rozin, Paul and Carol Nemeroff. "Sympathetic Magical Thinking: The Contagion and Similarity 'Heuristics'." In *Heuristics and Biases: The Psychology of Intuitive Judgment*, ed. Thomas Gilovic, Dale W. Griffin, and Daniel Kahneman. Cambridge: Cambridge University Press, 2002.

Ruskin, John: *The Seven Lamps of Architecture*. Project Gutenberg: http://www.gutenberg.org/files/35898/35898-h/35898-h.htm.

Russell, Bertrand. *The ABC of Relativity*. London: Allen and Unwin, 1969 [1925].

Rybczynski, Witold. *Now I Sit Me Down: From Klismos to Plastic Chair*. New York: Farrar, Straus, and Giroux, 2016.

Sagoff, Mark. "On Restoring and Reproducing Art." *Journal of Philosophy* 75:9 (September 1978): 453–470.

Saito, Yuriko. *Everyday Aesthetics*. New York: Oxford University Press, 2007.

Scarre, Geoffrey. "The Repatriation of Human Remains." In *The Ethics of Cultural Appropriation*, ed. James O. Young and Conrad Brunk. Malden, MA: Wiley-Blackwell, 2009: 72–92.

Searle, John. *The Construction of Social Reality*. New York: The Free Press, 1995.

Shakespeare, William. *The Complete Plays and Poems of William Shakespeare*. Ed. William Allen Neilson and Charles Jarvis Hill. Cambridge, MA: Houghton Mifflin, 1942.

Shanks, Michael. *Experiencing the Past: On the Character of Archaeology*. London: Routledge, 1992.

Sharpe, R. A. "The Empiricist Theory of Aesthetic Value." *Journal of Aesthetics and Art Criticism* 58:4 (Fall 2000): 321–332.

Shorto, Russell. *Descartes' Bones: A Skeletal History of the Conflict between Faith and Reason*. New York: Doubleday, 2008.

Shweder, Richard A. "Likeness and Likelihood in Everyday Thought: Magical Thinking in Judgments about Personality." *Current Anthropology* 18:4 (1977): 637–658.

Sibley, Frank. "Aesthetic Concepts." *Philosophical Review* 58 (1959): 421–450.

Sider, Theodore. "Against Vague Existence." *Philosophical Studies* 114 (2003): 135–146.

————. *Four Dimensionalism: An Ontology of Persistence and Time*. Oxford: Clarendon Press, 2001.

Simmel, Georg. "The Ruin." Trans. David Kettler. In *Georg Simmel, 1858–1915: A Collection of Essays*, ed. Kurt H. Wolff. Columbus: Ohio State University Press, 1959: 259–266.

Solomon, Robert. "Emotions, Thoughts, and Feelings: Emotions as Engagements with the World." In *Thinking about Feeling: Contemporary Philosophers on Emotions*, ed. Robert Solomon. New York: Oxford University Press, 2004: 76–89.

Soucek, Brian. "Personification of Art." *Encyclopedia of Aesthetics*, ed. Michael Kelly. 2nd ed. New York: Oxford University Press, 2014: Vol. 5: 116–119.

Starn, Orin. *Ishi's Brain: In Search of America's Last "Wild" Indian*. New York: W.W. Norton, 2004.

Stopford, Richard. "Preserving the Restoration of the *Pietà*." *British Journal of Aesthetics* 56:3 (2016): 301–315

Stokes, Dustin. "Cognitive Penetration and the Perception of Art." *Diacritica* 68:1 (2014): 1–34.

"Stolen Urn with Remains Finds Way to Pomfret Widow." *Buffalo News*. Sunday, February 10, 2013.

Thomasson, Amie. *Fiction and Metaphysics*. Cambridge: Cambridge University Press, 2008.

———. *Ordinary Objects*. New York: Oxford University Press, 2007.

Tokasz, Jay. "Separating History from Legend." *Buffalo News*. October 26, 2008: C2.

Trilling, Lionel. *Sincerity and Authenticity*. Cambridge, MA: Harvard University Press, 1971.

Tylor, Edward Burnett. *The Origins of Culture*. New York: Harper, 1958 [1871].

Ulrich, Laurel Thatcher, Ivan Gaskell, Sara J. Schechner, Sarah Anne Carter. *Tangible Things: Making History through Objects*. New York: Oxford University Press, 2015.

Urmson, J. O. "What Makes a Situation Aesthetic?" In *Art and Philosophy*, ed. W. E. Kennick. New York: St Martin's Press, 1964 [1957]: 552–564.

Vaillant, John. *The Golden Spruce: A True Story of Myth, Madness, and Greed*. New York: W.W. Norton, 2005.

———. *The Tiger: A True Story of Vengeance and Survival*. New York: Vintage Books, 2010.

Vonnegut, Kurt. *Mother Night*. New York: Random House, 1961.

Walton, Kendall. "Categories of Art." *Philosophical Review* 79 (1970): 334–367.

———. "How Marvelous! Toward a Theory of Aesthetic Value." *Journal of Aesthetics and Art Criticism* 51:3 (1993): 499–510.

———. *Mimesis as Make-Believe: On the Foundations of the Representational Arts*. Cambridge, MA: Harvard University Press, 1990.

Wicks, Robert. "Architectural Restoration: Resurrection or Replication?" *British Journal of Aesthetics* 34:2 (1994): 163–170.

Wiggins, David. *Sameness and Substance Renewed*. Cambridge: Cambridge University Press, 2001.

Wollheim, Richard. *Art and Its Objects*. 2nd edition. Cambridge: Cambridge University Press, 1980.

Wreen, Michael. "The Restoration and Reproduction of Works of Art." *Dialogue* 24 (1985): 91–100.

Zeimbekis, John and Athanassios Raftopoulis, eds. *The Cognitive Penetrability of Perception: New Philosophical Perspectives*. Oxford: Oxford University Press, 2015.

Zucker, Paul. *Fascination of Decay: Ruins: Relic—Symbol—Ornament*. Ridgewood, NJ: Gregg Press, 1968.

Websites

Biaterek tower in Astana, Kazakhstan: http://www.cnn.com/2012/07/13/world/asia/eye-on-kazakhstan-astana/.

Catholic analysis of relics: www.catholicdoors.com/faq/qu86.htm.

The Cloisters: http://www.metmuseum.org/about-the-museum/history-of-the-museum/the-cloisters-museum-and-gardens.

Cornell University bench: https://ezramagazine.cornell.edu/FALL13/CornellHistory.html.

Icelandic saga map: http://sagamap.hi.is/is/.

Feinstein, Roni. "Brancusi and the Space of Modern Sculpture," http://visual.uclaextension.edu/brancusi-and-the-space-of-modern-sculpture.

Inskeep, Steve. "Vacationing Family Finds Treasure Off Florida's Coast," July 30, 2015, National Public Radio Morning Edition. http://www.npr.org/2015/07/30/427648600/vacationing-family-finds-treasure-off-florida-s-coast.

Ise Jingu shrine: http://www.smithsonianmag.com/smart-news/this-japanese-shrine-has-been-torn-down-and-rebuilt-every-20-years-for-the-past-millennium-575558/?no-ist.

"Lincoln's Manuscripts Reveal a Constant Reviser," National Public Radio, February 12, 2009. At www.npr.org/templates/story/story.php?storyId=100531323.

Mojave National Preserve: https://nps.gov/moja/learn/nature/plants.htm.

PBS "Objects and Memory": http://www.pbs.org/program/objects-and-memory.

Palca, Joe. "Paging through History's Beautiful Science," National Public Radio Weekend Edition, Saturday, November 15, 2008. https://www.npr.org/templates/story/story.php?storyId=96957080.

Palmyra: http://whc.unesco.org/en/list/23; http://whc.unesco.org/en/news/1488; http://www.slate.com/blogs/the_slatest/2015/08/19/isis_kills_81_year_old_syrian_archaeologist_palmyra_expert_executed.html.

Parks, Rosa, house of: https://news.brown.edu/articles/2017/10/rosa-parks.

Simon, Scott, "Upon Reclaiming Palmyra, The Controversial Side of Digital Reproduction," interview with Roger Michel: NPR Weekend Edition, April 2, 2016: http://www.npr.org/programs/weekend-edition-saturday/2016/04/02/472784684/weekend-edition-saturday-for-april-2-2016?showDate=2016-04-02.

Smithsonian Institution repatriation site: http://anthropology.si.edu/repatriation/projects/ishi.htm.

Wright, Frank Lloyd: Darwin Martin House: http://www.darwinmartinhouse.org/restoration.cfm.

Xu Bing, *And Where Does the Dust Itself Collect?* https://mymodernmet.com/xu-bing-where-does-the-dust-itself-collect/

Index